A Research Agenda for Employee Engagement
in a Changing World of Work

Elgar Research Agendas outline the future of research in a given area. Leading scholars are given the space to explore their subject in provocative ways, and map out the potential directions of travel. They are relevant but also visionary.

Forward-looking and innovative, Elgar Research Agendas are an essential resource for PhD students, scholars and anybody who wants to be at the forefront of research.

Titles in the series include:

A Research Agenda for Knowledge Management and Analytics
Edited by Jay Liebowitz

A Research Agenda for Heritage Tourism
Edited by Maria Gravari-Barbas

A Research Agenda for Border Studies
Edited by James W. Scott

A Research Agenda for Sales
Edited by Fernando Jaramillo and Jay Prakash Mulki

A Research Agenda for Employee Engagement in a Changing World of Work
Edited by John P. Meyer and Benjamin Schneider

A Research Agenda for the Entrepreneurial University
Edited by Ulla Hytti

A Research Agenda for Place Branding
Edited by Dominic Medway, Gary Warnaby and John Byrom

A Research Agenda for Social Finance
Edited by Othmar M. Lehner

A Research Agenda for Employee Engagement in a Changing World of Work

Edited by

JOHN P. MEYER

> *Professor, Department of Psychology, The University of Western Ontario, London, Ontario, Canada and Adjunct Professor, Curtin Business School, Curtin University, Perth, Australia*

BENJAMIN SCHNEIDER

> *Professor Emeritus, University of Maryland, College Park, USA, Affiliated Research Scientist, Center for Effective Organizations, Marshall School of Business, University of Southern California, Los Angeles, USA and Lead Consultant, Employee Engagement and Organizational Diagnostics, Sarasota, USA*

Elgar Research Agendas

Edward Elgar
PUBLISHING

Cheltenham, UK • Northampton, MA, USA

Published by
Edward Elgar Publishing Limited
The Lypiatts
15 Lansdown Road
Cheltenham
Glos GL50 2JA
UK

Edward Elgar Publishing, Inc.
William Pratt House
9 Dewey Court
Northampton
Massachusetts 01060
USA

A catalogue record for this book
is available from the British Library

Library of Congress Control Number: 2021932263

This book is available electronically in the **Elgar**online
Business subject collection
http://dx.doi.org/10.4337/9781789907858

ISBN 978 1 78990 784 1 (cased)
ISBN 978 1 78990 785 8 (eBook)

Printed and bound by CPI Group (UK) Ltd, Croydon, CR0 4YY

For my grandchildren, Olive, Hugh, Thomas, Eleanor, Beth and Ewen. (JPM)

For Brenda, who has engaged me since that first day. (BS)

Contents

Figures

Contributors

Simon L. Albrecht Deakin University, Australia

Arnold B. Bakker Erasmus University Rotterdam, The Netherlands

John W. Boudreau University of Southern California, USA

Peter Cappelli The Wharton School, USA

Maike Czink University of Mannheim, Germany

Liat Eldor The Wharton School, USA

Alexis A. Fink Facebook, USA

Marylène Gagné Curtin University, Australia

Vicente González-Romá University of Valencia, Spain

Mark A. Griffin Curtin University, Australia

Jonathon R. B. Halbesleben University of Alabama, USA

Leaetta M. Hough The Dunnette Group, USA

David Litalien Université Laval, Canada

William H. Macey CultureFactors, USA

Matthew J. W. McLarnon Mount Royal University, Canada

John P. Meyer The University of Western Ontario, Canada, and Curtin University, Australia

Alexandre J. S. Morin Concordia University, Canada

Frederick L. Oswald Rice University, USA

Sharon K. Parker Curtin University, Australia

Alan M. Saks University of Toronto, Canada

Marisa Salanova Universitat Jaume I, Spain

Benjamin Schneider University of Maryland (Emeritus), USA

Sabine Sonnentag University of Mannheim, Germany

Monika Wiegelmann University of Mannheim, Germany

Despoina Xanthopoulou Aristotle University of Thessaloniki, Greece

Introduction

1. The promise of engagement

John P. Meyer and Benjamin Schneider

Few topics have captured the attention of both the academic and consulting communities like employee engagement. Although popularized by human resources consulting firms in the early 2000s (Macey & Schneider, 2008), the term "engagement" was first introduced to the academic literature by William Kahn in a 1990 *Academy of Management Journal* article. It has since been the subject of considerable research by both academics and practitioners. With the odd exception (e.g., Harter et al., 2002, 2020), research conducted within organizations or by consulting firms has been proprietary, so that our shared knowledge about engagement comes largely from the academic literature. Indeed, academic scholars have been prolific in their theorizing and research on the topic. This work has been summarized and critiqued in numerous books (e.g., Albrecht, 2010; Bakker & Leiter, 2010; Truss et al., 2009), special issues (Bakker & Albrecht, 2018; Shantz, 2017), narrative review articles (e.g., Bakker et al., 2014; Macey & Schneider, 2008; Saks & Gruman, 2014), and meta-analyses (e.g., Christian et al., 2011; Crawford et al., 2010; Halbesleben, 2010; Knight et al., 2016; Mackay et al., 2017; Young et al., 2018). So – bottom line – we have learned a great deal about engagement over the last few decades.

This book is about more than what we know about engagement; it is also about what we still need to know, and how we might go about learning more. It is about providing a research agenda set forth by the experts who have contributed much of what we have learned to date. It identifies important unanswered questions to stimulate those interested in beginning or advancing their own research on engagement. It is also about recent advances in methodology and data analytic techniques that can be used to address many of the unanswered questions, and stimulate still others.

To set the stage for what is to come, we first provide some context, starting with the basic questions: "What is engagement?"; "How is it measured?"; "How does it develop?"; "Why is it important?" Again, given the breadth of theory, research, and practical application, we can only scratch the surface here. Readers are encouraged to consult the more detailed reviews described above

3

for more detail. In addition, of course, the authors of each of the chapters in this book provide specific background as a basis for the research agenda they propose. So, as readers will see, the chapters in the book are about specific issues with regard to engagement research (facets of engagement, outcomes from engagement, multi-level issues in engagement research, and so forth) but here we introduce the reader to the broad engagement topic and its research history.

Background

What is engagement?

Although we typically recognize engagement when we see it, coming to a consensus on a precise definition of engagement is more difficult. There are several reasons for this, but arguably one of the most important is the background and perspective of the theorists who have been instrumental in popularizing the concept. For example, for Kahn (1990) the notion of engagement emerged from extensive observation and interviews with employees in two quite diverse organizations. Based on this research, Kahn defined engagement as "the harnessing of organizational members' selves to their work roles; in engagement, people employ and express themselves physically, cognitively, and emotionally during role performances" (p. 694). In contrast, for another international team of researchers, interest in engagement grew out of an earlier program of research on burnout (Bakker & Demerouti, 2017; Demerouti et al., 2001). Due in part to the positive psychology movement and its emphasis on well-being as opposed to ill-being (e.g., Seligman & Csikszentmihalyi, 2000, 2014), engagement was viewed as the antipode to burnout, and was defined as "as a positive, fulfilling, work-related state of mind that is characterized by vigor, dedication, and absorption" (Schaufeli & Bakker, 2004, p. 295). Still others working through the lens of self-determination theory (SDT; Deci & Ryan, 2000; Gagné & Deci, 2005), considered engagement to be synonymous with autonomous (self-determined) motivation (e.g., Meyer et al., 2010).

Another complicating factor is the fact that engagement can be viewed as a personal disposition (trait engagement), a psychological state (state engagement), or as a set of behaviors (behavioral engagement; Macey & Schneider, 2008). The definitions offered earlier by founders of this engagement endeavor tend to focus on the "state of being engaged," and set the stage for a program of research to identify personal (state engagement) and situational factors that contribute to (dis)engagement, as well as the outcomes (behavioral engagement) likely to result. We summarize some of this research later.

A third complicating factor in defining engagement concerns the target of engagement. We started this chapter by making reference to "employee engagement," and indeed this is a term that is commonly used because it locates the engagement within the person. However, other commonly used terms, such as "work engagement" and "job engagement," focus more on the setting in which the engagement is expressed. But engagement can also be described with reference to more specific targets to which it is addressed, such as "task engagement," "organizational engagement," "team engagement," or "project engagement," to name but a few.

A final complication is the need to distinguish engagement from related concepts such as job satisfaction, affective organizational commitment, and job involvement (see Meyer, 2017). Some scholars have argued that these concepts all reflect a common underlying positive attitude, or "A factor" (Newman et al., 2010), but others have provided meta-analytic evidence for the distinctiveness of the constructs (Christian et al., 2011). The conceptual overlap with other constructs is not limited to state engagement, but applies also to trait and behavioral engagement (Macey & Schneider, 2008). The key attraction of the engagement construct is its focus on energy, activation, and arousal. Regardless of the specific measures used to assess it, they all get at pieces of these. Further, analyses regarding outcomes reveal that engagement makes a significant incremental contribution to the prediction of employee effectiveness (Mackay et al., 2017).

How is engagement measured?

Just as there are multiple definitions of engagement, so too are there multiple measures. Two such measures were developed to reflect Kahn's (1990) definition, with subscales measuring cognitive, affective, and behavioral engagement (May et al., 2004; Rich et al., 2010). The most widely used measure in the academic literature is the Utrecht Work Engagement Scale (UWES: Schaufeli et al., 2002). Consistent with the earlier definition of Schaufeli and Bakker (2004), the UWES includes three subscales: vigor, dedication, and absorption. Other measures have been developed to reflect engagement to specific targets including the job and organization (Saks, 2006), and work and family (Rothbard, 2001).

The foregoing measures are generally completed by employees and the scores are linked to other variables of interest at an individual level of analysis.

However, these individual scores are sometimes aggregated to higher levels when researchers are interested in team, unit, or organizational engagement (e.g., Harter et al., 2002; Schneider et al., 2017). Alternatively, authors may use a "referent shift" (Chan, 1998) by rewording the items to refer to employees in the team or organization rather than the individual employee (e.g., Barrick et al., 2015). Items can also be reworded to measure engagement at "lower levels," such as a specific task or engagement at a specific time (e.g., Bakker & Bal, 2010; Bledow et al., 2011; Sonnentag, 2003). As discussed later, and elsewhere in this book, these adaptations of the engagement measures allow for higher- and cross-level analyses.

How does engagement develop?

Not surprisingly, this is also a complex question, and the answers depend on the theoretical framework guiding the research. One of the most well-established theories used to explain the development of engagement is the Job Demands-Resources (JD-R) model (Bakker & Demerouti, 2007, 2017). Job demands are the physical, psychological, social, and organizational aspects of the job that require sustained effort, and were initially considered to contribute to burnout (Demerouti et al., 2001). By contrast, resources are physical, psychological, social, and organizational aspects of the job that help to meet demands and contribute to engagement. However, it is now recognized that some demands can also contribute to engagement by stimulating the use of job and personal resources. The JD-R model has served as the impetus for a large body of engagement research (see Bakker & Demerouti, 2017) and is addressed in more detail in subsequent chapters.

SDT has also been a major impetus for engagement research and has been integrated within the JD-R model to elaborate on the mechanisms by which job resources contribute to engagement (e.g., Bakker & Demerouti, 2017; Schaufeli & Taris, 2014). According to SDT, employees are more likely to be engaged when conditions are conducive to the satisfaction of three core psychological needs: autonomy, competence, and relatedness. Thus, rather than focusing on specific conditions that contribute to the development of engagement, SDT offers need satisfaction as a "basic principle" underlying the engagement process (Meyer, 2013). There are many other well-established principles that can also be used to explain, or predict, the implications of specific interventions on employee engagement. These include, but are not limited to, person-environment fit, organizational support, trust, and justice.

Why does engagement matter?

The answer to this question is key to the strong interest in engagement among both academics and practitioners. Since the term was introduced by Kahn (1990), the "promise of engagement" was a motivated, happier, healthier, and more productive workforce. Evidence for these positive outcomes is provided by the findings reported in several meta-analyses (e.g., Christian et al., 2011; Crawford et al., 2010; Halbesleben, 2010; Mackay et al., 2017). Indeed, engagement has been consistently and significantly linked to job performance, absenteeism, retention, and well-being. Moving beyond the individual level of analysis, there is also evidence linking engagement to effectiveness at the team (Costa et al., 2014a, 2014b) and organizational (Barrick et al., 2015; Schneider et al., 2017) levels.

Of course, all of this evidence must be considered in context. Among other things, as we noted earlier, there remains some disagreement about the meaning and measurement of engagement. Most of the meta-analytic evidence for the positive outcomes associated with engagement comes from individual-level studies of "work engagement" measured at a single point in time. There are exceptions, but they are relatively rare. Higher- and cross-level studies are also relatively rare, as are diary and longitudinal studies, and studies focusing on engagement with other targets (e.g., tasks; projects). Questions also remain about the potential "dark side" of engagement (e.g., links to workaholism; work interfering with family). And perhaps most importantly, we cannot be sure that the promise of engagement will hold under the conditions of change in work, workers, and working that we will encounter in the coming decades. This book is about the future of engagement research, and the following is a brief roadmap to guide you through the chapters that follow.

A roadmap

Part I: Expanding traditional perspectives on engagement

The chapters in Part I address many of the ways that future research might expand upon the traditional perspectives on engagement just described. In Chapter 2, Alan Saks notes that the vast majority of engagement research has focused on job/work engagement with the employee as a referent (i.e., individual employees report on their own level of engagement with their job or work). This research has generated a wealth of information with practical implications. However, there are many other potential targets of engagement, and these can be measured from multiple perspectives. Saks offers a multidimensional model of engagement with five targets (tasks, job, team, business unit, and organization) and four referents (individual, team, unit, and organization). Thus, employees can be asked to what extent they or their team/ unit/organization members are engaged with their tasks, job, team, unit, or organization. Expanding the construct of engagement in this way raises a wide range of research questions pertaining to the measurement of engagement, the nomological network of antecedents and outcomes within targets, and relations among the various targets and referents.

In Chapter 3, Despoina Xanthopoulou and Arnold Bakker similarly argue for expansion of engagement research across levels. Working primarily within the JD-R theory framework (Bakker & Demerouti, 2017), they review research using the UWES at the stable individual level (i.e., across time) and adapted to the situational (time-delimited) and team/organizational levels. Again, raising the possibility that engagement is dynamic (i.e., can vary across time and situations) and can be operationalized at higher levels (e.g., team, organization) opens the door to a wide range of new questions. Xanthopoulou and Bakker focus particularly on the questions of isomorphism (similarity) in the antecedents and consequences of engagement at different levels and the processes that link engagement, its antecedents, and outcomes, across levels.

Perhaps attesting to its importance, Marisa Salanova also addresses engagement from a multi-level perspective in Chapter 4. She views engagement from a positive psychology perspective as an indicator of well-being at the individual, team, and organization levels. Using the HEalthy, Resilient Organization (HERO) model (Salanova et al., 2012) as a point of departure, she reviews research illustrating how healthy organizational resources and practices contribute to healthy employees (including engagement) and, in turn, to healthy organizational outcomes. Salanova places particular emphasis on her program of intervention research. While the findings have been largely supportive of the HERO Model, she identifies several new directions for research. To give but one example, she notes that interventions often have significant positive effects in the short term, but decline in the longer term. She calls for more research to identify strategies (e.g., designating well-being champions) that can be used to maintain and build upon initial gains.

Leaetta Hough and Frederick Oswald call for expansion of engagement research in a very different direction in Chapter 5. Most notably, they call for greater emphasis on the role of individual differences, particularly personality, in understanding the engagement process. They review research linking personality (e.g., Big 5 dimensions; core self-evaluation) to work engagement, proposing that they might serve as indicators of *engagement propensity* that can be incorporated into organizational selection systems. In this regard, they call for more research looking at facets of the Big 5 traits as general or situation-specific predictors of engagement. In a particularly unique twist to the individual-differences perspective, they note that the personality of leaders and co-workers might predict the engagement of those around them. Although they present some evidence to support this contagion effect (see also the Xanthopoulou and Bakker, and Salanova chapters), they argue for a much more systematic program of research using more sophisticated methodology and analytic techniques. Moreover, they call for greater use of follower engagement as a criterion in the evaluation of leader effectiveness.

Jonathon Halbesleben rounds out Part I of the book in Chapter 6 by expanding on the variety of potential outcomes of engagement. Not surprisingly, considerable attention has been given to the implications of employee engagement on retention and job performance, but there are many other potential outcomes that warrant investigation, including job crafting, innovation, creativity, safety and well-being, and work–life boundaries. Halbesleben uses conservation of resources theory (Hobfoll, 1989) to explain how and why engagement leads to these outcomes, as well as how the outcomes can in turn contribute to enhanced engagement to create a positive gain cycle. However, he also notes that there might be a "dark side" to engagement if, for example, it leads to excess emphasis on work to the detriment of work–life balance, or to "cutting corners" in the interests of efficiency with accompanying increases in risks to safety. Halbesleben suggests that one potential solution to the latter problem might be to foster engagement with the outcome-specific behaviors themselves (e.g., safety behaviors). This is in line with, and extends, the argument made by Saks for expansion of the targets of engagement, and is one of many of the directions for future research that he recommends.

Part II: Conceptualizing engagement in the changing world of work

While the chapters in Part I expand the concept of engagement in somewhat traditional ways, the chapters in Part II address the future of engagement theory, research, and practice in the changing world of work.

In Chapter 7, Peter Cappelli and Liat Eldor note that most engagement theory and research is premised on the notion of "standard employment" arrangements. However, there is a small, but increasing, percentage of individuals engaged in "gig" or contract work in its various shapes and sizes. Relationships between contractors and their clients are quite different from those between employers and employees, and are indeed regulated by contract law rather than employment law. These differences have implications for the meaning of engagement, what organizations (clients) might expect as a consequence of contract worker engagement, and what they can do to foster it. For example, as noted earlier, much of the theory and research pertaining to engagement deals with "work" or "job" engagement, both of which can have quite different meaning for standard employees and contract workers. Similarly, a common expectation for the engaged employee is that they will "go above and beyond" in the best interests of the employer, but the outcomes required of contractor workers are defined by the terms of the contract and any deviations may be neither expected nor desired. Finally, many of the initiatives that organizations might introduce to engage their employees (e.g., empowerment, training, mentoring) are either not relevant or may be in violation of contract law. However, rather than abandoning the construct as irrelevant for contract workers, Cappelli and Eldor suggest new ways of thinking about (a) the meaning of engagement for contract workers, (b) ways to foster such engagement, and (c) the benefits of doing so for both the contract worker and the client. These issues will become of increasing importance as contract work becomes more prevalent, but they have yet to be addressed systematically in theory, let alone research.

In addition to the changing employment relationships discussed by Cappelli and Eldor, work is increasingly being automated. In Chapter 8, John Boudreau discusses how both changing relationships and automation will create the need for continual "deconstruction and reinvention" of work. This process of deconstruction and reinvention involves the identification of "work elements" that make up a job. Once identified, decisions must be made about whether, and how, these elements should be automated or assigned to humans in standard and/or non-standard work arrangements. Importantly, these decisions are not of the either/or variety, but might include varying combinations of humans and automation. For example, some work elements might best be automated whereas others can only be performed by humans. In other cases, rather than "replacing" humans, automation might be used to "augment" human performance. In any case, Boudreau argues that, just as continuous change requires a shift in focus from jobs to work elements for purposes of job (re)design, there may need to be an accompanying shift in focus from job engagement to work-element (task) engagement. With this shift comes an opportunity to use work-element engagement as another important factor to consider in making decisions about how to reconfigure jobs. Although Boudreau is optimistic about our ability to apply existing engagement theory to research at the work-elements level, he acknowledges that this can only be determined with new research. Indeed, he poses a variety of interesting research questions about the nature, causes, correlates, and outcomes of engagement when viewed from a work-elements perspective.

Chapter 9 by Marylène Gagné, Sharon Parker, and Mark Griffin nicely complements the two preceding chapters by providing a theory-based conceptual framework to explain how the changing nature of work might impact employee engagement. The framework involves the integration of existing and emerging theory pertaining to work performance, motivation, and design. The authors begin with the premise that changes in work and the work environment will result in increased uncertainty, changes in the nature of interpersonal relationships, and the introduction of new technologies. Consequently, job performance will need to be reconceptualized to include not only task proficiency, but also adaptability and proactivity as change ensues. Employee engagement can be a key to success for all three components, but the potential effects of change on engagement can be both positive and negative. To explain these effects, Gagné et al. draw on SDT (Deci & Ryan, 1985; Gagné & Deci, 2005). First, they identify parallels between the concepts of employee engagement and autonomous motivation, and explain how autonomous motivation is affected by the satisfaction/frustration of three basic psychological needs (autonomy, competence, relatedness). Changes to work and the workplace can serve as a source of both need satisfaction and frustration, leading to increases or decreases in engagement. Finally, the authors draw on the SMART (stimulating, mastery-oriented, agentic, relational, tolerable) theory of work design being developed by Parker and her colleagues to illustrate how work can be (re)designed to increase the likelihood of need satisfaction and enhanced engagement. While grounded in established theory and research, the integrative framework breaks new ground and raises a wealth of important research questions of theoretical and practical relevance.

In Chapter 10, Simon Albrecht proposes a more targeted conceptual framework to link existing theory and research pertaining to organizational change and employee engagement. He notes that, to date, the two issues have largely been studied in isolation, with little cross-fertilization. With the nature, prevalence, and rapidity of change noted in the preceding chapters, it is important to understand how change can affect employee engagement, and how employee engagement might contribute to the effective implementation of change. Central to the conceptual framework is "climate for engagement" and "climate for change" within the organization. Albrecht conceptualizes climate in terms of the perceptions of individuals that team and/or organization members in general are engaged with their work and enthusiastic about change, respectively. In his framework, perceptions of engagement climate are expected to have their strongest and most direct effect on individual employees' own engagement, and perceptions of change climate should have their strongest and most direct effects on individuals' engagement in change. He also notes that cross-over and reciprocal relations are expected. Finally, while acknowledging the many other forces in play (see chapters in Part I), Albrecht places particular emphasis on the role of senior leadership in the creation of engagement and change climates. This effort to merge the engagement and change literatures is very timely and raises a plethora of new research questions awaiting answers.

Part III: Research strategies for the new agenda

Part III of the book provides a change of pace. While the authors of Parts I and II raised a wide range of interesting research questions about engagement, the authors of Part III introduce a set of relatively novel methods and data analytic tools to assist in answering these questions. Of course, they also raise still more interesting research questions that only become apparent once you unearth the tools needed to address them. All of the techniques described in these chapters are complex, and the space available to the authors did not allow them to do complete justice to the details. However, they all do an excellent job of introducing the methods, giving examples of their applications, suggesting how they might be used to address many of the important questions raised in earlier chapters, and, importantly, directing readers to other sources for more detail.

In Chapter 11, William Macey discusses the many different qualitative methods available to engagement researchers as they dig more deeply into the meaning of engagement, the ways it is experienced, how it develops, and the processes by which it influences employees' behavior and well-being. Of course, qualitative methods are not new, but their application by engagement researchers is surprisingly rare. This is curious given that the concept was introduced, at least to the academic community, by Kahn on the basis of qualitative investigations conducted in two quite diverse contexts. Many of the authors in earlier chapters suggest the need for more qualitative research as we begin to grapple with the implications of the changing world of work on employee engagement. Macey identifies a number of the qualitative techniques available for this purpose, along with examples of their application – including several cases involving engagement. Future applications of these techniques to address new questions pertaining to the changing world of work should generate a wealth of information in their own right, as well as raising important questions via inductive reasoning that might be addressed with the advanced quantitative techniques described in the subsequent chapters.

As noted above, much of engagement research has been conducted at the individual level of analysis. That is, it addresses the measurement of engagement in individuals along with the investigation of links between engagement and other variables, including those believed to be antecedents and consequences.

Indeed, these are the studies serving as the basis for the meta-analytic reviews described previously. Relatively few studies have been conducted at "higher" levels, such as the team, unit, or organization. Thinking about engagement at these levels raises new questions about the measurement of engagement, isomorphism in relations with antecedents and outcomes, and potential interactions across levels of analysis. In Chapter 12, Vicente González-Romá addresses all of these issues and more in a clear, concise, and engaging manner, with illustrative examples and additional sources for more detailed treatments including access to syntax.

In Chapter 13, Sabine Sonnentag, Monika Wiegelmann, and Maike Czink address the related issue of studying dynamic processes in engagement. As researchers begin to study variability (e.g., daily, weekly, seasonal) and changes (gradual or sudden increases or decreases) in engagement, time becomes a level of analysis nested within individuals. Sonnentag et al. explain how the concepts and methods used in multi-level research can be applied to the longitudinal data required to investigate variability and change in engagement. They too provide illustrative examples from the existing literature, describe the available methods and analytic tools available for future research, and direct readers to a wealth of additional resources for more detail on how to apply these methods and tools.

Most engagement research, whether conducted at the individual, unit, or organizational level and within or across time, has been variable-centered. That is, it focuses on how variables relate to one another within a sample. An underlying assumption of the analytic techniques used in this approach is that the parameters identified (e.g., means, variances, path coefficients) apply to the sample as a whole, and to the population from which it was generated. Moreover, the focus remains on the variables of interest (e.g., how does engagement as a variable relate to well-being as a variable?). In Chapter 14, Matthew McLarnon, Alexandre Morin, and David Litalien introduce readers to a complementary set of person-centered data analytic techniques. These person-centered techniques relax the assumption that a single set of parameters can describe a population as a whole, and allow for the possibility that a set of variables might combine differently across subpopulations. As a result, these techniques take a more holistic perspective by focusing on the person rather than the variables. For example, rather than considering how different targets of engagement (e.g., task, job, organization, family) might be related to one another within a population, a person-centered approach allows for the possibility that these engagements with these targets could relate differently to one another (and to other variables) across subpopulations. That is, individuals might have different "engagement profiles." Likewise, there could be differences across subpopulations in how one set of variables predicts another or in the trajectories of change in variables over time. McLarnon et al. introduce readers to the many person-centered analytic techniques available, and to the different kinds of questions they can be used to address.

Finally, in Chapter 15 Alexis Fink and William Macey explain how new technologies can provide access to data in quantities not previously imaginable. These data can be qualitative (e.g., web-based text) or quantitative (e.g., human resources information systems data) and can serve as input to the kinds of analyses described in the foregoing chapters. However, given the amount of data potentially available, new techniques for management and analysis are also required. Fink and Macey address these as well. Of course, with availability comes the responsibility to collect and use the data in morally and ethically responsible ways, an issue that Fink and Macey raise up front and continue to promote throughout the chapter. They also raise additional caveats regarding the relevance of the data available (e.g., through data scraping) to constructs of theoretical relevance and or practical value. Indeed, the chapter is a rich source of both possibilities and cautionary notes. This is a field that is arguably more familiar to scholars in the data sciences than to those in the social and management sciences, and is constantly changing. The opportunity seems ripe for collaboration among those in different disciplines to share ideas and expertise so that the best can be made of the vast amount of information that is being generated every day, or should we say every minute or second!

Summary

This is a book about engagement, and it is intended for new scholars, or those who are simply new to the topic. However, we expect that even the "seasoned" engagement researchers can learn something from the accomplished authors who contributed to this volume. As co-editors, we certainly did! The book provides an overview of what we already know about engagement but, more importantly, it also raises questions that still need to be answered, especially in the face of rapid and extensive changes in the world of work, workers, and working. It also identifies some of the relatively new methods and analytic techniques we can use to answer these questions. We hope you will find it engaging!

References

Albrecht, S.L. (Ed.) (2010). *Handbook of Employee Engagement: Perspectives, Issues, Research and Practice.* Cheltenham, UK, and Northampton, MA, USA: Edward Elgar Publishing.

Bakker, A.B., and Albrecht, S.L. (Eds.) (2018). Work engagement: Current trends. *Career Development International, 23*(1), 4–11.

Bakker, A.B., and Bal, P.M. (2010). Weekly work engagement and performance: A study among starting teachers. *Journal of Occupational and Organizational Psychology, 83,* 189–206.

Bakker, A.B., and Demerouti, E. (2007). The job demands-resources model: State of the art. *Journal of Managerial Psychology, 22,* 309–328.

Bakker, A.B., and Demerouti, E. (2017). Job demands-resources theory: Taking stock and looking forward. *Journal of Occupational Health Psychology, 22,* 273–285.

Bakker, A.B., Demerouti, E., and Sanz-Vergel, S.I. (2014). Burnout and work engagement: The JD-R approach. *Annual Review of Organizational Psychology and Organizational Behavior, 1,* 389–411.

Bakker, A., and Leiter, M. (Eds.) (2010). *Work Engagement: A Handbook of Essential Theory and Research* (pp. 102–117). New York, NY: Psychology Press.

Barrick, M.R., Thurgood, G., Smith, T., and Courtright, S. (2015). Collective organizational engagement: Linking motivational antecedents, strategic implementation, and firm performance. *Academy of Management Journal, 58*(1), 111–135.

Bledow, R., Schmitt, A., Frese, M., and Kühnel, J. (2011). The affective shift model of work engagement. *Journal of Applied Psychology, 96,* 1246–1257.

Chan, D. (1998). Functional relations among constructs in the same content domain at different levels of analysis: A typology of composition models. *Journal of Applied Psychology, 83*(2), 234–246.

Christian, M.S., Garza, A.S., and Slaughter, J.E. (2011). Work engagement: A quantitative review and test of its relations with task and contextual performance. *Personnel Psychology, 64,* 89–136.

Costa, P., Passos, A.M., and Bakker, A.B. (2014a). Team work engagement: A model of emergence. *Journal of Occupational and Organizational Psychology, 87,* 414–436.

Costa, P., Passos, A.M., and Bakker, A.B. (2014b). Empirical validation of the team work engagement construct. *Journal of Personnel Psychology, 13,* 34–45.

Crawford, E.R., LePine, J., and Rich, B.L. (2010). Linking job demands and resources to employee engagement and burnout: A theoretical extension and meta-analytic test. *Journal of Applied Psychology, 95,* 834–848.

Deci, E. L., and Ryan, R. M. (1985). *Intrinsic Motivation and Self-Determination in Human Behavior.* New York, NY: Plenum Press.

Deci, E.L., and Ryan, R.M. (2000). The "what" and "why" of goal pursuits: Human needs and the self-determination of behavior. *Psychological Inquiry, 11,* 227–268.

Demerouti, E., Bakker, A.B., Nachreiner, F., and Schaufeli, W.B. (2001). The job demands-resources model of burnout. *Journal of Applied Psychology, 86*(3), 499–512.

Gagné, M., and Deci, E.L. (2005). Self-determination theory and work motivation. *Journal of Organizational Behavior, 26,* 331–362.

Halbesleben, J.R.B. (2010). A meta-analysis of work engagement: Relationships with burnout, demands, resources, and consequences. In A.B. Bakker and M.P. Leiter (Eds.), *Work Engagement: A Handbook of Essential Theory and Research* (pp. 102–117). New York, NY: Psychology Press.

Harter, J.K., Schmidt, F.L., Agrawal, S., Plowman, S.K., and Blue, A.T. (2020). Increased business value for positive job attitudes during economic recessions: A meta-analysis and SEM analysis. *Human Performance, 33*(4), 307–330.

Harter, J.K., Schmidt, F.L., and Hayes, T.L. (2002). Business-unit level relationship between employee satisfaction, employee engagement, and business outcomes: A meta-analysis. *Journal of Applied Psychology, 87*, 268–279.

Hobfoll, S.E. (1989). Conservation of resources: A new attempt at conceptualizing stress. *American Psychologist, 44*, 513–524.

Kahn, W.A. (1990). Psychological conditions of personal engagement and disengagement at work. *Academy of Management Journal, 33*, 692–724.

Knight, C., Patterson, M., and Dawson, J. (2016). Building work engagement: A systematic review and meta-analysis investigating the effectiveness of work engagement interventions. *Journal of Organizational Behavior, 38*(6), 790–812.

Macey, W.H., and Schneider, B. (2008). The meaning of employee engagement. *Industrial and Organizational Psychology: Perspectives on Science and Practice, 1*, 3–30.

Mackay, M., Allen, J.A., and Landis, R.S. (2017). Investigating the incremental validity of employee engagement in the prediction of employee effectiveness: A meta-analytic path analysis. *Human Resource Management Review, 27*, 108–120.

May, D.R., Gilson, R.L., and Harter, L.M. (2004). The psychological conditions of meaningfulness, safety and availability and the engagement of the human spirit at work. *Journal of Occupational and Organizational Psychology, 77*, 11–37.

Meyer, J.P. (2013). The science–practice gap and employee engagement: It's a matter of principle. *Canadian Psychology, 54*, 235–245.

Meyer, J.P. (2017). Has employee engagement had its day: What's next and does it matter? *Organizational Dynamics, 46*, 87–95.

Meyer, J.P., Gagné, M., and Parfyonova, N.M. (2010). Toward an evidence-based model of engagement: What we can learn from motivation and commitment research. In S. Albrecht (Ed.), *Handbook of Employee Engagement: Perspectives, Issues, Research and Practice* (pp. 62–73). Cheltenham, UK, and Northampton, MA, USA: Edwin Elgar Publishing.

Newman, D.A., Joseph, D.L., and Hulin, C.L. (2010). Job attitudes and employee engagement: Considering the attitude "A-factor." In S.L. Albrecht (Ed.), *Handbook of Employee Engagement: Perspectives, Issues, Research and Practice* (pp. 43–61). Cheltenham, UK, and Northampton, MA, USA: Edward Elgar Publishing.

Rich, B.L., LePine, J.A., and Crawford, E.R. (2010). Job engagement: Antecedents and effects of job performance. *Academy of Management Journal, 53*, 617–635.

Rothbard, N.P. (2001). Enriching or depleting: The dynamics of engagement in work and family roles. *Administrative Science Quarterly, 46*, 655–684.

Saks, A.M. (2006). Antecedents and consequences of employee engagement. *Journal of Managerial Psychology, 21*, 600–619.

Saks, A.M., and Gruman, J.A. (2014). What do we really know about employee engagement? *Human Resource Development Quarterly, 25*, 155–182.

Salanova, M., Llorens, S., Cifre, E., and Martínez, I.M. (2012). We need a hero! Towards a validation of the HEalthy & Resilient Organization (HERO) Model. *Group & Organization Management, 37*(6), 785–822.

Schaufeli, W.B., and Bakker, A.B. (2004). Job demands, job resources, and their relationship with burnout and engagement: A multi-sample study. *Journal of Organizational Behavior, 25*(3), 293–315.

Schaufeli, W.B., Salanova, M., González-Romá, V., and Bakker, A.B. (2002). The meas-urement of engagement and burnout: A two sample confirmatory factor analytic approach. *Journal of Happiness Studies, 3,* 71–92.

Schaufeli, W.B., and Taris, T.W. (2014). A critical review of the job demands-resources model: Implications for improving work and health. In G. Bauer and O. Hamming (Eds.), *Bridging Occupational, Organizational and Public Health* (pp. 43–68). Dordrecht: Springer.

Schneider, B., Yost, A., Kropp, A., Kind, C., and Lam, H. (2017). Workforce engage-ment: What it is, what drives it, and why it matters for organizational performance. *Journal of Organizational Behavior, 39,* 462–480.

Seligman, M.E.P., and Csikszentmihalyi, M. (2000). Positive psychology: An introduc-tion. *American Psychologist, 55*(1), 5–14.

Seligman, M.E.P., and Csikszentmihalyi, M. (2014). Positive psychology: An introduc-tion. In M. Csikszentmihalyi (Ed.), *Flow and the Foundations of Positive Psychology* (pp. 279–298). New York, NY: Springer US.

Shantz, A. (Ed.) (2017). Coming full circle: Putting engagement into practice. *Organizational Dynamics, 46,* 65–66.

Sonnentag, S. (2003). Recovery, work engagement, and proactive behavior: A new look at the interface between nonwork and work. *Journal of Applied Psychology, 88,* 518–528.

Truss, C., Delbridge, R., Alfes, K., Shantz, A., and Soane, E. (Eds.) (2009). *Employee Engagement in Theory and Practice.* London: Routledge.

Young, H.R., Glerum, D.R., Wang, W., and Joseph, D.L. (2018). Who are the most engaged at work? A meta-analysis of personality and employee engagement. *Journal of Organizational Behavior, 39,* 1330–1346.

PART I

Expanding traditional perspectives on engagement

2. Multiple targets and referents of employee engagement

Alan M. Saks

Employee engagement continues to generate considerable interest from researchers, practitioners, and organizations. This is not surprising given the strong research evidence that highly engaged employees have more positive job attitudes, higher job performance, and better health and well-being, and organizations with more engaged employees have higher organizational performance (Barrick et al., 2015; Christian et al., 2011; Halbesleben, 2010; Rich et al., 2010; Schneider et al., 2017). However, most of what we know about employee engagement is based on only one target of engagement – the job, or what is generally known as *job engagement* or *work engagement*. As a result, we know very little or nothing about other targets of employee engagement. This represents a major shortcoming of employee engagement theory, research, and practice.

In this chapter, I argue for a multidimensional approach to employee engagement that considers multiple targets (e.g., the job, the organization) and referents (e.g., self, co-workers) of employee engagement. I first briefly discuss the meaning of employee engagement and how most research has focused on job or work engagement. I then discuss the meaning of and need for a multidimensional approach to employee engagement. This is followed by a review of the research on different targets and referents of employee engagement. The chapter concludes with directions for future research on employee engagement targets and referents.

The meaning of employee engagement

Kahn (1990) defined *personal* engagement as "the harnessing of organization members' selves to their work roles; in engagement, people employ and express themselves physically, cognitively, and emotionally during role performances" (p.694). He further states that engagement is the "simultaneous employment and expression of a person's 'preferred self' in task behaviors that promote connections to work and to others, personal presence (physical, cognitive, and emotional), and active, full role performance" (p.700). A key aspect of Kahn's (1990) definition of engagement is that it involves investing one's full and complete self in the performance of a role.

Rothbard (2001) also described engagement as a role-specific construct, or what she calls *role* engagement. According to her, role engagement refers to "one's psychological presence in or focus on role activities and may be an important ingredient for effective role performance" (p.656). She noted that "within the context of the organization, people often must engage in multiple roles to fulfill job expectations" (p.655). Rothbard conducted the first study to examine engagement in more than one role (job and family) and to demonstrate that engagement in one role can influence engagement in another role.

Most research on employee engagement, however, has focused on work or job engagement, and most studies have used Schaufeli et al.'s (2002) Utrecht Work Engagement Scale (UWES) to measure work engagement. In addition, several measures based on Kahn's (1990) definition of engagement have also been used to measure job engagement (May et al., 2004; Rich et al., 2010). Thus, most research on and measures of employee engagement have focused on job or work engagement to the exclusion of all other roles or targets of engagement.

Thus, we know a great deal about work and job engagement. However, most employees have to perform and engage in multiple roles in addition to their work or job role (Rothbard, 2001). Furthermore, employee engagement also varies in terms of the referent used to measure engagement. Most research has focused on the individual or oneself as the referent as opposed to other referents such as team members and co-workers. A consideration of different targets and referents of employee engagement requires a multidimensional approach to employee engagement research and practice.

A multidimensional perspective of employee engagement

A multidimensional approach to employee engagement acknowledges that employees have multiple roles and that they will bring different degrees or depths of themselves into the performance of each role. Thus, the extent or degree to which employees choose to employ and express themselves physically, cognitively, and emotionally will vary across the different roles that they occupy. In addition, employee engagement can also vary with respect to the referent used to measure engagement (e.g., oneself versus one's co-workers).

Research on the target of employee engagement focuses on an individual's engagement in a specific role. For example, Saks (2006) asked participants to indicate the extent to which they are engaged in their job (e.g., "I really 'throw' myself into my job") and in their organization (e.g., "Being a member of this organization makes me come 'alive'."). Similarly, Rothbard (2001) asked participants to indicate their engagement in their work (e.g., "I focus a great deal of attention on my work") and their family (e.g., "I focus a great deal of attention on my family").

Research on the referent of employee engagement focuses on whose engagement is being considered regardless of the target. For example, Costa et al. (2014) asked individuals to respond to questions about the work engagement of their group (e.g., "At our work, we feel bursting with energy"). Similarly, Barrick et al. (2015) measured collective organizational engagement by asking participants to indicate the job engagement of their co-workers (e.g., "My co-workers and I really 'throw' ourselves into our work"). Thus, in these examples the target of engagement is the job, and the referent is one's team and co-workers, respectively.

As shown in Table 2.1, a multidimensional approach to employee engagement considers at least five targets of engagement (the task, job, team, business unit, and organization), and four referents of engagement (oneself, team members, business-unit members, and organization members). Thus, as shown in Table 2.1, there are a total of 20 possible target–referent combinations, although as described below, most research on employee engagement has focused on just one of these combinations (the target being the job, and the referent being oneself).

Table 2.1   A multidimensional approach to employee engagement

		Engagement	Referent	
Target of Engagement	Oneself	Team members	Business-unit members	Organization members
Task	Task–Oneself	Task–Team members	Task–Business unit members	Task–Organization members
Job	Job–Oneself	Job–Team members	Job–Business unit members	Job–Organization members
Team	Team–Oneself	Team–Team members	Team–Business unit members	Team–Organization members
Business unit	Business unit–Oneself	Business unit–Team members	Business unit–Business unit members	Business unit–Organization members
Organization	Organization–Oneself	Organization–Team members	Organization–Business unit members	Organization–Organization members

Note: In each cell the engagement score can be calculated at the individual level or aggregated at the team, business-unit, or organizational level.

In summary, research on employee engagement is at best incomplete and at worse misleading given that it has primarily focused on work or job engagement with the referent usually being oneself and it has neglected other targets and referents of employee engagement. This is a serious omission because different targets and referents of employee engagement are likely to be differentially related to antecedents and consequences. Thus, a more complete understanding and theory of employee engagement requires more attention to multiple targets and referents of employee engagement.

Targets and referents of employee engagement

Employees have numerous roles and responsibilities in their organization. Thus, for each role they may vary in the extent to which they are engaged or disengaged (Saks & Gruman, 2014). In this section, I discuss research on the following targets of employee engagement: one's job, specific job tasks, one's team or work group, the business unit or department that one belongs to, and the organization itself.

Work/job engagement

Most research on employee engagement has been on job or work engagement and most studies have used the UWES to measure work engagement. The results of several meta-analyses have found that job resources and job demands predict work/job engagement, and work/job engagement is related to employee attitudes, behavior, and performance. For example, Christian et al. (2011) found that job characteristics (autonomy, task variety, task significance, and feedback), as well as problem solving, job complexity, and social support were positively related to engagement, and physical demands (the amount of physical effort required by the job) and work conditions such as health hazards and noise were negatively related to engagement. Crawford et al. (2010) found that nine types of resources (autonomy, feedback, opportunities for development, positive workplace climate, recovery, rewards and recognition, support, job variety, and work role fit) were positively related to work engagement. They also found that challenge demands (job responsibility, time urgency, and workload) were positively related to work engagement, while hindrance demands (administrative hassles, emotional conflict, organizational politics, resource inadequacies, role conflict, and role overload) were negatively related. Work engagement has also been found to be positively related to job satisfaction, organizational commitment, task, and contextual performance, and negatively related to turnover intentions (Christian et al., 2011; Halbesleben, 2010).

The referent for most studies on work or job engagement has been oneself. An exception is the study by Barrick et al. (2015) on collective organizational engagement (a shared perception among organizational members about how engaged members of the organization are when they perform their job) that was conducted in 83 small to medium-sized credit unions. In this study, the target of engagement was the job, and the referent was one's co-workers. Barrick et al. (2015) used items that correspond to Rich et al.'s (2010) Job Engagement Scale that refer to work and the job, and they changed the referent to one's co-workers and oneself ("My co-workers and I ..."). In addition, they averaged employee ratings within each credit union to obtain a collective organizational engagement score for each firm.

Task engagement

One of the limitations of research on work/job engagement is that all tasks performed by an employee are subsumed into one general measure of work engagement. However, most jobs are multifaceted and consist of a variety of tasks, projects, and assignments, and employees are likely to vary in terms of how engaged they are when they perform each task. As a result, general or overall measures of work engagement represent a composite of all the tasks that an employee performs. For example, consider a professor who is highly engaged in research but disengaged in teaching and service (or vice versa). A general measure of work/job engagement will obscure these differences and produce a moderate work engagement score. This means that overall engagement scores might be misleading to the extent that employees are forced to give one response based on the various tasks they perform when they are responding to questions about their overall work or job engagement.

Newton et al. (2020) define task engagement as "the degree to which individuals invest their physical, cognitive, and emotional energies into a specific task that composes part of their work role" (p.3). They measured task engagement by changing the target from "job" to "task" and using oneself as the referent. Across two studies, they found that task engagement on one task influences task engagement and performance on a subsequent task and this influence can be positive or negative. Task engagement on one task was found to have a positive effect on task engagement and performance on a second task through positive affect, and a negative effect through attention residue (ruminative thinking about a prior task while engaged in a subsequent task). The negative effect through attention residue, however, was mitigated when the first task was viewed as having been completed. This study represents the first to measure task engagement and to demonstrate that engagement on one task can influence engagement on another task. Thus, changes in work tasks are likely to be important for understanding task engagement (see Boudreau, this volume).

Team engagement

Costa et al. (2014) define team work engagement (TWE) as a "shared, positive and fulfilling, motivational emergent state of work-related well-being" (p.35). They further note that like individual-level work engagement, TWE consists of three dimensions: team vigor, team dedication, and team absorption. Costa et al. (2014) demonstrated that TWE is a valid construct that is distinct but related to individual-level work engagement. TWE is more strongly related to team-level variables (e.g., collective efficacy) and "it is dependent on the interaction and dynamics that occur within the team and not so much on individual characteristics" (Costa et al., 2014, pp.35–36). Torrente et al. (2012) conducted one of the first studies on TWE and found that TWE mediated the relationship between team social resources such as a supportive team climate and team performance.

However, because the UWES has been used to measure TWE, the target of TWE research has been the job or work engagement, not team engagement. What makes this research team-related is the use of the team as the referent and the aggregation of TWE scores to the team level (Costa et al., 2014; Torrente et al., 2012). Thus, research on TWE has not measured engagement in team-specific roles or activities. The target is the job, and the referent is the work group. There are no studies at this time that have used the team as the target of engagement.

Business-unit engagement

Harter et al. (2002) published the first study on business-unit employee engagement. Their study involved a meta-analysis that included close to 8,000 business units in 36 organizations. They found significant positive correlations between employee engagement aggregated at the business-unit level and business outcomes (customer satisfaction, profitability, productivity, retention, and safety). However, a limitation of this study is that the measure of employee engagement was the Gallup Workplace Audit (GWA), which includes items that measure employee perceptions of work characteristics which are more like antecedents of engagement (e.g., opportunities to learn and grow) than engagement itself. As noted by the authors, the GWA items are "antecedents of personal job satisfaction and other affective constructs" (p.269). Thus, although the referent was oneself, the target was not the business unit. Rather, the authors averaged scores on the GWA for each business unit.

In another study on business-unit engagement, Salanova et al. (2005) investigated the relationship between organizational resources, work engagement, and service climate in a sample of 114 service units from hotels and restaurants. Although the focus of this study was business-unit engagement, the engagement measure used was the UWES, so the engagement target was the job, and the referent was oneself. Thus, rather than measure business-unit engagement, the authors measured work engagement and aggregated scores at the business-unit level.

In summary, although the focus of these two studies was the business unit, the job or one's work, not the business unit, was the engagement target. At this time, no previous study has measured employee engagement in which the business unit is the target.

Organization engagement

In the first study on organization engagement, Saks (2006) tested a model that included both job engagement and organization engagement. He designed measures of job engagement and organization engagement in which the target was the job and the organization, and the referent for both measures was oneself. Saks (2006) found that although the two targets of engagement were significantly positively correlated ($r = 0.62$, p < 0.001), there was a significant difference between them with job engagement (M = 3.06) being higher than organization engagement (M = 2.88). He also found differences in both the antecedents and consequences of job and organization engagement. For example, while perceived organizational support (POS) was a significant predictor of job and organization engagement, job characteristics predicted job engagement but not organization engagement, and procedural justice predicted organization engagement but not job engagement. With respect to the consequences, both job and organization predicted job satisfaction, organizational commitment, intention to quit, and organizational citizenship behavior towards the organization; however, only organization engagement predicted organizational citizenship behavior towards individuals.

In a follow-up study that used single-item measures of overall job engagement ("I am highly engaged in this job") and organization engagement ("I am highly engaged in this organization"), Saks (2019) found that job engagement was a stronger predictor of job-related consequences (i.e., job satisfaction and intention to quit one's job), and organization engagement was a stronger predictor of organization-related consequences (i.e., organizational commitment and organizational citizenship behaviors).

Several other studies have measured organization engagement using the Saks (2006) measure in which the target is the organization, and the referent is oneself. For example, Malinen et al. (2013) found that trust in senior management and procedural justice perceptions were positively related to organization engagement, and organization engagement partially mediated the relationship between trust in senior management and procedural justice with intention to quit. Juhdi et al. (2013) found that human resource (HR) practices were significantly related to organization engagement, and organization engagement partially mediated the relationship between HR practices and turnover intention. Mahon et al. (2014) found that shared personal vision, shared positive mood, and perceived organizational support (POS) were positively related to organization engagement, and the positive relationships between shared personal vision and POS with organization engagement were stronger for participants with higher emotional intelligence.

Only two studies besides Saks (2006) measured organization engagement and job engagement in the same study. Farndale et al. (2014) used an adapted version of the Saks (2006) measure of organization engagement and the UWES to measure work engagement. For both measures the referent was oneself. Farndale et al. (2014) found that both work engagement and organization engagement were significantly related to affective commitment, active learning, initiative, organizational citizenship behavior towards the organization, and perceived organizational performance, and organization engagement was also positively related to job satisfaction. Further, work engagement was more strongly related to active learning and initiative, while organization engagement was more strongly related to affective commitment and job satisfaction.

Suhartanto and Brien (2018) adapted Saks' (2006) and Farndale et al.'s (2014) scales to measure job engagement and organization engagement. Thus, the target was the job and the organization, and the referent was oneself. They found that both job engagement and organization engagement were positively related to job performance and job satisfaction; however, the relationships for job engagement were stronger. Further, job engagement was also related to employee perceptions of store performance and the relationship was partially mediated by job performance.

Finally, Schneider et al. (2017) examined workforce engagement using an aggregate measure of the experiences of individual employees in organizations. They measured workforce engagement using four items in which the target was the job, and the referent was oneself (e.g., "I look forward to coming to work each day"). Individual engagement scores were aggregated at the organizational level. Thus, although the focus of this study was the engagement at the organization level, the target of engagement was not the organization. Rather, the authors used a direct consensus model which "aggregates personally framed items to form an aggregate index" (p.467).

In summary, several studies have measured organization engagement in which the organization is the target, and the referent is oneself. Overall, these studies suggest that organization-related factors such as trust in senior management, procedural justice perceptions, HR practices, and POS are important predictors of organization engagement, and organization engagement is related to work outcomes even when job engagement is included as a predictor variable. However, because only three studies measured both job engagement and organization engagement, it is not possible to make definitive conclusions about how they differ with respect to antecedents and consequences. Nonetheless, Farndale et al. (2014) concluded that work and organization engagement are "distinct constructs, with different strengths of relationship with other constructs in the work outcomes and perceived organization performance nomological network" (p.170).

Summary

Research on employee engagement has been limited when it comes to targets and referents of employee engagement. With respect to different targets of engagement, most studies have used the job as the target. There has only been one study on task engagement, no studies on team engagement or business-unit engagement, and several studies on organization engagement. With respect to the referent used to measure engagement, the referent used in most studies has been oneself, although in several studies the referent has been one's work group or team, and in one study the referent was one's co-workers (Barrick et al., 2015).

Thus, of the 20 possible target–referent combinations in Table 2.1, most research has been on the "job target–oneself referent" combination. In addition, several studies have aggregated the data at the team (Costa et al., 2014; Torrente et al., 2012), business-unit (Harter et al., 2002; Salanova et al., 2005) and organization level (Barrick et al., 2015; Schneider et al., 2017). Thus, in addition to the target and referent of engagement, a third factor to consider is the level of aggregation. Thus, for each of the 20 cells in Table 2.1, the engagement score can be for individuals or it can be aggregated at the team, business-unit, or organizational level.

A research agenda for employee engagement targets and referents

Given that so few studies have investigated different targets of employee engagement and most studies have used oneself as the referent, there is much to study and learn about employee engagement targets and referents. Particular attention should be given to measurement, nomological networks of engagement targets, relationships between employee engagement targets, and relationships between employee engagement targets and referents.

Measurement of employee engagement

An important topic for future research is the measurement of different targets and referents of employee engagement. There are several approaches to consider. The most straightforward is to adapt and reword scale items of existing measures of work and job engagement. For example, items from the Job Engagement Scale (Rich et al., 2010), such as "I devote a lot of energy to my job" and "I am enthusiastic about my job," can be used for other targets of engagement by changing "job" to "team," "business unit/department," or "organization." This is in fact how Newton et al. (2020) measured task engagement. They adapted an existing measure of job engagement by changing the target from "job" to "task." In addition, the referent can be changed from oneself to the team, business unit/department, or organization by replacing "I" with "My team/business unit/department/organization" to measure the engagement of one's team, business unit/department, or organization for any particular target.

One measure that seems especially adaptable for use with any target of engagement is the scale designed by Rothbard (2001). She used the same two measures (attention and absorption) for work and family engagement by inserting "family" and "work" in each item (e.g., "I spend a lot of time thinking about my work/family"). These items can be used to measure any target of engagement by inserting the desired target (e.g., "I spend a lot of time thinking about my task/team/business unit/organization") and any referent by replacing "I" with "members of my team/business unit/organization."

A second approach is to preface engagement items with a statement that informs respondents about what they should be thinking about when answering each question (e.g., a certain task, their job, their work group/team, their department, their organization). For example, an opening statement might ask participants to answer each question thinking about their team. The actual items can be based on an existing scale such as Rich et al. (2010) with the word "job" removed (e.g., "I exert my full effort," "I devote a lot of energy," "I feel positive," "My mind is focused," "I am absorbed"). This approach can be used to measure more than one target at a time using the same items. The referent can also be adjusted so that the respondent answers the questions thinking about themselves or members of their team, business unit, or organization.

A final approach is to develop separate scales for each target of engagement. For example, Saks (2006) developed scales to measure job engagement (e.g., "This job is all-consuming; I am totally into it") and organization engagement (e.g., "One of the most exciting things for me is getting involved with things happening in this organization"). The items can be based on the main components of engagement (e.g., physical, emotional, and cognitive dimensions) but refer to a specific target. This type of scale can then be used to measure employee engagement for any target and adjusted to refer to the desired referent (e.g., "One of the most exciting things for me/my team/members of my department/members of my organization is getting involved with things happening in this job/team/department/organization").

A more specific approach might involve identifying the main activities and behaviors associated with the performance of a specific role. For example, if the target is the team, one would identify the main activities that team members perform independent of their actual job. Participants would then be asked to indicate the extent to which they fully and completely immerse and engage themselves in each activity or behavior (e.g., meet with my team to discuss problems) that must be performed by all team members. While this might restrict the use of such a scale to the context in which it is developed, it would be more specific than existing scales of work and job engagement.

Nomological networks of engagement targets

Although we have learned a great deal about the nomological network of work/ job engagement, we know very little about the nomological network of other targets of engagement. Therefore, future research is needed to measure team, business-unit, and organization engagement to learn about their predictors and consequences. It would seem that each target of engagement will be more strongly related to target-relevant predictors and outcomes (e.g., task engagement will predict task performance).

Research is required that not only examines each target of engagement, but also examines several targets of engagement in the same study. This is necessary to identify the antecedents and consequences that are unique to each target of engagement. For example, some antecedents (e.g., positive affect) might be universal and predict all targets of engagement, while other antecedents (e.g., job characteristics) might be more strongly related to one target of engagement (e.g., job/work engagement). Thus, it is important to identify both the unique and common antecedents of different targets of engagement (see Xanthopoulou & Bakker, this volume). It is also important to know the consequences of each target of engagement as it is likely that each target will differ in terms of how strongly related it is to various work outcomes.

Relationships between employee engagement targets

Several studies have shown that different targets of engagement are related and might influence other targets of engagement (e.g., Rothbard, 2001). One area of research that is especially important and interesting is how engagement in one role can influence engagement in other roles. Thus, a key research question is: Does employee engagement in one role or target spill over and foster (or deplete) engagement in other roles and targets?

The results of Rothbard (2001) as well as Newton et al. (2020) suggest that engagement in one target can have a positive or negative effect on engagement in other targets. Future research is needed to examine the extent to which engagement in one target influences engagement in other targets and the conditions and mechanisms (e.g., positive affect) that are responsible for positive and negative spill over effects.

The concept of residual engagement is also worth examining as it suggests that employees who are highly engaged in one target might continue to be engaged in another target to the extent that the positive emotion and feelings engendered when engaged in one target carry or spill over to engagement of other targets. This has important implications for practice as it suggests that employees should first perform a highly engaging role prior to performing a less engaging role so that the second role benefits from the positive affect experienced when performing the first more engaging role. Thus, it might be possible to improve employee work engagement on some tasks by first providing employees with new tasks that are designed to be more engaging (see Boudreau, this volume). The concept of attention residue is also worth investigating as it suggests that some employees might be less engaged in a role if it is difficult to remove themselves from a previous role in which they were highly engaged (Newton et al., 2020).

It would also be worthwhile to test Rothbard's (2001) model of engagement in multiple roles for possible depletion and enrichment effects. For example, if an employee is highly engaged in their work role, will this deplete or enrich their engagement in organization and team roles? Rothbard (2001) developed a testable model of the dynamics of engagement in multiple roles; however, to date it has only been tested for work and family engagement. Future research should test her model and the dynamics of engagement in various roles. Rothbard (2001) noted that her findings indicate that "engagement in multiple roles can be enriching, not just depleting" (p.681). However, until this is tested across multiple roles it remains specific to work and family engagement. Thus, there is much to learn about how employee engagement might increase, decrease, or stay the same during role transitions. Although these dynamic relationships can be investigated using the traditional variable-centered approach used by Rothbard (2001), researchers might also consider a person-centered approach that allows for the identification of groups with different configurations (profiles) of engagement across targets (see McLarnon et al., this volume).

Relationships between targets and referents of employee engagement

The linkages between employee engagement targets and referents is a topic that has not received very much attention. As indicated earlier, only work engagement has been studied using oneself, team members, and co-workers as referents. Future research on targets of engagement should consider different referents as there are many potential linkages within and across targets.

For example, research on different targets of engagement might investigate the extent to which work engagement when oneself is the referent is related to work engagement when the team and members of one's department or organization are the referent. This research is important for understanding how engagement of oneself might translate into engagement for different referents as well as the extent to which the engagement of different referents might influence engagement of oneself.

In addition, research on different targets and referents of engagement might consider the extent to which engagement in one target is related to another target of engagement when the referent is oneself or one's co-workers. For example, if the referent of work engagement is oneself, to what extent is it related to team engagement (or business-unit or organization engagement) when the referent is oneself, the team, the business unit, or the organization? This research might also consider different levels of aggregation and the extent to which engagement at the individual level translates into engagement at higher levels for various targets and referents of engagement. Crossing the targets of engagement with employee engagement referents presents many new avenues for future research on multiple targets and referents of employee engagement which has implications for multi-level and cross-level analysis (see González-Romá, this volume).

Conclusion

We have learned a great deal about work and job engagement over the last two decades, but very little about the extent to which employees are engaged in specific tasks, team-related activities, their business unit, and the organization. Therefore, there is a need for employee engagement research to investigate different targets and referents of employee engagement. This research should not only identify the antecedents and consequences of different targets of engagement, but it should also investigate the relationships between different targets and referents of engagement, and the extent to which engagement in one role has a positive or negative effect on engagement in other roles as well as the mechanisms involved. If employee engagement research is to continue to develop and evolve, future research needs to pay more attention to the targets and referents of employee engagement at different levels of aggregation and take a multidimensional approach to employee engagement research, theory, and practice.

References

Barrick, M. R., Thurgood, G. R., Smith, T. A., and Courtright, S. H. (2015). Collective organizational engagement: Linking motivational antecedents, strategic implementation, and firm performance. *Academy of Management Journal, 58*, 111–135.

Christian, M. S., Garza, A. S., and Slaughter, J. E. (2011). Work engagement: A quantitative review and test of its relations with task and contextual performance. *Personnel Psychology, 64*, 89–136.

Costa, P., Passos, A. M., and Bakker, A. (2014). Empirical validation of the team work engagement construct. *Journal of Personnel Psychology, 13*, 34–45.

Crawford, E. R., LePine, J. A., and Rich, B. L. (2010). Linking job demands and resources to employee engagement and burnout: A theoretical extension and meta-analytic test. *Journal of Applied Psychology, 95*, 834–848.

Farndale, E., Beijer, S. E., Van Veldhoven, M. J. P. M., Kelliher, C., and Hope-Hailey, V. (2014). Work and organization engagement: Aligning research and practice. *Journal of Organizational Effectiveness: People and Performance, 1*, 157–176.

Halbesleben, J. R. B. (2010). A meta-analysis of work engagement: Relationships with burnout, demands, resources, and consequences. In A. B. Bakker and M. P. Leiter (Eds), *Work Engagement: A Handbook of Essential Theory and Research* (pp.102–117). Hove: Psychology Press.

Harter, J. K., Schmidt, F. L., and Hayes, T. L. (2002). Business-unit level relationship between employee satisfaction, employee engagement, and business outcomes: A meta-analysis. *Journal of Applied Psychology, 87*, 268–279.

Juhdi, N., Pa'wan, F., and Hansaram, R. M. K. (2013). HR practices and turnover intention: The mediating roles of organizational commitment and organizational engagement in a selected region in Malaysia. *International Journal of Human Resource Management*, 24, 3002–3019.

Kahn, W. A. (1990). Psychological conditions of personal engagement and disengagement at work. *Academy of Management Journal*, 33, 692–724.

Mahon, E. G., Taylor, S. N., and Boyatzis, R. E. (2014). Antecedents of organizational engagement: Exploring vision, mood and perceived organizational support with emotional intelligence as a moderator. *Frontiers in Psychology*, 5, 1–11.

Malinen, S., Wright, S. and Cammock, P. (2013). What drives organizational engagement? A case study on trust, justice perceptions and withdrawal attitudes. *Evidence-Based HRM: A Global Forum for Empirical Scholarship*, 1, 96–108.

May, D. R., Gilson, R. L., and Harter, L. M. (2004). The psychological conditions of meaningfulness, safety and availability and the engagement of the human spirit at work. *Journal of Occupational and Organizational Psychology*, 77, 11–37.

Newton, D. W., LePine, J. A., Kim, J. K., Wellman, N., and Bush, J. T. (2020). Taking engagement to task: The nature and functioning of task engagement across transitions. *Journal of Applied Psychology*, 105, 1–18.

Rich, B. L., LePine, J. A., and Crawford, E. R. (2010). Job engagement: Antecedents and effects of job performance. *Academy of Management Journal*, 53, 617–635.

Rothbard, N. P. (2001). Enriching or depleting: The dynamics of engagement in work and family roles. *Administrative Science Quarterly*, 46, 655–684.

Saks, A. M. (2006). Antecedents and consequences of employee engagement. *Journal of Managerial Psychology*, 21, 600–619.

Saks, A. M. (2019). Antecedents and consequences of employee engagement revisited. *Journal of Organizational Effectiveness: People and Performance*, 6, 19–38.

Saks, A. M., and Gruman, J. A. (2014). What do we really know about employee engagement? *Human Resource Development Quarterly*, 25, 155–182.

Salanova, M., Agut, S., and Peiro, J. M. (2005). Linking organizational resources and work engagement to employee performance and customer loyalty: The mediation of service climate. *Journal of Applied Psychology*, 90, 1217–1227.

Schaufeli, W. B., Salanova, M., González-Romá, V., and Bakker, A. B. (2002). The measurement of engagement and burnout: A two sample confirmatory factor analytic approach. *Journal of Happiness Studies*, 3, 71–92.

Schneider, B., Yost, A. B., Kropp, A., Kind, C., and Lam, H. (2017). Workforce engagement: What it is, what drives it, and why it matters for organizational performance. *Journal of Organizational Behavior*, 39, 462–480.

Suhartanto, D., and Brien, A. (2018). Multidimensional engagement and store performance: The perspective of frontline retail employees. *International Journal of Productivity and Performance Management*, 67, 809–824.

Torrente, P., Salanova, M., Llorens, S., and Schaufeli, W. B. (2012). Teams make it work: How team work engagement mediates between social resources and performance in teams. *Psicothema*, 24, 106–112.

3. Antecedents and consequences of work engagement: a multilevel nomological net

Despoina Xanthopoulou and Arnold B. Bakker

Most studies on employee work engagement have treated the concept as a relatively persistent work-related motivational state, characterized by vigor, dedication, and absorption (Schaufeli & Bakker, 2010). Engaged employees feel full of energy, are enthusiastic about their work, and often lose track of time when they are working. The typical work engagement study uses a survey design to identify employees scoring high on engagement – an observation that is assumed to be consistent across time and work contexts. However, research over the past two decades has indicated that even employees who are generally highly engaged may have off-days during which they have limited energy, little enthusiasm for their work, and lack of concentration (Sonnentag et al., 2010). Thus, it is currently acknowledged that work engagement can be conceived as a rather stable concept that allows distinguishing engaged from disengaged employees, *and* as a dynamic concept that varies considerably within the same employee across time and situations. The situational approach allows determining when employees exceed or fall behind their average engagement levels (Xanthopoulou & Bakker, 2013). Lately, scholars argued that work engagement can also be defined at the organizational or team level of analysis as a "shared, positive and fulfilling, motivational state of work-related well-being" (Costa et al., 2014a; p. 418), enabling a distinction between highly versus less engaged teams and organizations. Hence, it follows that the antecedents and consequences of collective, individual (i.e., stable) and situational (i.e., variable) work engagement can be found at different – yet interrelated – levels of analysis, namely the organizational/team level (that concerns differences between groups), the person level (that concerns differences between employees), and the situation level (that concerns short-term, within-employee variations), respectively.

To capture this triple nature of work engagement, scholars have adopted a multilevel perspective to determine how more fixed (e.g., organizational resources, team work, personality traits) but also more dynamic (i.e., job-related, socio-emotional, behavioral) factors may explain work engagement, and which are the psychological processes that link its antecedents and consequences across levels of analysis (Bakker, 2015; Bakker & Demerouti, 2018; Daniels, 2006). This multilevel perspective is in line with job demands-resources (JD-R) theory (Bakker & Demerouti, 2017, 2018), which suggests that the characteristics of the work environment that determine work engagement can be found at different, hierarchical levels of analysis. In this chapter, we draw on this theorizing and review existing empirical evidence in order to (1) detect the meaning as well as the predictors and outcomes of work engagement (i.e., its nomological net) at the organizational/team, individual, and situational level of analysis; and (2) unravel the cross-level psychological processes and boundary conditions that explain how factors from different analytical levels interrelate in determining work engagement and its outcomes.

Addressing the first issue is relevant to better understand the multilevel nature of the construct. If the meaning of the concept and the links between work engagement and its predictors and outcomes are not isomorphic across analytical levels, it may mean that collective, individual, and situational engagement capture unique conditions explained by different psychological processes. For example, employees working in a resourceful work environment may generally be more engaged than those working in a suboptimal environment, and perform better because they are generally able and willing to invest considerable effort in their work. However, during episodes when employees are more engaged and absorbed in their task than usual, they may disregard information in the environment that may be particularly relevant for the execution of the task – thus failing to fulfill the task in the best possible way. This potential lack of isomorphism will require reconsideration of the conceptual definition of work engagement, as well as the theorizing explaining its antecedents and consequences at different analytical levels (Kozlowski & Klein, 2000). Addressing the second issue will reveal how factors from different analytical levels may contribute to explain work engagement. By discussing these two issues, our central goal is to identify gaps in our understanding of the multilevel nature of work engagement that may guide future studies.

Antecedents and outcomes of work engagement: a short overview

During the past two decades, JD-R theory (Bakker & Demerouti, 2017, 2018) has dominated research on the predictors and outcomes of work engagement. Accordingly, job resources (i.e., organizational, social, physical, or psychological aspects of one's job that facilitate goal attainment and promote personal growth, learning, and development) and personal resources (i.e., personal beliefs about the control employees can exert on their work environment) are the main drivers of work engagement. The underlying assumption is that employees who have access to high levels of job resources (e.g., autonomy, skill variety, feedback) and who possess personal resources (e.g., self-efficacy, optimism) are likely to find meaning in their work, feel responsible for their work outcomes, and know where they stand at work (Hackman & Oldham, 1980). These critical psychological states satisfy employees' basic needs for autonomy, competence, and belongingness (Deci & Ryan, 2008). When basic psychological needs are satisfied, employees feel autonomously motivated (i.e., engaged), which has a positive impact on job performance and productivity, as well as health and well-being. Another central proposition of JD-R theory is that job and personal resources are particularly relevant for work engagement when they are most needed – namely, when employees are confronted with high levels of job demands. In demanding work conditions, employees are urged to make better use of the available resources, thus boosting their work engagement.

The most recent version of JD-R theory (Bakker & Demerouti, 2017, 2018) also acknowledges that employees are active agents in their work environment and, as such, they make attempts to craft their job characteristics in order to achieve a better job–person fit and find meaning in their work. Accordingly, employees who try to increase the structural (e.g., autonomy) and social (e.g., colleague support) resources in their work environment, to optimize their demands, and to increase their challenges, are likely to become more engaged and perform better. Job crafting results in a more enriched work environment, while it also strengthens employees' personal resources and volition. Further, JD-R theory assumes that engaged employees are more likely to use such job-crafting strategies producing a positive reinforcing cycle.

Previous empirical studies on work engagement provided strong support for the main assumptions of JD-R theory (Bakker & Demerouti, 2017, 2018). For instance, meta-analytical evidence showed that job and personal resources are the core antecedents of work engagement (Crawford et al., 2010), and that engagement relates to enhanced performance and well-being (Christian & Slaughter, 2007; Halbesleben, 2010; Nahrang et al., 2011). Furthermore, recent meta-analyses (Lichtenthaler & Fischbach, 2019; Oprea et al., 2019; Rudolph et al., 2017) revealed that job crafting in the form of increasing job, structural, and social resources and increasing challenges relates positively to work engagement and job performance. In contrast, job crafting in the form of reducing (instead of optimizing) job demands relates negatively to work engagement and job performance. Also, Lichtenthaler and Fischbach (2019) found that engaged employees are more likely to actively increase their job resources and look for more challenges at work. Although these meta-analyses used evidence from both between- and within-person studies, they did not account for the relationships between work engagement and its antecedents and outcomes across different levels of analysis.

Numerous studies have investigated the antecedents and outcomes of collective, individual (i.e., stable) and situational (i.e., variable) work engagement. At the collective level, Costa et al. (2015) showed common perceptions of team members' job resources to relate positively with collective (i.e., team) work engagement and consequently, to team performance. Similarly, Barrick et al. (2015) found motivating work design, human resources management (HRM) practices, and CEO leadership to relate positively with collective organizational engagement, which associated positively to firm performance. At the individual (i.e., stable) level, there is evidence suggesting that relatively stable organizational resources (e.g., psychosocial safety climate, organizational support; see Albrecht, this volume) and individual characteristics that function as personal resources (see Hough & Oswald, this volume) enhance employees' stable work engagement that, in turn, contributes positively to job performance and overall employee well-being (see Halbesleben and also Salanova, this volume). Finally, at the situational level, evidence reveals that on days employees have access to or actively seek job resources, they are more engaged in their work and perform better (for a review, see Bakker, 2014). In addition, on interesting and challenging workdays (Tadić Vujčić et al., 2017), on days employees feel recovered from previous-days' effort (Sonnentag, 2003), or on days they take short recovery breaks during work (Kühnel et al., 2017), employees report higher levels of vigor, dedication, and absorption.

Despite the relevance of this empirical evidence within levels, studies on work engagement across different levels of analysis (i.e., organizational/team, individual, and situational level) are still scarce. In the following sections, we review empirical evidence with the aim to address certain emerging multilevel issues. Do collective, individual (i.e., stable), and situational (i.e., variable) work engagement mean the same? Are the causes and consequences of engagement at each level similar? How do psychological processes unfold across different levels of analysis in explaining work engagement, and under which boundary conditions are these processes more likely to occur?

Multilevel work engagement: investigating the nomological net

When trying to understand the concept of work engagement from a multilevel perspective, it is important to account for two issues. The first is to address the factorial invariance of the work engagement construct across levels of analysis. The second is to determine the antecedents and consequences of engagement at the different analytical levels.

When it comes to the issue of factorial invariance, studies that operationalized work engagement as a motivational state characterized by vigor, dedication, and absorption have used the Utrecht Work Engagement Scale (UWES; Schaufeli et al., 2006) to measure the construct as a collective experience, as a stable individual experience, and as a variable, situational state. The UWES includes three items for each of the three underlying dimensions: vigor (e.g., "At my work, I feel strong and vigorous"), dedication (e.g., "I am enthusiastic about my work"), and absorption (e.g., "I am immersed in my work"). Since the scale was initially developed to capture work engagement as a rather stable experience, items ask how employees *generally* feel regarding their work. However, the scale items have been adapted to capture within-person variations in work engagement either on a weekly (e.g., "Last week at work, I felt strong and vigorous"; Bakker & Bal, 2010), daily (e.g., "Today at work, I felt strong and vigorous"; Sonnentag, 2003), or even momentary (e.g., "Right now, I feel strong and vigorous in my work"; Bledow et al., 2011) level. Also, the UWES items have been adapted to capture collective experiences of vigor (e.g., "At our work, we feel strong and vigorous"), dedication (e.g., "We are proud of the work we do"), and absorption (e.g., "We get carried away when we are working") within teams that were then aggregated to the team level of analysis (Costa et al., 2014b). Thus, the question is whether the construct captured with the general version of the UWES means the same as the constructs captured with the situational and collective versions.

To answer this question, Breevaart et al. (2010) performed a multilevel factor analytic study on the situational version of the UWES. The authors pooled data from three different diary studies among a total of 271 Dutch employees, where situational (i.e., daily) work engagement was assessed with an adaptation of the UWES across five workdays. Results of multilevel confirmatory factor analyses revealed that the model that captured the proposed three-factor structure across levels of analysis (i.e., the between-person and within-person levels) was the best-fitting model. Furthermore, factor loadings and factor correlations were significant and in the expected direction at both levels, while partial metric invariance across levels of analysis was also supported. Support for partial metric invariance indicates that employees generally perceive the UWES items assessing stable work engagement in the same way as the UWES items assessing situational (i.e., variable) work engagement. Thus, the concept of work engagement, as measured with the UWES, means the same across the individual and situational levels of analysis.

However, when it comes to the factorial invariance of work engagement across individuals and teams, research evidence is not straightforward. Costa et al. (2014b) adapted the UWES scale at the team level (e.g., "In our work, we feel bursting with energy") and used aggregated scores of individual employees to test the factor structure of the instrument. They found that, at the team level, the one-factor structure fit better to the data than the hypothesized three-factor structure. These findings question whether individual and collective work engagement are the same constructs. However, although Costa and colleagues tested the factor structure of team work engagement (by using aggregated scores), they did not test factorial invariance across analytical levels (team vs individual) by means of multilevel confirmatory factor analysis. Thus, studies that use more elaborate statistical techniques are needed to shed light on the invariance of the collective work engagement construct.

As concerns evidence on the predictors and outcomes of work engagement across analytical levels, we were only able to locate two studies that simultaneously tested the same relationships between work engagement and its predictors across teams (i.e., work units) and individuals. Huhtala et al. (2015) investigated whether an organization's ethical culture related to work engagement at both the individual and the work-unit levels. They collected data from more than 2,000 employees working in 245 different work units in one public sector organization. Results of multilevel structural equation modeling (MSEM) analyses revealed that shared perceptions of ethical culture related positively (standardized estimate = 0.81, $p < 0.001$) to shared experiences of work engagement at the work-unit level, while individual perceptions of ethical culture related positively to individual work engagement (standardized estimate = 0.40, $p < 0.001$) at the individual level of analysis. Watanabe and Yamauchi (2018), in their study among over 1,000 nurses nested in 54 wards in four hospitals in Japan, investigated the reasons why nurses work overtime and how this relates to their work engagement. MSEM results showed that involuntary overtime work due to high workload related negatively to engagement both at the ward (standardized estimate = -0.44, $p < 0.05$) and at the individual (standardized estimate = -0.11, $p < 0.05$) level. However, involuntary overtime work due to conformity pressure (i.e., overtime generated from implicit pressures from supervisors/colleagues) associated negatively to engagement at the individual level (standardized estimate = -0.12, $p < 0.05$), but was unrelated to engagement at the ward level (standardized estimate = 0.05, $p > 0.05$). All in all, these findings suggest that the favorable role of organizational ethical culture for work engagement holds across levels of analysis. This is in line with JD-R theory (Bakker & Demerouti, 2017, 2018) since ethical culture is an organizational resource that may promote employee motivation and engagement. However, results are mixed when it comes to the role of demanding work aspects, suggesting that job demands may matter differently for work engagement at different analytical levels (for a further discussion, see Xanthopoulou & Bakker, 2013).

Given the relevance of work engagement for employees and organizations, it was surprising to find only two empirical studies that simultaneously tested the same antecedents of work engagement across levels and no studies on the invariance of the relationship between work engagement and its outcomes across analytical levels. Hence, it is not possible to make safe conclusions as to whether the links between engagement, its antecedents, and its consequences are invariant across analytical levels. Based on JD-R theory (Bakker & Demerouti, 2017, 2018), we would expect isomorphic relationships across levels of analysis. However, given the very small body of research to date, future studies should shed light on the issue of isomorphism of the operational definition, as well as the causes and consequences (i.e., the nomological net), of work engagement across levels of analysis by investigating whether different findings across levels are true or attributed to methodological artifacts (e.g., use of only self-report measures instead of combining different sources of information across levels). To this end, it is necessary to test the investigated processes simultaneously across the different levels of analysis by using advanced MSEM techniques (see González-Romá, this volume).

Cross-level processes and boundary conditions

Our second aim with this chapter is to unravel the psychological processes and boundary conditions that explain how causes from different analytical levels interrelate in determining work engagement and its outcomes. To this end, we focused on empirical studies that investigated cross-level mediating processes, and cross-level moderators in explaining work engagement.

Cross-level mediating processes

As concerns the mediating processes that develop across levels of analysis in explaining work engagement, as well as its causes and consequences, empirical studies have mainly supported theoretical propositions that endorse a multilevel framework in their analysis (e.g., Bakker & Demerouti, 2018; Daniels, 2006). For instance, Daniels (2006) distinguished job characteristics into latent (i.e., institutional, social, or technological developments that refer to the macro level), perceived (i.e., employees' overall perceptions of the work environment that refer to the individual level) and enacted (i.e., events and activities at work as they happen that capture the situation level). Further, he suggested that latent job characteristics form employees' overall perceptions of their job that – in turn – stimulate them to endorse those characteristics that they think are part (or should be part) of their job, determining how they feel at a specific moment. Similarly, Bakker and Demerouti (2018) suggested that high performance HR practices may promote a positive organizational climate and enhance organizational performance, and that this positive process at the organizational level of analysis may promote resources at the team level of analysis (e.g., quality coaching from the leader, that may in turn determine team members' work engagement levels).

In line with these theoretical propositions, studies accounting for cross-level effects showed that resources at the organizational/team level of analysis, such as empowering leadership as measured by the leaders (Tuckey et al., 2012) or authentic leadership rated by leaders (Penger & Černe, 2014) and by both leaders and employees (Hsien & Wang, 2015), enhanced individual team members' work engagement through the enrichment of their work environment (e.g., increases in cognitive resources, challenges, perceived support, or trust). Similarly, a study among 511 employees nested in 88 teams showed that the quality of the leader–member exchange relationship (rated by the followers) mediated the positive link between leader work engagement and followers' work engagement, while followers' engagement was consequently related to enhanced follower performance and reduced turnover intentions (Gutermann et al., 2017). Tims et al. (2013) studied the consequences of job crafting at the team level, using the referent-shift model. Their study among 525 employees working in 54 teams showed that seeking resources and challenges at the team level stimulated team work engagement, which, in turn, facilitated individual team performance through the enhancement of individual vigor. In a weekly diary study, van Woerkom et al. (2016) found that support for strengths use from the organization (i.e., employees' overall beliefs regarding the extent to which the organization supports them actively to use their strengths at work) improved employees' weekly actual strengths' use, which, in turn, promoted their weekly self-efficacy beliefs, work engagement, and proactive behaviors.

Importantly, a few studies indicated that work engagement at lower levels of analysis may explain engagement and performance at higher levels of analysis. For instance, Bakker and Oerlemans (2019) in their study of work episodes found that daily job-crafting strategies of seeking job resources facilitated employees' momentary basic need satisfaction that, in turn, enhanced momentary work engagement which related positively to work engagement at the day level. Also, Ogbonnaya and Valizade (2018) used secondary data from the British National Health Service and showed that the negative relationship between high-performance work practices and staff absenteeism (both assessed at the organizational level of analysis) was mediated by work engagement and job satisfaction at the individual level.

In sum, with regard to cross-level mediating processes research evidence so far suggests that resourceful working conditions at the collective and the individual level may explain collective-, individual-, and situational-level outcomes through the enhancement of individual or situational (i.e., variable) work engagement. Importantly, it is also evident that resourceful working conditions at the situational (i.e., variable) level of analysis may enhance employees' stable work engagement via an increased frequency of work engagement episodes.

Cross-level moderators

The role of moderators is important for theory development because it helps understanding under which conditions work engagement is more likely to occur, or more likely to result in favorable outcomes for employees and organizations. First, leadership style seems to be a relevant moderator that determines when (job and personal) resources are particularly relevant for employee engagement. Zhang et al. (2017) studied 324 employees nested in 74 groups of high-technology companies in China and found that employees' core self-evaluations (i.e., personal resources) related positively to their work engagement particularly when their leaders had higher (vs lower) levels of psychological capital (i.e., hope, self-efficacy, resilience, and optimism). Thus, mutually high levels of personal resources in leaders and employees boosted employees' work engagement. Tuckey et al. (2012) came to similar conclusions after they found evidence for a three-way interaction effect suggesting that follower work engagement was highest under conditions of high follower cognitive demands, high cognitive resources, and simultaneously high empowering leadership (as rated by the leaders).

Second, employee individual differences have been found to moderate the within-person processes explaining variations in engagement. In line with the main assumptions of JD-R theory (Bakker & Demerouti, 2017, 2018), this evidence generally suggests that job and personal resources may reinforce or substitute for each other in explaining work engagement, and that they are particularly relevant when combined with job or individual demands. Bakker et al. (2019b) followed 87 Norwegian naval cadets for 30 consecutive workdays and found a three-way interaction suggesting that daily strengths' use (i.e., use of those individual characteristics that allow goal attainment) related positively to daily work engagement, particularly for those cadets characterized by lower levels of neuroticism and higher levels of extraversion (see Hough & Oswald, this volume). Also, Bakker et al. (2019a) conducted a weekly diary study in which they followed 185 employees who had experienced a major life event in the previous year (e.g., health problem, death of a family member, divorce). They found a three-way interaction suggesting that weekly self-efficacy (i.e., personal resource) related positively to weekly work engagement only for those employees who experienced high detachment from the major life event that week and who generally considered work a central component of their lives. Finally, scholars showed that weekly job-crafting strategies (i.e., increasing social and structural job resources and challenging job demands) related positively to weekly work engagement for those employees who were characterized by higher (vs lower) levels of occupational role salience (i.e., one's belief that one's work is an important determinant of self-definition; Petrou et al., 2017), and lower (vs higher) impression-management motives (i.e., employees' efforts to present a favorable image to others; Rofcanin et al., 2019).

In summary, as concerns cross-level moderators, studies suggest that resource availability at the collective level of analysis boosts the positive relationship between resources and work engagement at the individual level of analysis. Also, individual characteristics or experiences may determine the strength or the direction of the relationship between situational antecedents and variations in work engagement.

A cross-level model guiding future research on work engagement

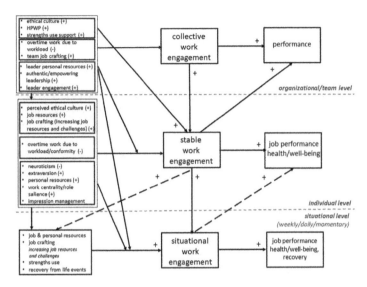

Figure 3.1   Work engagement: a multilevel nomological net

Note: Solid lines represent relationships that have been supported by empirical data from cross-levels studies presented in this chapter. Dotted lines represent theory-based relationships that are yet to be tested. HPWP = high-performance work practices.

Figure 3.1 summarizes the presented evidence on cross-level mediating processes that explain how engagement unfolds across levels of analysis, as well as the boundary conditions (i.e., moderators) that determine when engagement is more or less likely to occur. Solid lines in Figure 3.1 correspond to relationships that have been supported by empirical evidence presented in this chapter. Dotted lines represent effects that have not yet been tested with empirical data but are relevant from a theoretical point of view. For instance, it seems plausible that individual (i.e., stable) levels of work engagement may enhance situational (e.g., daily) work engagement and performance via the improvement of daily job and personal resources. Furthermore, high levels of situational (i.e., daily or momentary) work engagement may be generalized to the individual level, promoting overall performance and physical and psychological health and well-being. Similarly, it is important to test collective resources (e.g., HRM practices) that have been found to enhance collective engagement as moderators of the relationships between individual- and situational-level resources and work engagement (see Barrick et al., 2015). Hence, the nomological net presented in Figure 3.1 may be used as a basis for future studies aiming to further support the proposed relationships across the different levels of analysis, as well as to extend this net by pointing out additional links that will advance our understanding of the development of the construct across analytical levels.

Next to extending these within- and cross-level relationships, future studies should also shed light on the issue of invariance of work engagement across analytical levels. The issue of invariance concerns both the operational definition of engagement across the collective level, the individual level, and the situational level, and the invariance of the relationships linking work engagement with its causes and consequences. As concerns the former, the empirical evidence presented in this chapter suggests that work engagement has the same factorial structure (i.e., means the same) across the individual and situational level of analysis. However, evidence of invariance across the collective and individual levels is weak since no study so far has addressed the factorial structure of engagement across these two levels simultaneously. Therefore, future empirical endeavors should address this gap in the literature. As concerns the latter issue, the studies that test the invariance of the same psychological processes across different levels of analysis simultaneously are very limited. Thus, scholars should apply elaborate methodological and statistical approaches (see González-Romá, this volume) and should preferably make use of data from different sources (e.g., objective organizational indicators, leaders, individual employees) whenever possible to test not only whether the same causes and consequences relate in a similar way with work engagement across levels, but also whether the strength of these relationships varies across levels. Such evidence is necessary in order to conclude whether relationships are isomorphic or not across analytical levels and whether a shift in the theoretical paradigm of work engagement is needed or not (Kozlowski & Klein, 2000).

Overall conclusion

In this chapter, we reviewed recent studies on the multilevel nature of work engagement in order to determine the state of art. We synthesized this evidence in a multilevel nomological model outlining how various predictors at the organizational/team, individual, and situational levels interrelate in explaining work engagement and the resulting outcomes at different levels of analysis. Based on our review of the literature, we identified gaps in our understanding of the multilevel nature of work engagement. We hope that our analysis will stimulate cross-level studies that will address these gaps and help organizations and employees to stay energized and enthusiastic at work.

References

Bakker, A.B. (2014). Daily fluctuations in work engagement: An overview and current directions. *European Psychologist, 19*, 227–236.

Bakker, A.B. (2015). Towards a multilevel approach of employee well-being. *European Journal of Work and Organizational Psychology, 24*, 839–843.

Bakker, A.B., and Bal, P.M. (2010). Weekly work engagement and performance: A study among starting teachers. *Journal of Occupational and Organizational Psychology, 83*, 189–206.

Bakker, A.B., and Demerouti, E. (2017). Job demands-resources theory: Taking stock and looking forward. *Journal of Occupational Health Psychology, 22*, 273–285.

Bakker, A.B., and Demerouti, E. (2018). Multiple levels in job demands-resources theory: Implications for employee well-being and performance. In E. Diener, S. Oishi, and L. Tay (Eds), *Handbook of Wellbeing*. Salt Lake City, UT: DEF.

Bakker, A.B., Du, D., and Derks, D. (2019a). Major life events and family life, work engagement, and performance: A test of the work-home resources model. *International Journal of Stress Management, 26*, 238–249.

Bakker, A.B., Hetland, J., Kjellevold Olsen, O., and Espevik, R. (2019b). Daily strengths use and employee well-being: The moderating role of personality. *Journal of Occupational and Organizational Psychology, 92*, 144–168.

Bakker, A.B., and Oerlemans, W.G.M. (2019). Daily job crafting and momentary work engagement: A self-determination and self-regulation perspective. *Journal of Vocational Behavior, 112*, 417–430.

Barrick, M.R., Thurgood, G.R., Smith, T.A., and Courtright, S.H. (2015). Collective organizational engagement: Linking motivational antecedents, strategic implementation, and firm performance. *Academy of Management Journal, 58*(1), 111–135. http://dx.doi.org/10.5465/amj.2013.0227.

Bledow, R., Schmitt, A., Frese, M., and Kühnel, J. (2011). The affective shift model of work engagement. *Journal of Applied Psychology, 96*, 1246–1257.

Breevaart, K., Bakker, A.B., Demerouti, E., and Hetland, J. (2010). The measurement of state work engagement: A multilevel factor analytic study. *European Journal of Psychological Assessment, 28*, 305–312.

Christian, M.S., and Slaughter, J. (2007). Work engagement: A meta-analytic review and directions for research in an emerging area. *Academy of Management Proceedings, 1*, 1–6.

Costa, P., Passos, A.M., and Bakker, A.B. (2014a). Team work engagement: A model of emergence. *Journal of Occupational and Organizational Psychology, 87*, 414–436.

Costa, P., Passos, A.M., and Bakker, A.B. (2014b). Empirical validation of the team work engagement construct. *Journal of Personnel Psychology, 13*, 34–45.

Costa, P., Passos, A.M., and Bakker, A.B. (2015). Direct and contextual influence of team conflict on team resources, team work engagement, and team performance. *Negotiation and Conflict Management Research, 8*, 211–227.

Crawford, E.R., LePine, J., and Rich, B.L. (2010). Linking job demands and resources to employee engagement and burnout: A theoretical extension and meta-analytic test. *Journal of Applied Psychology, 95*, 834–848.

Daniels, K. (2006). Rethinking job characteristics in work stress research. *Human Relations, 59*, 267–290.

Deci, E.L., and Ryan, R.M. (2008). Self-determination theory: A macrotheory of human motivation, development and health. *Canadian Psychology, 49*, 182–185.

Gutermann, D., Lehmann-Willenbrock, N., Boer, D., Born, M., and Voelpel, S.C. (2017). How leaders affect followers' work engagement and performance: Integrating leader-member exchange and crossover theory. *British Journal of Management, 28*, 299–314.

Hackman, J.R., and Oldham, G.R. (1980). *Work Redesign*. Reading, MA: Addison Wesley.

Halbesleben, J.R.B. (2010). A meta-analysis of work engagement: Relationships with burnout, demands, resources, and consequences. In A.B. Bakker and M.P. Leiter (Eds), *Work Engagement: A Handbook of Essential Theory and Research* (pp. 102–117). New York: Psychology Press.

Hsien, C.-C., and Wang, D.-S. (2015). Does supervisor-perceived authentic leadership influence employee work engagement through employee-perceived authentic leadership and employee trust? *International Journal of Human Resource Management, 26*, 2329–2348.

Huhtala, M., Tolvanen, A., Mauno, S., and Feldt, T. (2015). The associations between ethical organizational culture, burnout, and engagement: A multilevel study. *Journal of Business Psychology, 30*, 399–414.

Kozlowski, S.W.J., and Klein, K.J. (2000). A multilevel approach to theory and research in organizations: Contextual, temporal, and emergent processes. In K.J. Klein and S.W.J. Kozlowski (Eds), *Multilevel Theory, Research, and Methods in Organizations: Foundations, Extensions, and New Directions* (pp. 3–90). San Francisco: Jossey-Bass.

Kühnel, J., Zacher, H., de Bloom, J., and Bledow, R. (2017). Take a break! Benefits of sleep and short breaks for daily work engagement. *European Journal of Work & Organizational Psychology, 26*, 481–491.

Lichtenthaler, P.W., and Fischbach, A. (2019). A meta-analysis on promotion- and prevention-focused job crafting. *European Journal of Work & Organizational Psychology, 28*, 30–50.

Nahrang, J.D., Morgeson, F.P., and Hofmann, D.A. (2011). Safety at work: A meta-analytical investigation of the link between job demands, job resources, burnout, engagement, and safety outcomes. *Journal of Applied Psychology, 96*, 71–94.

Ogbonnaya, C., and Valizade, D. (2018). High performance work practices, employee outcomes and organizational performance: A 2–1–2 multilevel mediation analysis. *International Journal of Human Resource Management, 29*, 239–259.

Oprea, B.T., Barzin, L., Vrîgă, D., Iliescu, D., and Rusu, A. (2019). Effectiveness of job crafting interventions: A meta-analysis and utility analysis. *European Journal of Work & Organizational Psychology, 28*, 723–741.

Penger, S., and Černe, M. (2014). Authentic leadership, employees' job satisfaction and work engagement: A hierarchical linear modeling approach. *Economic Research, 27*, 508–526.

Petrou, P., Bakker, A.B., and van den Heuvel, M. (2017). Weekly job crafting and leisure crafting: Implications for meaning-making and work engagement. *Journal of Occupational and Organizational Psychology, 90*, 129–152.

Rofcanin, Y., Bakker, A.B., Berber, A., and Gölgeci, I. (2019). Relational job crafting: Exploring the role of employee motivate with a weekly diary study. *Human Relations, 72,* 859–886.

Rudolph, C.W., Katz, I.M., Lavigne, K.N., and Zacher, H. (2017). Job crafting: A meta-analysis of relationships with individual differences, job characteristics, and work outcomes. *Journal of Vocational Behavior, 102,* 112–138.

Schaufeli, W.B., and Bakker, A.B. (2010). Defining and measuring work engagement: Bringing clarity to the concept. In A.B. Bakker and M.P. Leiter (Eds), *Work Engagement: A Handbook of Essential Theory and Research* (pp. 10–24). New York: Psychology Press.

Schaufeli, W.B., Bakker, A.B., and Salanova, M. (2006). The measurement of work engagement with a short questionnaire: A cross-national study. *Educational and Psychological Measurement, 66,* 701–716.

Sonnentag, S. (2003). Recovery, work engagement, and proactive behavior: A new look at the interface between nonwork and work. *Journal of Applied Psychology, 88,* 518–528.

Sonnentag, S., Dormann, C., and Demerouti, E. (2010). Not all days are created equal: The concept of state work engagement. In A.B. Bakker and M.P. Leiter (Eds), *Work Engagement: A Handbook of Essential Theory and Research* (pp. 25–38). New York: Psychology Press.

Tadić Vujčić, M., Oerlemans, W.G.M., and Bakker, A.B. (2017). How challenging was your work today? The role of autonomous work motivation. *European Journal of Work & Organizational Psychology, 26,* 81–93.

Tims, M., Bakker, A.B., Derks, D., and van Rhenen, W. (2013). Job crafting at the team and individual level: Implications for work engagement and performance. *Group & Organizational Management, 38,* 427–454.

Tuckey, M.R., Bakker, A.B., and Dollard, M.F. (2012). Empowering leaders optimize working conditions for engagement: A multilevel study. *Journal of Occupational Health Psychology, 17,* 15–27.

Van Woerkom, M., Oerlemans, W., and Bakker, A.B. (2016). Strengths use and work engagement: A weekly diary study. *European Journal of Work and Organizational Psychology, 25,* 384–397.

Watanabe, M., and Yamauchi, K. (2018). The effect of quality of overtime work on nurses' mental health and work engagement. *Journal of Nursing Management, 26,* 679–688.

Xanthopoulou, D., and Bakker, A.B. (2013). State work engagement: The significance of within-person fluctuations. In A.B. Bakker and K. Daniels (Eds), *A Day in the Life of a Happy Worker* (pp. 25–40). Hove: Psychology Press.

Zhang, L., Zhang, N., and Qui, Y. (2017). Positive group affective tone and employee work engagement: A multilevel investigation. *Social Behavior and Personality, 45,* 1905–1918.

4. Work engagement: a key to HEROs – healthy and resilient organizations

Marisa Salanova

Pablo Picasso, a Spanish painter and sculptor who was born in 1881 in Malaga, had a curious way of referring to himself when he was absorbed in his art: "When I paint, the brush paints alone." Obviously, it is not literally possible for the "brush to paint alone". There is an actor (Pablo Picasso) who drives it, gives it life. Picasso was a genius and loved his job; painting was his life's purpose – indeed, he was "work engaged". However, it is not necessary to be Picasso to experience work engagement. This psychological experience is more common than it may seem at first glance, and researchers have been busy documenting it in recent years, as shown in this inspiring book. However, work engagement is also a collective experience that occurs in today's organizations, and it is a crucial element in so-called HEROs (healthy and resilient organizations) – that being the topic of this chapter.

Positive organizational psychology and work engagement

From its beginnings, psychology has basically focused on the study of pathologies and disorders, and this negative orientation, based on the traditional medical model, has given rise to a theoretical framework of a *pathogenic* nature, focused on remedy and recovery. In Positive Psychology, begun in 1998 when Professor Martin Seligman delivered his speech as president of the American Psychological Association (APA), a new framework emerged emphasizing positive psychological characteristics and human strengths. Adapted to a work context, Positive "Organizational" Psychology (POP) is the scientific study of the optimal functioning of people in organizations at different levels of analysis. The study of POP at work aims to describe, explain, and predict optimal performance at individual, group, leader and organizational (IGLO) levels by cultivating organizational well-being (Salanova, 2020a; Salanova et al., 2016, 2019). The ultimate goal of POP is to discover the characteristics of a "full organizational life" at the IGLO levels. To this end, it seeks to answer two key questions: How do employees experience positive organizations, and what are the attributes of positive organizations?

Based on previous research, I consider engagement to be a key indicator of employee health, specifically work-related psychological well-being, at all IGLO levels of analysis. Some researchers consider "health" and "well-being" in a broader sense, sometimes referring to both mental and physical attributes as a single entity, while others explicitly see them as separate constructs. In this chapter, I use the terms "health" and "well-being" interchangeably as they apply at all IGLO levels of analysis. And, to repeat, I consider employee engagement to be a key indicator of such well-being. The vast research literature on generic health and well-being takes into account different facets of health/well-being like physical (physical symptoms and physical illnesses and diseases), psychological (mental/emotional, like positive/negative emotional states, satisfaction, strain, burnout, thriving, and engagement), and social well-being (i.e., fairness, positive relationship, social support). While that breadth is attractive at a molar level of thinking, consistent with the theme of this book, I focus in this chapter on engagement as a key indicator of well-being, and seek to identify antecedents, consequences, and correlates at IGLO levels of analysis.

Work engagement is an indicator of, and a key facet of, organizational well-being in the HERO Model I will explore here. In that sense, I agree with Bakker et al. (2008), who defined work engagement as: "a positive, fulfilling affective-motivational state of *work-related well-being* that is characterized by vigor, dedication, and absorption" (p. 187; emphasis added). Thus, work engagement is a facet of organizational well-being because this "positive state" integrates the motivational and affective-cognitive components identified by Bakker et al.

Vigor is characterized by high levels of energy and resilience while working, the willingness to invest effort in one's work, and persistence in work activity, even in the midst of difficulties. Dedication refers to being strongly involved in one's work and experiencing a sense of transcendence, enthusiasm, inspiration, pride, and challenge. Finally, absorption is characterized by the person fully concentrating while working and enjoying the activity such that time "flies by" and they have difficulty disconnecting from work. In accord with this conceptualization of work engagement, the Utrecht Work Engagement Scale (UWES) was developed and has been used widely (Schaufeli et al., 2002, 2006), revealing good psychometric properties (Schaufeli & Bakker, 2020). We have used the UWES extensively in our work to measure engagement at multiple levels.

Work engagement can also be shared by team members as an index of (collective) team engagement (Schaufeli & Salanova, 2011; Torrente et al., 2012). This sharedness of engagement can occur through an emotional contagion process defined as "the tendency to automatically imitate and synchronize facial expressions, vocalizations, postures, and movements with those of another person and, therefore, to converge together" (Hatfield et al., 1994). We have shown the existence of team engagement in studies of more than 200 work units and their leaders. This research reveals that team engagement is activated by the presence of social resources shared by the team (i.e., coordination, teamwork, social support) and results in high in-role and extra-role performance (Cruz et al., 2013; Gracia et al., 2013; Salanova et al., 2011; Torrente et al., 2012, 2013). Individual as well as collective team engagement are key elements of HEROs; that is the topic we turn to next.

HEROs and work engagement

HEROs are defined as

> those organizations that make systematic, planned, and proactive efforts to improve employees' and organizational processes and outcomes … [and] that involve carrying out healthy organizational resources and practices aimed at improving the work environment at the levels of (a) the task (autonomy, feedback), (b) the interpersonal (social relationships, transformational leadership), and (c) the organization (HR practices), especially during turbulence and times of change. (Salanova et al., 2012, p. 788)

HEROs are hypothesized to be able to not only survive but to thrive in turbulent periods such as economic crises, critical internal changes, or even a pandemic like Covid-19. They do this by having resilient employees, groups, and leaders who are able to learn so that the organization can emerge even stronger (healthier) from these situations (Salanova, 2020b). HEROs are hypothesized to be resilient because they are able to effectively confront challenging circumstances and be strengthened by being effective in adverse situations. That is, they not only adjust to the turbulence, but also develop the ability to identify the need and to take action for change to meet future challenges (Salanova et al., 2012; 2019; see also Albrecht, this volume).

The HERO Model serves as a heuristic for both research and practice from a holistic, comprehensive, positive, and multi-level (i.e., IGLO) perspective. In practice, the HERO methodology is co-creative and participative, meaning that different stakeholders (i.e., executives, supervisors, employees, and customers) are important partners in the assessment, implementation, and data-dissemination process. Importantly, this process is followed up with the development of healthy action-research programs to influence organizational policies and eventually organizational culture. As shown in Figure 4.1, the HERO Model has three main interrelated components: (a) healthy cross-level organizational resources and practices, (b) healthy employees, and (c) healthy cross-level organizational outcomes (Salanova et al., 2012), as described below.

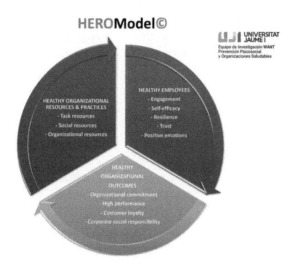

Figure 4.1   The HERO Model (Salanova et al., 2012)

1. *Healthy cross-level organizational resources and practices* include task resources (e.g., autonomy, variety), social environment (e.g., social support, transformational leadership), and organizational practices (e.g., work–life balance, equity and inclusion, wellness programs).
2. *Healthy employees* are characterized by engagement, resilience, self-efficacy, trust, and positive affect, with engagement being of central importance.
3. *Healthy cross-organizational outcomes* include in-role and extra-role performance along with other indicators of effectiveness (e.g., service quality, objective financial performance, commitment, customer loyalty), and positive relationships with the environment and the community.

Data on the HERO Model are collected from different respondents at multiple (IGLO) levels in an organization (e.g., CEOs, teams' immediate supervisors, employees, and customers). In-role and extra-role performance are assessed by team members and immediate supervisors, while organizational performance is assessed using quantitative (questionnaires) and qualitative (interviews and focus groups) methods, as well as with objective performance indicators (of quality, of financial outcomes) (Llorens et al., 2013).

Because of HEROs' multi-level focus, care is taken in data-gathering to reflect those different levels (see González-Romá, this volume). For example, survey items are worded to reflect the specific level of interest, such as the work unit (e.g., "In my work unit, we are coordinated with each other") or organization (e.g., "In this company there are practices to facilitate the workers' work–family balance"). Such care in assessment permits establishing linkages among different levels in the HERO Model based on team/organizational perceptions and experiences over time. Gathering these kinds of IGLO data permits the use of multi-level models in order to test within- and cross-level relationships among variables of the HERO Model (see Xanthopoulou & Bakker, this volume). The following provides some examples.

At the *individual level*, Lisbona et al. (2018) showed that employee engagement is a relevant driver of positive individual outcomes in organizations such as personal initiative, which, in turn, influences individual job performance. Indeed, Lisbona et al. also showed an indirect effect of employee engagement on individual performance through personal initiative in two different studies, one cross-sectional and the other longitudinal. In both studies, high levels of engagement led to higher personal initiative, which, in turn, led to higher individual job performance.

Focusing on the *group level*, Torrente et al. (2012) showed that team social resources (such as social support climate, coordination, and teamwork) were significant antecedents of team aggregate engagement. This project involved data on 533 employees nested within 62 teams and 13 organizations. In combination, the aggregate antecedents of team engagement might be said to form a kind of engagement climate (Albrecht, this volume). Also at the team level of analysis, Rodríguez-Sánchez et al. (2017) showed that team work engagement is an important mediator in explaining how team cohesion leads to team performance in creative tasks over time. This longitudinal team-level simulation project involved 18 project teams (composed of 605 individuals).

At the *organizational level* of analysis, Gracia et al. (2013) studied a sample of 107 Spanish tourist establishments involving 615 service workers and 2,165 customers. The purpose of this project was to explore engagement as a mediator of the relationship between organizational resources provided to workers (i.e., training opportunities, autonomy, and technical support) and customers' perceptions of service quality. The results revealed that when organizations are seen as providing employees with sufficient resources this (a) leads to aggregate feelings of engagement, which in turn result in (b) collective feelings of competence (more empathic with the customer and more extra-role behaviors), and (c) customers' perceptions of superior service quality. Also, using multi-level models, we showed that organizational practices (i.e., improving psychosocial health and developing team workers' skills and careers) at the organizational level are positively associated with team work engagement (at the group level) (Acosta et al., 2013).

We have also done more work on multi-level models now involving the *leaders level*. In multi-level modeling, issues at one level can influence issues at other levels (González-Romá, this volume). For example, Martínez et al. (in press), in a study of 1,079 employees nested in 124 work teams, found significant cross-level effects of leadership (at the leader level) on individual-level work engagement. When employees feel emotionally overloaded, there are leader behaviors that relieve the potential negative impact on follower levels of engagement. Also, we showed that transformational leadership (at the leader level) has a significant effect on team-level work engagement, which in turn is directly related to team performance (Cruz et al., 2013).

In summary, work engagement plays an important role in the IGLO model of multi-level well-being (along with self-efficacy and resilience) and is, therefore, a key element of HEROs. Research at each level of analysis reveals the multiple roles that work engagement can play, sometimes as a direct correlate of outcomes, sometimes as a mediator of antecedents in relationship to outcomes, and sometimes as a moderator of relationships.

Enhancing work engagement through Positive Psychological Interventions based on the HERO Model

The research on the HERO Model presented so far leads to questions as to how they might be put into practice. For the present purposes, I focus on the potential impact of Positive Psychology Interventions (PPIs) on multi-level (IGLO) engagement. PPIs include the design and application of multi-level strategies implemented by individuals, teams, leaders, and the organization as a whole to promote organizational performance, through improving multi-level well-being including work engagement (Salanova et al., 2013).

In their review of generic intervention studies, Knight et al. (2019) have shown that there are benefits of workplace interventions to improve employee engagement. They presented the results of 40 intervention studies, such as: development of personal resources (N=5), development of job resources (N=12), leadership training (N=3), health promotion (N=18), and joint development of job and personal resources (N=2). Twenty (50 percent) of the studies they reviewed showed positive and significant effects on engagement. The most successful interventions to increase engagement were bottom-up interventions, particularly job crafting, and health promotion (specifically mindfulness interventions). While they identified some moderators of these encouraging findings, they note that more such research is needed.

In what follows I review some of the intervention work we have been doing in our WANT-Research Team (www.want.uji.es). We have been conducting PPIs using controlled and randomized designs with at least one intervention group and a waiting-list control group. In addition, we have been collecting baseline and post-intervention follow-up data.[1] I briefly review results about PPIs that specifically impacted work engagement as a key element of the HERO Model at the individual, group, and leadership levels of analysis.

In a quasi-experimental longitudinal study (i.e., control group with baseline and post-intervention measures) on work stress, Cifre et al. (2011) implemented an intervention program for work team redesign. The program involved numerous changes, such as supervisor role redesign and changes in job demands and resources for better fit, as well as improved training and increased information about the company. These interventions collectively produced improvements in personal resources (self-efficacy and perceived competences) and job resources (innovation team climate) that increased work engagement at the individual and team levels in a manufacturing company.

Several additional quasi-experimental studies on mindfulness programs at the individual level (Coo & Salanova, 2018, 2020) have also been conducted. The first of these studies was conducted with 35 nurses and consisted of three sessions based on the traditional eight-week Mindfulness-Based Cognitive Therapy (MBCT) program (Kuyken et al., 2010). Results indicated that the program was successful in promoting happiness at work, work engagement, and performance, as well as improving nurses' ability to pay attention to the present moment in an open and non-judgmental way (Mindfulness). The intervention in the second study consisted of eight MBCT sessions, and the results indicated that the program was successful in increasing the participants' levels of emotional intelligence and work engagement at the individual level of analysis. Similar results have been obtained by Coo et al. (2020), where they showed that the MBCT intervention increased participants' perceptions of the personal resources they bring to work such as psychological capital.

Finally, we recently conducted experimental studies of coaching programs (Peláez et al., 2019, 2020) in an international automotive company in Spain. The first study was conducted at the individual level of analysis with 60 staff employees who participated in a team coaching session followed by three individual sessions. Results indicated that, compared to the controls, the intervention program significantly increased all the study variables at the end of the program and three months later, including individual levels of work engagement. The second study was conducted at the individual, leader, and group levels of analysis. In it we implemented the coaching program with 41 executives and managers who first received 360-degree feedback (about positive leadership, engagement, psychological capital, and performance), and then over three months received the group-coaching leadership workshop (with five weekly, four-hour sessions), and three individual sessions. Follow-up 360s indicated that the intervention program was successful in producing significant differences against the controls in leadership skills, psychological capital, work engagement, and performance at the individual, leader, and team levels of analysis.

In summary, it is clear from our experimental and quasi-experimental research, as well as others' research (Knight et al., 2019) that interventions can produce the desired effects on individual, team, and leader behavior and work engagement. Such intervention studies add experimental evidence to the existing findings based on largely concurrent and correlational studies in support of the HERO Model. However, there are many research questions that remain to be answered.

Challenges for future research on work engagement

In this chapter, I explained how and why work engagement is a key psychological concept in understanding HEROs as positive organizations, and provided supporting evidence using a variety of methods in varying contexts. In this section, I propose some challenges for future research on work engagement as a key to HEROs.

First, more research is needed to understand how work engagement relates to other key indicators of employee health, particularly self-efficacy and resilience. Engagement, self-efficacy, and resilience appear to operate in tandem as indicators of health. However, it would be interesting to explore whether self-efficacy also operates as an individual difference variable that contributes to a propensity to engage, as suggested by Hough and Oswald (this volume). This issue could also be explored at the team and leadership and organizational levels of analysis.

The interest in resilience is based not only on the research summarized here but also on Cooke et al. (2016), who showed that resilient employees not only sustain effort through challenges, but also cultivate self-efficacy regarding their own competences as well as engagement (de Lucena Carvalho et al., 2006; Mache et al., 2014; Malik & Garg, 2020; Wang & Li, 2017). Further research on this nesting of resilience, self-efficacy, and engagement and their antecedents and consequences could prove important for use as a basis for additional intervention studies.

Salanova (2020b) has proposed specific areas of future research that may be particularly important in the time of Covid-19. It is recommended, for example, that it would be important to study the kinds and combinations of resources for resilience that might help to maintain, or even enhance, work engagement during crises. For example, is it psychological resources (i.e., positive emotions, self-efficacy, optimism, meaningful work, mental flexibility, emotional styles), social resources (i.e., positive social relationship among co-workers, teams and leaders, fairness, trust) and/or organizational resources (i.e., work–life balance, wellness, and positive communication programs) that have the most important effects?

Research on the following multi-level questions would also be important: (1) what are the personal and social psychological processes and variables that influence contagion of engagement in teams? For instance, one might study diversity (in age, in culture, for example) to answer questions about the degree to which more or less diverse groups experience emotional contagion vis-à-vis engagement; and (2) how might engagement change at multiple levels during organizational change, vis-à-vis use of new technologies (see Boudreau, this volume)?

The issue of the methods used for studies also requires attention. That is, most of the organizational studies on work engagement are quantitative in nature, and there is a need for more qualitative studies (see Macey, this volume). We found in our HERO studies that qualitative data (mostly interviews) with various individuals and groups (e.g., the CEO, immediate supervisors, employees, and customers, among others) revealed quite different perspectives (Acosta et al., 2015). For example, differences were observed on such issues as: (a) the number and type of policies, practices, and resources in the organization to support engagement, and (b) the level of employee and team engagement and how well-being programs are or are not connected with organizational success and performance. In short, from a practical perspective, combining qualitative and quantitative sources of information can give us a more complete conceptual map about the drivers and consequences of work engagement to enhance a more engaged workforce.

The last challenge for future research on work engagement and HEROs is related to interventions and the durability of their effects over time. To date, the longest follow-ups have been three months, so research over longer periods of time is required; we know they work but we do not know for how long. The fact that positive effects are mainly found immediately after interventions translates into the imperative to investigate the tactics/interventions and mechanisms required to sustain the effects of positive interventions effects over time. We now need to provide answers to such questions as:

- If job autonomy is increased for front-line workers, will they engage in more job-crafting to enhance engagement over time?
- If coaching is implemented on an on-going basis rather than as a short-lived experiment, will leaders be more continuously engaged and will that engagement, through contagion, yield more engaged teams and employees?
- Is it possible to train employees to be well-being champions who could actively reinforce the effects of the interventions to facilitate transfer of training to the daily routine of the workplace over time?
- To what degree do improvements in work engagement yield effects for people outside of the workplace (see Saks, this volume)?

In conclusion, the HERO Model in its current multi-level form identifies a complex set of issues targeted at the full range of well-being with an intense focus on work engagement as a key element. Positive consequences seem to follow from well-being, specifically engagement, at multiple levels of analysis. Nevertheless, additional research needs to be undertaken to further reinforce and extend what has been learned and how it can be applied to create more HEROs.

Note

1. We work within the framework of competitive projects at the national level (both in companies and in the government) and R&D contracts with surrounding organizations. In addition, just this year we started a European project in the framework of Horizon 2020, a European Union research programme, on multi-level interventions to improve mental health at work in small and medium enterprises (SMEs) and public institutions. In this project, we will include work engagement as a key indicator of health and well-being; please see the website for more information. We are actively participating in nine European countries and 14 institutions from those countries. The support we have received suggests we are responding to a felt need for these kinds of interventions across much of Europe.

References

Acosta, H., Cruz, V., Salanova, M., and Llorens, S. (2015). Healthy organization: analysing its meaning based on the HERO Model [Organizaciones saludables: analizando su significado desde el Modelo HERO]. *International Journal of Social Psychology*, *30*(2), 323–350.

Acosta, H., Torrente, P., Llorens, S., and Salanova, M. (2013). Prácticas organizacionales saludables: un estudio de su impacto relativo sobre el engagement con el trabajo. [Healthy organizational practices: a study about their impact on work engagement]. *Revista Peruana de Psicología y Trabajo Social*, *2*, 107–12.

Bakker, A., Schaufeli, W.B., Leiter, M., and Taris, T.W. (2008). Work engagement: an emerging concept in occupational health psychology. *Work & Stress*, *22*(3), 187–200.

Cifre, E., Salanova, M., and Rodríguez-Sánchez, A.M. (2011). Dancing between theory and practice: enhancing work engagement through work stress intervention. *Human Factors and Ergonomics in Manufacturing*, *21*(3), 269–286.

Coo, C., Ortega, A., and Salanova, M. (2020). Practice makes the master: a diary study of a positive intervention program at work and its effects on wellbeing and performance. Manuscript submitted for publication.

Coo, C., and Salanova, M. (2018). Mindfulness can make you happy-and-productive: a mindfulness controlled trial and its effects on happiness, work engagement and performance. *Journal of Happiness Studies*, *19*(6), 1691–1711.

Coo, C., and Salanova, M. (2020). Development of Mindfulness Signature Strengths program to promote emotional intelligence, work engagement and well-being. Manuscript submitted for publication.

Cooke, F.L., Cooper, B., Bartram, T., Wang, J., and Mei, H. (2016). Mapping the relationships between high-performance work systems, employee resilience and engagement: a study of the banking industry in China. *International Journal of Human Resource Management*, *30*(8), 1239–1260.

Cruz, V., Salanova, M., and Martínez, I.M. (2013). Liderazgo transformacional y desempeño grupal: unidos por el engagement grupal. *Revista de Psicología Social*, *28*(2), 183–196.

De Lucena Carvalho, V.A.M., Calvo, B.F., Martín, L.H., Campos, F.R., and Castillo, I.C. (2006). Resiliencia y el modelo burnout-engagement en cuidadores formales de ancianos [Resilience and the burnout-engagement model informal caregivers of the elderly]. *Psicothema*, *18*(4), 791–796.

Gracia, E., Salanova, M., Grau, R., and Cifre, E. (2013). How to enhance service quality through organizational facilitators, collective work engagement, and relational service competence. *European Journal of Work and Organizational Psychology*, *22*(1), 42–55.

Hatfield, E., Cacioppo, J.T., and Rapson, R.L. (1994). *Emotional Contagion*. New York: Cambridge University Press.

Knight, C., Patterson, M., and Dawson, J. (2019). Work engagement interventions can be effective: a systematic review. *European Journal of Work and Organizational Psychology*, *28*(3), 348–372.

Kuyken, W., Watkins, E., Holden, E., White, K., Taylor, R.S., Byford, S., Evans, A., Radford, S., Teasdale, J.D., and Dalgleish, T. (2010). How does mindfulness-based cognitive therapy work? *Behaviour Research and Therapy*, *48*(11), 1105–1112.

Lisbona, A., Palaci, F., Salanova, M., and Frese, M. (2018). The effects of work engagement and self-efficacy on personal initiative and performance. *Psicothema*, *30*(1), 89–96.

Llorens, S., Salanova, M., Torrente, P., and Acosta, H. (2013). Interventions to promote healthy & resilient organizations (HERO) from positive psychology. In G.F. Bauer and G.J. Jenny (Eds), *Salutogenic Organizations and Change: The Concepts Behind Organizational Health Intervention Research* (pp. 91–106). Zurich: Springer.

Mache, S., Vitzthum, K., Wanke, E., Groneberg, D.A., Klapp, B.F., and Danzer, G. (2014). Exploring the impact of resilience, self-efficacy, optimism and organizational resources on work engagement. *Journal of Prevention, Assessment & Rehabilitation*, *47*(4), 491–500.

Malik, P., and Garg, P. (2020). Learning organization and work engagement: the mediating role of employee resilience. *International Journal of Human Resource Management*, *31*(8), 1071–1094.

Martínez, I., Salanova, M., and Cruz, V. (in press). Our boss is a good boss! The cross-level effects of transformational leadership on work engagement in service jobs. *Journal of Work and Organizational Psychology*.

Peláez, M.J., Coo, C., and Salanova, M. (2019). Facilitating work engagement and job performance through strengths-based micro-coaching: a controlled trial study. *Journal of Happiness Studies*. First online. https://doi.org/10.1007/s10902-019-00127 -5.

Peláez, M.J., Salanova, M., and Martínez, I.M. (2020). Coaching-based leadership intervention program: a controlled trial study. *Frontiers in Psychology*, *10*, 3066.

Rodríguez-Sánchez, A., Devloo, T., Rico, R., Salanova, M., and Anseel, F. (2017). What makes creative teams tick? Cohesion, engagement, and performance across creativity tasks: a three-wave study. *Group & Organization Management*, *42*(4), 521–547.

Salanova, M. (2020a). Cultivar el Bienestar Organizacional (BO) en tiempos de la Covid-19 [Cultivate organizational wellbeing in times of Covid-19]. *Capital Humano*, in press.

Salanova, M. (2020b). How to survive COVID-19? Notes from organizational resilience. In Moya et al., Social Psychology in the face of COVID-19 (special issue), *International Journal of Social Psychology*. First online. https://doi.org/10.1080/ 02134748.2020.1795397.

Salanova, M., Llorens, S., Acosta, H., and Torrente, P. (2013). Positive interventions in positive organizations. *Terapia Psicológica*, *31*(1), 101–113. www.redalyc.org/ articulo.oa?id=785/78559051009.

Salanova, M., Llorens, S., Cifre, E., and Martínez, I.M. (2012). We need a hero! Towards a validation of the Healthy & Resilient Organization (HERO) Model. *Group & Organization Management, 37*(6), 785–822.

Salanova, M., Llorens, S., and Martínez, I.M. (2016). Contributions from positive organizational psychology to develop healthy and resilient organizations. *Papeles del Psicólogo, 3*(37), 177–184.

Salanova, M., Llorens, S., and Martínez, I.M. (2019). *Organizaciones Saludables: Una mirada desde la Psicología Positiva* [Healthy Organizations: An Overview from Positive Psychology]. Madrid: Aranzadi, Thomson Reuters.

Salanova, M., Lorente, L., Chambel, M.J., and Martínez, I.M. (2011). Linking trans-formational leadership to nurses' extra-role performance: the mediating role of self-efficacy and work engagement. *Journal of Advanced Nursing, 67*(10), 2256–2266.

Schaufeli, W.B., and Bakker, A. (2020). Work engagement: a critical assessment of the concept and its measurement. In W.R. Tuch, A.B. Bakker, L. Tay, and F. Gander (Eds), *Handbook of Positive Psychology Assessment*. Göttingen: Hogrefe. In press.

Schaufeli, W.B., Bakker, A.B., and Salanova, M. (2006). The measurement of work engagement with a short questionnaire: a cross-national study. *Educational and Psychological Measurement, 66*, 701–716.

Schaufeli, W.B., and Salanova, M. (2011). Work engagement: on how to better catch a slippery concept. *European Journal of Work and Organizational Psychology, 20*(1), 39–46.

Schaufeli, W.B., Salanova, M., González-Romá, V., and Bakker, A. (2002). The meas-urement of burnout and engagement: a confirmatory factor analytic approach. *Journal of Happiness Studies, 3*, 71–92.

Torrente, P., Salanova, M., and Llorens, S. (2013). Spreading engagement: on the role of similarity in the positive contagion of teamwork engagement. *Journal of Work and Organizational Psychology, 29*, 153–159.

Torrente, P., Salanova, M., Llorens, S., and Schaufeli, W.B. (2012). Teams make it work: how teamwork engagement mediates between social resources and performance in teams. *Psicothema, 24*(1), 106–112.

Wang, Z., Li, C., and Li, X. (2017). Resilience, leadership and work engagement: the mediating role of positive affect. *Social Indicators Research, 132*(2), 699–708.

5. Personality determinants of employee engagement

Leaetta M. Hough and Frederick L. Oswald

Employee engagement has multiple individual, interpersonal, and situational factors of influence, and this chapter focuses specifically on personality. Employee engagement includes relatively stable characteristics or *traits* that differentiate employees, such as typical employee levels of zest, vitality, energy, and human agency. It also includes psychological *states* that may change within employees over time, such as employees' daily work involvement and affective commitment to coworkers, customers, and to the organization. Finally, these states and traits often involve *behaviors* as signals of engagement and affective commitment beyond the formal expectations of the job, behaviors such as volunteering, supporting others, defending the organization, and other forms of organizational citizenship behaviors (OCBs).

Many researchers and practitioners have argued that although these three components – traits, states, and behaviors – fall under a single umbrella of engagement, they are better considered as conceptually distinct from one another (e.g., Macey & Schneider, 2008). We wholeheartedly agree, and we therefore urge our readers to consider and investigate the nomological nets or patterns of the many constructs that are antecedents of engagement (such as personality), those that are central to the construct of engagement, and the outcomes of engagement that are of importance to both organizations and employees. Only then can we understand the appropriate level of aggregation for thinking about and measuring the components and process of employee engagement. In this vein, and for the purposes of summarizing the literature on personality correlates of engagement, the nomological net for employee engagement that we have cast in this chapter is wide. In support for our approach, we point to research that suggests a strong "A-factor" (attitude) among various definitions of employee engagement in the literature (Newman et al., 2010).

Before we discuss personality in greater detail, we point out that employee engagement is best considered a broader framework of functional elements involving the individual, the environment, and the interaction between the two. More specifically:

1. *Employee characteristics*: Reflects personality (our focus), interests, motivation and energy/vitality, and other employee characteristics pertaining to other factors that contribute not merely to what employees "can do" with their skills and abilities, but to what they actually "will do" with their skills and abilities (Sackett et al., 1988). In this latter sense, employee engagement is a reflection of motivation and behavior under typical work conditions.
2. *Environmental characteristics*: Reflects task-based and team-based characteristics of the work itself; the characteristics of coworkers (e.g., supervisors, peers, teams/groups); human resources policies and practices; and organizational culture, mission, values. A multilevel perspective (see González-Romá, this volume) is helpful for considering and organizing the types of environmental characteristics that help or hinder employee engagement in individuals and teams.
3. *Interactional characteristics*: Reflects the dynamic interplay between the aforementioned individual and environmental characteristics. This interaction is not merely a statistical concept but rather reflects the substantive unfolding *process* of employee engagement (see McLarnon et al., this volume). Thanks to new time-intensive data collection and analysis technologies (see Fink & Macey, this volume), these sorts of dynamics can be measured, understood, and perhaps changed more quickly now than ever in the past.

Keeping this broader framework firmly in mind for context, our chapter focuses on employees' *personality reflecting the propensity for being and feeling engaged* at work. We rely on meta-analysis to summarize the available empirical evidence for personality traits predicting employee engagement. Because personality traits reflect relatively stable attributes of people over time and across situations and cultures (McCrae et al., 2002), organizations can usefully measure them in job applicants to help determine whether they have a propensity for being and feeling engaged at work. Incorporating predictors of engagement within the selection process can be worthwhile even in the presence of subsequent organizational interventions intended to improve employee engagement even further.

We review research showing that coworker and immediate supervisor behaviors relate to, and presumably have a causal influence on, employees' level of engagement. Extrapolating from that research, we identify coworker and supervisor personality characteristics that appear likely to engender engagement in others.

Our chapter is divided into three sections. The first section focuses on individual differences as a source of employee engagement; more specifically, the personality characteristics underlying *propensity for being and feeling engaged* that an employee brings to work. The second section focuses on interpersonal activity as a source of engagement; more specifically, the behaviors and personality characteristics of teammates and supervisors that underlie the *propensity to engender engagement in others*. The third and final section focuses on synthesis-driven ideas and future directions for research and practice involving the role and importance of personality in employee engagement.

Personality as a determinant of employee engagement: the individual employee

As some scholars have hypothesized and researched (e.g., Kahn, 1990; Macey & Schneider, 2008), personality variables that reflect some combination of zest, vitality, energy, and human agency are likely to correlate positively with and contribute to employee engagement. The definition of employee engagement as a construct often incorporates the concepts of energy and active involvement, so perhaps this is no surprise. However, this very fact illustrates an important point: Personality-based determinants of employee engagement need to be made distinct from environmental determinants.

Thus, in this section, we focus on the direct effect of how personality characteristics affect employee engagement. This direct effect does not preclude – and in fact encourages – readers to think further about important mediators and processes – indirect effects – where an employee's engagement affects interactions, teamwork, and the work of organizations, and this in turn further affects the engagement of all parties involved.

Personality and employee engagement are related

We have located four meta-analyses in the past ten years that address the relationship between personality variables and employee engagement (i.e., Christian et al., 2011; Halbesleben, 2010; Inceoglu & Warr, 2011; Young et al., 2018). These meta-analyses are consistent with our earlier point that energy is the construct that pervades theorizing and nomological nets involving personality traits (predictors) that relate to employee engagement (the criterion). We summarize these meta-analytic findings in Table 5.1, where we also identify two other relevant studies: one study published after these meta-analyses (i.e., Grobelna, 2019) and another study with a focus on core self-evaluation (i.e., Rich et al., 2010).

Table 5.1   Personality correlates of employee engagement

Personality characteristic	Engagement (Overall)						Engagement component (Facets)												
							Absorption				Dedication				Vigor			
	k	N	r	SDr	ρ	SDρ	k	N	ρ	SDρ	k	N	ρ	SDρ	k	N	ρ	SDρ
Five-factor model																		
Conscientiousness																		
Christian et al. (2011)	12	5 821	0.36	0.08	0.42[1]													
Inceoglu and Warr (2011)[3]																		
Achievement Orientation	3	741	0.35	–	–	–												
Dependability	3	741	0.24	–	–	–												
Young et al. (2018)	57	25 424	0.30	–	0.39[2]	0.13	20	7 668	0.35	0.10	20	7 667	0.34	0.13	20	7 665	0.40	0.11
Extraversion																		
Inceoglu and Warr (2011)[3]																		
Affiliation	3	741	0.20	–	–	–												
Social Potency	3	741	0.31	–	–	–												
Young et al. (2018)	44	20 471	0.32	–	0.40[2]	0.14	19	5 791	0.29	0.08	20	6 363	0.33	0.13	20	6 362	0.39	0.14
Emotional Stability																		
Inceoglu and Warr (2011)[3]	3	741	0.27	–	–	–												
Young et al. (2018)[4]	43	21 699	0.27		0.35[2]	0.09	15	5 196	0.19	0.08	16	5 768	0.34	0.14	17	5 830	0.40	0.14

Personality characteristic	Engagement (Overall)						Engagement component (Facets)												
							Absorption				Dedication				Vigor				
	k	N	r	SDr	ρ	SDρ	k	N	ρ	SDρ	k	N	ρ	SDρ	k	N	ρ	SDρ	
Agreeableness																				
Inceoglu and Warr (2011)[3]	3	741	0.16	-	-	-													
Young et al. (2018)	33	17 626	0.21	-	0.28[2]	0.13	13	4 813	0.18	0.11	13	4 813	0.24	0.14	13	4 812	0.24	0.14	
Openness to experience																				
Inceoglu and Warr (2011)[3]	3	741	0.15	-	-	-													
Young et al. (2018)	31	15 262	0.21	-	0.28[2]	0.16	12	4 322	0.22	0.15	12	4 322	0.21	0.14	12	4 321	0.23	0.12	
Other personality variables																				
Core Self-Evaluation																				
Rich et al. (2010)	1	245	0.34	-	-	-													
Optimism																				
Halbesleben (2010)	5	1 799	0.37	0.12	0.44[1]	0.13													
Proactive Personality																				
Christian et al. (2011)	6	4 304	0.35	0.07	0.44[1]														
Young et al. (2018)	20	8 339	0.37	-	0.49[2]	.10	7	2 888	0.48	0.08	7	2 888	0.40	0.06	7	2 888	0.45	0.05	
Self-Efficacy (Generalized)																				
Halbesleben (2010)	17	5 163	0.50	0.16	0.59[1]	0.18													

Personality characteristic	Engagement (Overall)						Engagement component (Facets)																
							Absorption				Dedication				Vigor								
	k	N	r	SDr	ρ	SD ρ	k	N	ρ	SD ρ	k	N	ρ	SD ρ	k	N	ρ	SD ρ					
Affective/mood variables																							
Positive Affectivity																							
Christian et al. (2011)	14	6 715	0.37	0.16	0.43[1]																		
Grobelna (2019)	1	222	0.45	–	–	–																	
Young et al. (2018)	33	12 107	0.52	–	0.62[2]	0.13	12	4 282	0.52	0.09	13	4 741	0.59	0.11	14	4 793	0.59	0.11					
Negative Affectivity																							
Young et al. (2018)	34	10 072	-0.22	–	-0.25[2]	0.13	8	2 604	0.12	0.00	11	3 260	-0.25	0.00	9	3 063	-0.26	0.03					

[1] Corrected for measurement unreliability in both the predictor and criterion.

[2] Corrected for both predictor range restriction and measurement unreliability in both the predictor and criterion.

[3] Inceoglu and Warr (2011) reported SHL *Occupational Personality Questionnaire (OPQ)* scale-level validities organized according to factors of the Five-Factor model of personality. We summarized (averaged the absolute values of the observed validities reported) within each factor. By contrast, note that other researchers (e.g., Hough & Ones, 2001) consider several of the OPQ scales to be compound variables made up of more than one Big Five factor; they categorize several of the specific OPQ scales into Big Five factors that are somewhat different than Inceoglu and Warr.

[4] Correlations reported in this meta-analysis are reversed to be consistent with the others; that is, for Neuroticism reversed to indicate Emotional Stability.

Note: For data reported in this table, see Christian et al. (2011), Table 4, p. 108; Grobelna (2019), Table 3, p. 360; Halbesleben (2010), Table 8.2, p. 109; Inceoglu and Warr (2011), Table 1, p. 178; Rich et al. (2010), Table 1, p. 2010; and Young et al. (2018), Table 2, p. 1337, and Table 4, p. 1338.

Meta-analytic results indicate that several personality variables correlate in the 0.40s and 0.50s with employee engagement, some even as high as the .60s. These correlations should be interpreted carefully, in light of the potential effects of (a) measurement error variance (which attenuates correlations), (b) method variance due to self-report (which accentuates correlations), and (c) construct proliferation (as some of these personality traits may require more evidence for discriminant validity; Shaffer et al., 2016). The specific personality characteristics that demonstrated these high levels of validity are:

- *Positive Affectivity*, a composite of primarily Big Five Extraversion, but also Conscientiousness (especially the Achievement Orientation facet), and to a lesser degree Agreeableness (see Watson & Clark, 1992). Regarding the relationship between Positive Affectivity and engagement, Young et al. (2018) reported a corrected meta-analyzed validity of 0.62 ($k = 33$, $N = 12,107$), and Christian et al. (2011) reported a corrected meta-analyzed validity of 0.43 ($k = 14$, $N = 6,715$).
- *Generalized Self-Efficacy*, a general belief regarding how much one tends to have the requisite knowledge, skills, ability, and motivation to execute action and follow-through to accomplish any given outcome successfully (Bandura, 1982). Halbesleben (2010) reported corrected meta-analytic validity of 0.59 ($k = 17$, $N = 5,163$) between Generalized Self-Efficacy and engagement.
- *Proactive Personality*, a composite of Achievement Orientation and Social Potency (Hough & Ones, 2001). A person high in Proactive Personality tends to show initiative, seek opportunities to manipulate and control the environment effectively, take action, and persevere until the desired effect or change has occurred (Bateman & Crant, 1993). Two studies reported corrected, meta-analyzed validities of 0.49 ($k = 20$; $N = 8,339$) and 0.44 ($k = 6$, $N = 4,304$) – Young et al. (2018) and Christian et al. (2011), respectively – between Proactive Personality and engagement.
- *Optimism*, a compound variable consisting of Big Five factors of Emotional Stability and Extraversion (see Hough & Ones, 2001). Halbesleben (2010) reported corrected meta-analytic validity of 0.44 ($k = 5$, $N = 1,799$) between Optimism and engagement.
- *Conscientiousness*, especially the Achievement Orientation facet, which involves both striving to meet internal goals (mastery orientation) and striving to meet external comparisons and outcomes (performance orientation). Three meta-analyses report validities of approximately 0.40 between Conscientiousness and engagement (i.e., Christian et al., 2011; Inceoglu & Warr, 2011; and Young et al., 2018).
- *Extraversion*, especially the Social Potency facet, which refers to the desire to show agency or leadership to influence others. Two studies reported

meta-analyzed validity of approximately 0.40 between Extraversion and engagement (i.e., Inceoglu & Warr, 2011; and Young et al., 2018).

An important observation of the relationships shown in Table 5.1 is that three compound personality variables – Positive Affectivity, Generalized Self-Efficacy, and Proactive Personality – all correlate strongly with overall engagement. Further examination indicates that personality variables best predict the engagement facet of Vigor, one of three work engagement facets measured by the Utrecht Work Engagement Scale (UWES) (Schaufeli & Bakker, 2006). Note that Agreeableness (a Big Five factor) correlates only modestly with engagement compared with other personality traits; however, Agreeableness might be important for improving the engagement of others, an idea that we will discuss later.

Clearly, meta-analytic and individual study-based evidence converge to support the conclusion that personality characteristics correlate positively and practically with employee engagement. Given the considerable evidence that employee engagement ultimately has important financial consequences for an organization, such as by increasing satisfaction, teamwork, and even company-level financial returns (Schneider et al., 2017), it follows that organizations would generally benefit from selecting job applicants on a suite of reliably measured personality traits that are related to employee engagement.

Indeed, consultants and in-house industrial-organizational psychologists have done just that, having developed and validated measures of traits that relate to or resemble the *propensity to be engaged*. To provide a couple of specific practice-based examples, David Jones reports useful validities for the Eager to Engage scale and its use with clients (HirePayoff, 2013); and Joe Garcia of the Home Depot also reports useful levels of validity for personality characteristics predicting its Associate Commitment Index, a measure of engagement (Garcia, 2019). In line with these examples, we predict a steady increase, if not a surge, in the numbers and types of organizations using talent management assessments, personality and otherwise, for the express purpose of increasing employee engagement in those hired. Producing this hoped-for outcome requires efforts that apply to any selection battery of measures. That is, organizations should not use measures because an eye-catching website or flyer simply *claims* to reflect the personality and engagement constructs of interest; instead, organizations should demand something much more important and much less glamorous: *research evidence* demonstrating solid support for reliability, validity, and fairness, in ways enumerated by the Society for Industrial and Organizational Psychology's *Principles for the Validation and Use of Personnel Selection Procedures* (2018).

Coworker and supervisor personality characteristics

Determinants of employee engagement

As anyone who has ever worked with other people knows, the actions and interactions of coworkers (teammates, supervisors, and leaders) critically affect the engagement for all workers involved, no matter what the job, organization, or industry. This follows the classic tenet by Schneider that "people make the place" (Schneider, 1987), and so we must ask: What employee personality characteristics help shape engagement for all employees in an organization? Some thoughts and research on this question are provided below.

Coworkers affect employee engagement: relevant coworker personality characteristics

Coworkers are omnipresent for most employees, serving as a constant and important influence on employee work engagement. Yet surprisingly little research is available on the impact of coworker personality on any given employee's level of engagement. This is true for research about personality measured at the individual coworker level, at the team level, and over time. Some important exceptions are enumerated below.

Team and supervisor personality: effects on employee engagement

Definitions about the nature and effectiveness of teams or leaders inevitably include a statement that they influence individual employee engagement. In other words, teams and supervisors are inherently responsible for developing and maintaining employee engagement, just as much as employees themselves.

Regarding team effects on employee engagement, Team Proactive Personality has been a situational characteristic of research interest. In their multilevel study, Wang et al. (2017) concluded that higher team-level proactivity triggered a given team member's increase in individual proactivity and engagement; in fact, team proactivity was a positive buffer to promote engagement when employees were feeling lower organizational support.

Regarding supervisor support influencing employee engagement, abundant theory and research on leader–follower relationships are supportive. For example, the theory of Leader–Member Exchange (LMX) emphasizes the unique dyadic relationships that develop over time (Graen & Uhl-Bien, 1995). Correlational meta-analyses find that quality of the supervisor–subordinate relationship, as reflected by LMX, does indeed relate positively to employee engagement ($\rho = 0.31$, $k = 4$, $N = 4,695$; Christian et al., 2011).

Turning to personality, research has also found that the *follower* personality characteristics of Positive Affectivity and Locus of Control correlated positively with LMX (e.g., Dulebohn et al., 2012; $\rho = 0.31$, $k = 12$, $N = 2,482$, and $\rho = 0.26$, $k = 8$, $N = 1,653$, respectively). Together, these and the previous meta-analytic findings cited point to the potential importance of employee personality variables as determinants of their own engagement, as partially mediated via LMX – the quality of leader–member relationships.

Other studies have investigated the *leader* personality as a direct determinant of follower engagement. For example, a joint research effort by Hogan Associates and Sirota found that being sociable, curious, and altruistic – but not hedonistic, not overly cautious, and not overly skeptical – reflects a general profile of leader characteristics that contributes to subordinate engagement (Hogan Associates & Sirota, 2015; Howell, 2017). In addition, a meta-analysis by Bono and Judge (2004) found correlations in the low 0.20s between leader Extraversion, Openness, and Agreeableness with transformational leadership. This is useful to know, given that a different meta-analytic study focusing on transformational leadership found strong and positive correlations with employee engagement (Hoch et al., 2018), thus empirically fleshing out a mediational pathway from leader personality, to transformational leadership style, to employee engagement (for one investigation of the full model, see Wefald et al., 2011).

Directions for future research

As a field, we have barely scratched the surface in understanding the role and importance of personality variables in determining and predicting engagement. Below we provide additional research and thinking needed to understand more fully the many roles personality plays in engagement. Overall, these points attempt to break the bonds of cross-sectional, self-report, and coarse measurement and methodologies, moving the field into more longitudinal, multi-method, and other more refined approaches.

Innovative longitudinal research examining the dynamic nature of engagement

We need research that examines the role of personality in coworker support and trust as it influences engagement across multiple employees operating in teams and informal coworker networks. Also important is identifying personality characteristics of employees who, over time, effectively and consistently re-engage in the task or team over time. We thus need more intensive longitudinal designs where we can reliably measure and model employee engagement (e.g., Wang et al., 2016). Such research promises to help us better understand the reality of employment engagement processes and therefore make better predictive inferences about them.

Increased consensus regarding the key components or dimensions of employee engagement

Modern technologies and tools give us the opportunity to collect real-time data and determine how many dimensions of employee engagement are detectable, empirically distinguishable, and psychologically interpretable, and how such data and findings might extend traditional engagement theories and measures – or even supplant them.

Inclusion of facet-level personality measures and facet-level employee engagement measures in validation studies

Erring on the side of a facet-level data-driven approach can help determine where and when the data (e.g., correlational patterns) might detect refined vs broad patterns of relationships between personality facets and engagement facets (vs factors). This approach is reflected in the nomological web clustering approach offered by Hough et al. (2015; see also McLarnon et al., this volume). We and others have argued over many years (see especially Hough et al., 2015; O'Neill & Paunonen, 2013) that broad, compound, and complex personality variables can show *that* relationships are evident, but may not tell the entire story about *why* those relationships exist in terms of interpretable patterns of facet-level relationships with criteria. Of course, it is an ongoing empirical question whether facet-level discoveries and patterns will pan out, and whether a lack of relationship reflects a measurement problem or a theoretical problem; but we cannot even begin to try without some serious focus on the matter.

Examination of personality-engagement relationships within occupational types or organizational settings

For instance, Generalized Self-Efficacy and its close cousin, Core Self-Evaluation, might predict engagement across jobs in a relatively similar manner, whereas other personality facets might be expected to predict engagement differently across different types of occupations or organizational settings. For example, as one speculative hypothesis, Affiliation, a facet of Extraversion, might correlate with engagement in people-oriented occupations, but not in technical occupations. Measuring employees and occupations on their vocational interests to determine person–environment fit might be helpful for predicting employee engagement in job applicants (Oswald et al., 2019), just as such measurement has been useful for predicting employee effort or persistence, job performance, and other organizational outcomes (Nye et al., 2012; Van Iddekinge et al., 2011).

Additional multilevel and social network research on personality and engagement

Research could usefully investigate how the personality traits of supervisors reflect important cross-level characteristics that relate to fostering individual and team engagement, in tandem with the aggregated (mean-level) personality traits and engagement levels of teams and individual team members. (See González-Romá, this volume.) Social network analyses might also prove useful when researchers seek to examine how engagement develops and spreads through a network over time (e.g., how formal leaders vs employees compare in fostering the intensity and frequency of employee engagement within their networks; how intra- and inter-team networks of competition and cooperation promote or hinder employee engagement).

Examination of leader "dark side" personality characteristics that relate to engagement/disengagement

Narcissism and Machiavellianism are dark-side personality characteristics that positively correlate with leader ineffectiveness (Hogan & Hogan, 2001) and counterproductive work behavior (O'Boyle et al., 2012). We suggest that supervisor mistrust and corresponding employee disengagement are important contributors to these relationships, and thus, further research can examine whether employees who are otherwise projected to be engaged will nonetheless disengage at work when managers and coworkers possess dark-side personality characteristics.

Expanding the criterion space for supervisory effectiveness to include subordinate and team engagement

Employee engagement needs to be considered more often as an indicator of supervisory effectiveness, because it is an outcome that is often more proximal to supervisory behavior than any financial bottom line. For instance, as part of multi-source or 360-degree feedback processes (Church et al., 2019), subordinates could provide input into the appraisal of their supervisor's ability to engage teams and employees. These supervisory data, in turn, could be related to employee engagement data, both at the individual level and at more aggregated levels (e.g., teams or units; see González-Romá, this volume). And as already alluded to, modern technologies and machine-learning algorithms, together, might collect and analyze this engagement information across roles in the organization more quickly and effectively, to be used for subsequent organizational interventions on both supervisors and employees (e.g., individual and team development, timely acknowledgements and rewards, team and role restructuring). Engagement is both a top-down and bottom-up phenomenon that happens at all levels and involves the personality traits of those involved. Engagement (good, bad, and otherwise) is a function of personality and can be contagious between supervisors and teams, between teams and employees, across teams and across supervisors, and so on (see Xanthopoulou and Bakker, this volume).

Examination of the role of coworker personality in dyadic relationships and its effect on engagement

For example, we suggest that coworker Agreeableness (and its facets, Trust and Altruism) might predict a focal employee's engagement, for two reasons. First, theories and models suggest that coworker trust is critical for employees to experience the high level of psychological safety required for their engagement (Schneider et al., 2010). Second, Agreeableness correlates positively with behavioral criterion measures involving interpersonal effectiveness (Hogan & Holland, 2003). Taking these two points together, network modeling would seem like a very appropriate way to understand personality networks as they relate to employee engagement networks dynamically, dyadically, and within larger groups.

Examination of team personality variables and engagement

In support of this research direction, past research has discovered that Team Agreeableness (operationalized as the mean of team members' scores on Agreeableness) correlates 0.56 with Workload Sharing (Barrick et al., 1998), which in turn should serve to improve employee engagement (which was not measured in this cited study). Using meta-analysis to study relationships between team-level personality variables and team performance, Bell (2007) found mean Team Agreeableness and mean Team Conscientiousness correlate in the mid 0.30s with team performance in field studies. Interestingly, the lowest team member score on Agreeableness and Conscientiousness correlated at about that same level with team performance; but the correlations were much lower for the maximum team member score. These findings tentatively suggest that one member with an undesirable level of a trait can negatively affect employee engagement (as many of us have experienced firsthand).

Assessment of relative contributions of personality vs situational characteristics with engagement

The relative contributions of personality traits are useful, also separating these relative contributions by source (e.g., employees, teams, and leaders), and also comparing these contributions to those from situational factors in organizations that affect engagement. For example, a recent unpublished study examined the contributions of both personality and job characteristics to employee engagement (Lei et al., 2020). The highest personality-based predictor was Proactive Personality ($r = 0.54$), a construct we defined earlier; and the best job characteristics predictor of engagement was Learning Opportunities ($r = 0.67$). One could imagine that these two variables might interact, reflecting the impact of person–environment fit on employee engagement. Related to this static operationalization of fit, one could also readily imagine how these two variables relate to one another and to engagement dynamically over time. But even better than imagining, more process-oriented research along these lines is needed, and it is possible given new measurement and machine-learning capabilities.

Examination of the transitory versus stable nature of engagement

Longitudinal research is needed to understand *distributions and dynamics* of employee engagement, where the trait is the mean, and deviations from the trait over time and across situations reflect states (similar to how Fleeson, 2001, conceptualized traits as distributions). Note that even if such within-person studies indicate that employee engagement reliably differs from time to time (see Sonnentag et al., this volume), reasonably high intra-class correlations indicate stable mean differences between employees in their engagement, which again is critically tied to our recommendation to consider personality traits within broader selection and promotion systems that are related to employee engagement (see McLarnon et al., this volume).

Concluding thoughts

Evidence from the meta-analyses and primary studies cited within this chapter cumulates to support the conclusion that personality characteristics should be attended to as important determinants of employee work engagement. Furthermore, a supervisor's personality traits might also be considered as part of a rich profile of organizational factors that meaningfully affects both employee- and team-level engagement. Supervisor personality traits have a direct effect on employee engagement, and also an indirect effect, by influencing their own leadership and management behaviors that ultimately foster employee engagement. This indirect effect is ripe for further study, given greater availability of intensive longitudinal data for examining organizational processes, and given that engagement is truly an intra- and inter-personal process.

Although a significant amount of research to-date relates personality characteristics to employee engagement at work, the underlying data largely come from concurrent self-report measures. Also, in most of these self-report studies, researchers create and correlate composites of personality (related to energy or vitality) with composites of employee engagement. This approach may increase one's confidence in obtaining at least some level of stable prediction across settings and over time. However, the composite approach also hedges one's predictive bets, potentially obscuring more specific and more powerful predictions, as well as a more precise understanding of how the variables contributing to each composite are interrelated (assuming each constituent measure is well developed and reliable).

We might continue with the practicality of the composite approach, while *also* encouraging innovative research involving an expanded set of measures of facet-level personality and employee engagement constructs. That way, perhaps different and more efficient predictor composites could be tailored to different jobs, teams, supervisors, and future job requirements, as has been discussed when taking a synthetic validity approach to personality and personnel selection (Hough et al., 2015). Moving forward methodologically, advancing our understanding of employee engagement and its implications for selection will critically require multilevel, network-based, and other dynamic longitudinal research designs, and a correspondingly creative reframing of engagement issues important to organizations (see González-Romá, this volume). Perhaps in the future we will find that intensive real-time measurement using big-data-oriented technologies and analytics (see Fink & Macey, this volume), as implemented by substantively oriented researchers and practitioners, will help capture and capitalize on some of these dynamics (e.g., for real-time interventions that improve employee engagement).

This chapter examined the measurement and understanding of personality as another important tool in the toolbox of an organization's efforts to increase its employee engagement, particularly within selection/promotion processes that include reliable, valid, fair, and job-relevant assessments. Using personality measures as a personnel selection tool for employee engagement is becoming a popular innovation, suggesting that today's innovative artificial-intelligence-based selection technologies have the potential to enhance this approach (Gonzalez et al., 2019). To reach this goal, we hope that researchers in this arena will remain as engaged as the employees they influence.

References

Bandura, A. (1982). Self-efficacy mechanism in human agency. *American Psychologist*, *37*, 122–147.

Barrick, M. R., Stewart, G. L., Neubert, M. J., and Mount, M. K. (1998). Relating member ability and personality to work-team processes and team effectiveness. *Journal of Applied Psychology*, *83*, 377–391.

Bateman, T. S., and Crant, J. M. (1993). The proactive component of organizational behavior: A measure and correlates. *Journal of Organizational Behavior*, *14*, 103–118.

Bell, S. (2007). Deep-level composition variables as predictors of team performance: A meta-analysis. *Journal of Applied Psychology*, *92*, 395–615.

Bono, J. E., and Judge, T. A. (2004). Personality and transformational and transactional leadership: A meta-analysis. *Journal of Applied Psychology*, *89*, 901–910.

Christian, M. S., Garza, A. S., and Slaughter, J. E. (2011). Work engagement: A quantitative review and test of its relations with task and contextual performance. *Personnel Psychology*, *64*, 89–136.

Church, A. H., Bracken, D. W., Fleenor, J. W., and Rose, D. S. (Eds) (2019). *The Handbook of Strategic 360 Feedback*. Oxford: Oxford University Press

Dulebohn, J. H., Bommer, W. H., Liden, R. C., Brouer, R. L., and Ferris, G. R. (2012). A meta-analysis of antecedents and consequences of Leader–Member Exchange: Integrating the past with an eye toward the future. *Journal of Management*, *38*, 1715–1759.

Fleeson, W. (2001). Toward a structure-and process-integrated view of personality: Traits as density distributions of states. *Journal of Personality and Social Psychology*, *80*, 1011–1027.

Garcia, J. (2019). *Employee Engagement, Customer Service, and Business Results*. Home Depot, unpublished manuscript.

Gonzalez, M. F., Capman, J. F., Oswald, F. L., Theys, E. R., and Tomczak, D. L. (2019). Where's the I-O? Artificial intelligence and machine learning in talent management systems. *Personnel Assessment and Decisions*, *5*, 33–44.

Graen, G. B., and Uhl-Bien, M. (1995). Relationship-based approach to leadership: Development of Leader–Member Exchange (LMX) theory of leadership over 25 years: Applying a multi-level multi-domain perspective. *Leadership Quarterly, 25,* 219–247.

Grobelna, A. (2019). Effects of individual and job characteristics on hotel contact employees' work engagement and their performance outcomes. *International Journal of Contemporary Hospitality Management, 31,* 349–369.

Halbesleben, J. R. B. (2010). A meta-analysis of work engagement: Relationships with burnout, demands, resources, and consequences. In A. B. Bakker and M. P. Leiter (Eds), *Work Engagement: A Handbook of Essential Theory and Research* (pp. 102–117). New York: Psychology Press.

HirePayoff (2013, November). Finding the right candidate reduces an employer's cost of "growing employee engagement". Retrieved January 11, 2020 from https://HirePayoff.com.

Hoch, J. E., Bommer, W. H., Dulebohn, J. H., and Wu, D. (2018). Do ethical, authentic, and servant leadership explain variance above and beyond transformational leadership? A meta-analysis. *Journal of Management, 44,* 501–529.

Hogan, J., and Holland, B. (2003). Using theory to evaluate personality and job performance relations: A socioanalytic perspective. *Journal of Applied Psychology, 88,* 100–112.

Hogan, R., and Hogan, J. (2001). Assessing leadership: A view from the dark side. *International Journal of Selection and Assessment, 9,* 40–51.

Hogan Associates and Sirota (2015). *Building an Engaged Workforce: How to Grow Employee Engagement Using Personality.* Unpublished manuscript. Sirota Consulting, LLC.

Hough, L. M., and Ones, D. S. (2001). The structure, measurement, validity, and use of personality variables in industrial, work, and organizational psychology. In N. R. Anderson, D. S. Ones, H. K. Sinangil, and C. Viswesvaran (Eds), *Handbook of Industrial, Work & Organizational Psychology,* Vol. 1 (pp. 233–277). London and New York: Sage.

Hough, L. M., Oswald, F. L., and Ock, J. (2015). Beyond the big five: New directions for personality research and practice in organizations. *Annual Review of Organizational Psychology and Organizational Behavior, 2,* 183–209.

Howell, A. (2017). Engagement starts at the top: The role of a leader's personality on employee engagement. *Strategic HR Review, 16,* 144–146.

Inceoglu, I., and Warr, P. (2011). Personality and job engagement. *Journal of Personnel Psychology, 10,* 177–181.

Kahn, W. A. (1990). Psychological conditions of personal engagement and disengagement at work. *Academy of Management Journal, 33,* 692–724.

Lei, X., Rhodes, D., and Borden, C. (2020). The importance of job factors versus personality for boosting workplace engagement. Poster session at the 35th annual conference of the Society for Industrial and Organizational Psychology, Online. Austin, TX.

Macey, W. H., and Schneider, B. (2008). The meaning of employee engagement. *Industrial and Organizational Psychology, 1,* 3–30.

McCrae, R. R., Costa, P. T., Jr., Terracciano, A., Parker, W. D., Mills, C. J., De Fruyt, F., and Mervielde, I. (2002). Personality trait development from age 12 to age 18: Longitudinal, cross-sectional and cross-cultural analyses. *Journal of Personality and Social Psychology, 83,* 1456–1468.

Newman, D. S., Joseph, D. L., and Hulin, C. L. (2010). Job attitudes and employee engagement: Considering the "A-factor". In S. L. Albrecht (Ed.), *Handbook of Employee Engagement: Perspectives, Issues, and Practice* (pp. 43–61). Cheltenham, UK, and Northampton, MA: Edward Elgar Publishing.

Nye, C. D., Su, R., Rounds, J., and Drasgow, F. (2012). Vocational interests and performance: A quantitative summary of over 60 years of research. *Perspectives on Psychological Science, 7*, 384–403.

O'Boyle, E. H., Jr., Forsyth, D. R., Banks, G. C., and McDaniel, M. A. (2012). A meta-analysis of the dark triad and work behavior: A social exchange perspective. *Journal of Applied Psychology, 97*, 557–579.

O'Neill, T. A., and Paunonen, S. V. (2013). Breadth in personality assessment: Implications for the understanding and prediction of work behavior. In N. Christiansen and R. P. Tett (Eds), *Handbook of Personality at Work* (pp. 299–333). New York: Routledge.

Oswald, F. L., Hough, L. M., and Zuo, C. (2019). Personnel selection and vocational interests: Recent research and future directions. In C. D. Nye and J. Rounds (Eds), *Vocational Interests in the Workplace: Rethinking Behavior at Work*. New York: Routledge.

Rich, B. L., LePine, J. A., and Crawford, E. R. (2010). Job engagement: Antecedents and effects on job performance. *Academy of Management Journal, 53*, 617–635

Sackett, P. R., Zedeck, S., and Fogli, L. (1988). Relations between measures of typical and maximum job performance. *Journal of Applied Psychology, 73*, 482–486.

Schaufeli, W. B., and Bakker, A. B. (2006). The measurement of work engagement with a short questionnaire: A cross national study. *Educational and Psychological Measurement, 66*, 701–716.

Schneider, B. (1987). The people make the place. *Personnel Psychology, 40*, 437–453.

Schneider, B., Macey, W. H., Barbera, K. M., and Young, S. A. (2010). The role of employee trust in understanding employee engagement. In S. L. Albrecht (Ed.), *Handbook of Employee Engagement: Perspectives, Issues, Research and Practice*. Hoboken: Wiley-Blackwell.

Schneider, B., Yost, A. B., Kropp, A., Kind, C., and Lam, H. (2017). Work engagement: What it is, what drives it, and why it matters for organizational performance. *Journal of Organizational Behavior, 39*(4), 462–480.

Shaffer, J. A., DeGeest, D., and Li, A. (2016). Tackling the problem of construct proliferation: A guide to assessing the discriminant validity of conceptually related constructs. *Organizational Research Methods, 19*, 80–110.

Society for Industrial and Organizational Psychology (2018). *Principles for the Validation and Use of Personnel Selection Procedures*, 5th ed. Cambridge, MA: Cambridge University Press.

Van Iddekinge, C. H., Roth, P. L., Putka, D. J., and Lanivich, S. E. (2011). Are you interested? A meta-analysis of relations between vocational interests and employee performance and turnover. *Journal of Applied Psychology, 96*, 1167–1194.

Wang, M., Zhou, L., and Zhang, Z. (2016). Dynamic modeling. *Annual Review of Organizational Behavior and Organizational Psychology, 3*, 241–266.

Wang, Z., Zhang, J., Thomas, C. L., Yu, J., and Spitzmueller, C. (2017). Explaining benefits of employee proactive personality: The role of engagement, team proactivity composition and perceived organizational support. *Journal of Vocational Behavior, 101*, 90–103.

Watson, D., and Clark, L. A. (1992). On traits and temperament: General and specific factors of emotional experience and their relation to the Five-Factor Model. *Journal of Personality, 60*, 441–476.

Wefald, A. J., Reichard, R. J., and Serrano, S. A. (2011). Fitting engagement into a nomological network: The relationship of engagement to leadership and personality. *Journal of Leadership & Organizational Studies, 18*, 522–537.

Young, H. R., Glerum, D. R., Wang, W., and Joseph, D. L. (2018). Who are the most engaged at work? A meta-analysis of personality and employee engagement. *Journal of Organizational Behavior, 39*, 1330–1346.

6. Individual-level outcomes of employee engagement: a conservation of resources framework

Jonathon R. B. Halbesleben

In the three decades since Kahn's (1990) seminal work on employee engagement, empirical research has been quite consistent in demonstrating the value of employee engagement for employees, teams, and organizations (Bailey et al., 2017; Harter et al., 2002; Xanthopoulou et al., 2009). In fact, those relationships have been so consistent that some authors have labeled engagement "the key to improving performance" (Markos & Sridevi, 2010, p. 89) and a "driver of organizational effectiveness" (Sundaray, 2011, p. 53). As a result, several authors have proposed and tested interventions designed to increase employee engagement (Gustomo et al., 2019; Seppälä et al., 2018; Wingerden et al., 2016), with some evidence that interventions can have a positive return on investment for organizations (Knight et al., 2017; Mueller, 2019).

The focus of much of the research on outcomes of engagement has been on job performance (e.g., Christian et al., 2011; Macey & Schneider, 2008; Mäkikangas et al., 2016; Rich et al., 2010) and turnover/retention (Agarwal & Gupta, 2018; Halbesleben & Wheeler, 2008; Rafiq et al., 2019). In fact, Dalal et al. (2012) found that engagement, along with job satisfaction and trait negative affect, was the best predictor of employee job performance. However, emerging research has demonstrated that engagement impacts a number of other important outcomes. This chapter focuses on individual-level outcomes of employee engagement, with an emphasis on relatively recent research on novel outcomes that extend the literature beyond performance and retention. In addition to synthesizing recent research trends, the chapter includes future research directions to enhance the literature.

Framing the relationship between engagement and outcomes

In order to better understand the relationship between engagement and its outcomes, it is helpful to understand the theoretical frames that have guided much of the research.

Several theoretical perspectives have been applied in the study of employee engagement, including self-determination theory (Gagné et al., this volume; Meyer & Gagné, 2008; Meyer et al., 2010) and the job demands-resources (JD-R) model (Albrecht et al., 2018). Among the most commonly applied theories to address the consequences of engagement has been conservation of resources (COR) theory (Hobfoll, 1988, 1989). COR theory describes the processes related to resources, broadly defined as states, objects, and character-istics that are valued because they help achieve goals (Halbesleben et al., 2014; Hobfoll, 1988). COR theory is built on two primary ideas: (1) humans seek to attain and protect resources, and (2) we invest the resources we have in order to attain more resources (Hobfoll et al., 2018). Resources, and more specifically resource investment, are keys to understanding the consequences of employee engagement. Several researchers have suggested that engaged employees have more than adequate, or even excess, resources to address the demands of their jobs (Gorgievski & Hobfoll, 2008; Halbesleben & Wheeler, 2008). According to COR theory, as we gain resources, our ability to invest resources in ways that benefit us increases (Hobfoll, 2001). Therefore, employees higher in engagement are better positioned to invest their resources in ways that lead to positive outcomes because they have excess resources and thus can focus less on minimizing resource losses (Halbesleben, 2011). This creates resource gain cycles, whereby the existence of higher levels of resources leads to more resources in the future (Hobfoll, 2001; Laguna et al., 2017).

While very similar, COR theory differs slightly from the JD-R model in that COR theory does not explicitly separate out demands from resources. In COR theory, demands are represented by resource investment and loss. In other words, whereas the JD-R model might consider "writing this chapter" a task that could be more or less of a demand depending on the author, COR theory would conceptualize this situation in terms of whether the author had ade-quate resources (e.g., time; relevant knowledge, skills, and abilities) to write the chapter. Simply possessing resources is not enough; to be a resource it has to be relevant in helping an employee achieve goals (Halbesleben et al., 2014). The excess time I may have had to write this chapter will not lead to engagement in writing if that time is not coupled with the relevant knowledge needed to write the chapter. Further, my knowledge and skill with regard to home brewing will hold little value when faced with writing a chapter about engagement.

COR theory provides an intuitive understanding of the relationship between engagement and a wide variety of outcomes. If engaged employees have excess resources, it is logical that they will invest those resources to improve job performance, particularly if performance leads to rewards that they are seeking. Further, if they are able to attain those rewards, it makes sense that employees would be less likely to leave a job in which they experience high levels of engagement. In the following sections, I review existing research on outcomes that have extended engagement research in new directions beyond performance and retention, identifying themes consistent with COR theory.

Emerging research on outcomes of engagement

Job crafting

Job crafting refers to changes that employees make to their work, whether physical or cognitive, to better align the work with their goals or preferences (Tims et al., 2012; Wrzesniewski & Dutton, 2001). Nearly a decade ago, Bakker et al. (2011) proposed that engaged employees would be more likely to craft their jobs in order to create a virtuous cycle of increasing resources, based on work suggesting engaged employees were more likely to seek out feedback and professional development opportunities that could increase resources (Hakanen et al., 2008; Hyvonen et al., 2009).

As will be a theme in this chapter, engagement leads to higher job crafting, but a number of studies have found that job crafting can also lead to higher levels of engagement (e.g., Bakker et al., 2012; Dubbelt et al., 2019; Kooij et al., 2017). Mäkikangas et al. (2016) found that job crafting served as a moderator of the relationship between work engagement and team performance, such that the relationship was stronger when job crafting was higher. This, of course, suggests that job crafting created additional resources that could be invested in performance.

The reciprocal relationship between job crafting and engagement represents a resource gain cycle. Specifically, when an employee has extra resources to invest in work (as is the case for engaged employees), he or she can invest those resources in ways that alter their job in order to create opportunities to gain even more resources. Those additional resources further perpetuate the employee's engagement and increase the likelihood that he or she will continue to seek out ways to increase resources through job crafting.

Innovation and creativity

An emerging body of time-lagged and longitudinal studies suggests that engagement is associated with higher levels of creativity and innovation in organizations (cf. Asif et al., 2019; Henker et al., 2015; Park et al., 2014). In a study of 400 Korean employees, Kim and Park (2017) found that work engagement was associated with higher levels of knowledge sharing and innovative work behavior. Interestingly, it appears that the impact that engagement has on innovative behavior is greater among employees with more experience in their positions (Zhang & Bartol, 2010); experience thus seems to be a resource that is useful, at least in this case.

This literature also reinforces the notion of resource gain cycles. As employees invest their excess resources in creative and innovative activities, it is likely to increase their work engagement. In a sample of about 350 employees in five public organizations at two data collection points, Gawke et al. (2017) found that work engagement was associated with higher levels of employee intrapreneurship behaviors; they also found that higher levels of employee intrapreneurship behaviors at the first data collection point were associated with higher levels of engagement at the second data collection point. These findings also apply to gain cycles leading to higher levels of innovativeness at the group level (Hakanen et al., 2008).

Safety and well-being

Increasingly, engagement has been examined as a key factor in understanding safety outcomes for employees (McCaughey et al., 2014; Mullins, 2018; Nahrgang et al., 2011). For example, Wachter and Yorio (2014) examined the relationship between safety-specific engagement and a variety of safety outcomes among safety managers, employees, and supervisors. They found that the relationship between various safety management programs and safety outcomes, including accident rates, was mediated by safety engagement. While more research is needed, particularly studies using designs that could support causal conclusions, their work suggests that the impact of safety programs on safety outcomes could be a function of whether those programs are effective in providing the resources necessary for them to invest in safer behaviors.

Integrating the literature on engagement, safety, and creativity, Halbesleben and Bellairs (2015) offered an alternative way of thinking about how engagement could impact safety behaviors, suggesting that engagement had the potential to also *increase* unsafe incidents. They suggested that highly engaged employees might develop creative shortcuts, termed workarounds, to get around barriers in work process (cf. Halbesleben et al., 2008), but that by engaging in workarounds they might increase exposure to safety hazards for themselves or others. Their proposal highlights an emerging theme in the literature that may be important in understanding outcomes of engagement – the differentiation between general employee engagement and engagement with specific, and potentially competing, facets of one's job (Saks, this volume). This may be particularly relevant in safety settings, as engagement related to safety may lead to safer work practice, whereas engagement that is more in line with productivity or performance may not align with engaging in safety behaviors (Halbesleben, 2011). Put another way, employees with higher levels of safety engagement are probably less likely to engage in workarounds, whereas employees with higher levels of general engagement with their work may be more likely to utilize workarounds as they prioritize performance over safety.

Continuing the trend, there is some evidence of a reciprocal relationship between engagement and workplace safety (Radic, 2019). For example, in a mixed-method study of construction workers and supervisors, Whiteoak and Mohamed (2016) found that when employees feel safer, they are more likely to report general engagement in their work. While more research is needed on this topic, it appears that a positive gain cycle may exist for engagement and safety outcomes when the resources are focused on safety and not on productivity.

The work–life boundary

Similar to the work on engagement and workarounds in the context of safety, the emerging research stream regarding engagement and the work–life interface has further exposed a potential "dark side" of engagement. Halbesleben et al. (2009) found that work engagement was associated with higher work–family interference. That work has been replicated and extended in a number of ways (e.g., Iqbal et al., 2017); for example, finding that access to and use of electronic communication technologies as a resource for work accomplishment in non-work hours is more common among engaged employees and associated with higher work–family conflict (Boswell & Olson-Buchanan, 2007; Derks et al., 2015).

There is an interesting nuance in this literature that will serve as a segue to a broader discussion of research needs on the outcomes of engagement. Hakanen and Peeters (2015) conducted a seven-year study that found that engagement was related to *lower* work–family conflict. While contrary to previous findings, this suggests the need to explore how individuals might adapt to the resources they have over time in ways that foster engagement without negatively impacting family (cf. Matthews et al., 2014). This seems likely, particularly given that Hakanen and Peeters also found that workaholism was related to higher work–family conflict. In other words, having the resources necessary to be psychologically engaged with work over extended periods of time may not have as negative an impact on family if that engagement does not lead to behaviors that interfere with family.

Future research on outcomes of engagement

To conclude this chapter, I will discuss a number of issues that require further exploration in order for us to better understand the relationship between engagement and its outcomes. The dynamics of resources, engagement, and its outcomes from COR theory offer some insight into ways future research can help us better understand the relationship between engagement and its outcomes. Specifically, COR would suggest that many of the outcomes associated with engagement are because employees are in a better position to invest their excess resources; however, we do not fully understand how sustainable those investments are over time or whether investment strategies change during one's career. Moreover, there is still much work that is needed to fully understand the boundary conditions, or moderators, to the investment of resources that drives the relationship between engagement and its outcomes.

As with many concepts in organizations (Shipp & Cole, 2015), the role that time plays in understanding the relationship between engagement and outcomes is important but under-studied (Hobfoll et al., 2018). While theories suggest that engagement can grow over time because of gain cycles, it is not clear how long such cycles are sustainable in the short or long term (Sonnentag et al., this volume). For example, time pressure to complete tasks leads to higher levels of engagement if that time pressure is short-lived; however, that time pressure can lead to reduced engagement if the pressure lingers for longer periods of time (Baethge et al., 2018). Looking at even longer-term outcomes, employees may not be able or willing to sustain high engagement and performance while working in an environment where there is no ability for them to grow in their jobs/careers.

Moreover, it is not clear how much adaptation impacts the relationship between engagement and outcomes over time (cf. Ford et al., 2014; Matthews et al., 2014). As engaged employees continue to invest resources that lead to higher job performance, one might expect that higher job performance becomes expected, both of the employee and those he or she works for. More research is needed on how employees perceive both engagement and its outcomes over time in order to better understand how these perceptions change and how that impacts the relationship between engagement and outcomes.

An important variant on our understanding of time in the context of engagement's outcomes is the experience of engagement over one's lifespan. Bakker and Hakanen (2019) suggested that the experience of engagement may change as employees age, in large part because their experiences of resources change. These changes in engagement over time would almost certainly impact outcomes of engagement and raise some very interesting questions. For example, several studies have suggested that coaching and performance feedback from supervisors is associated with higher levels of engagement and subsequent outcomes (e.g., Lee et al., 2019; Xanthopoulou et al., 2009). However, it would seem that the nature of that feedback and the timing could be important and worth additional study. It would seem that coaching and positive feedback earlier in one's career may build up self-efficacy and increase the likelihood of an employee investing the excess resources associated with engagement in positive outcomes. On the other hand, getting negative feedback about those investments early in one's career may lead to lower engagement and different, more conservative, investments in resources that may not only lead to fewer positive outcomes, but reduce the impact of positive feedback later in one's career.

Further, given the potential for positive reciprocal relationships between engagement and several of the outcomes discussed earlier in this chapter, it is unclear how engagement and its outcomes play out during retirement. That is, while one might assume that work engagement declines prior to retirement (perhaps contributing to the decision to retire), empirical evidence has been mixed (Frins et al., 2016; Leijten et al., 2017). Following retirement, initial evidence suggests that very high levels of passion for work, a concept with similarities to engagement, can lead to lower psychological adjustment to retirement (Houlfort et al., 2015). Interestingly, it seems that employees with high levels of engagement in multiple life domains have better adjustment to retirement (Hamm et al., 2019), reinforcing the notion that examining specific targets of engagement may be increasingly important to future studies (Saks, this volume).

Further, there are a number of potential moderators to the relationship between engagement and its outcomes that require additional investigation.

Halbesleben et al. (2009) suggested that conscientiousness may play an important role in how engaged employees manage their resources (see also Hough & Oswald, this volume; Russell et al., 2017). Halbesleben et al. (2009) suggested, for example, that conscientious employees may be more effective at managing their time so that they can remain engaged in work in ways that create less conflict between work and family (e.g., working over lunch to be able to attend a child's soccer game later). Broadly speaking, it appears that moderators that impact one's ability to appropriately manage resources should impact the relationship between engagement and outcomes, since those moderators may impact the ability of the employee to translate the excess resources associated with engagement into positive outcomes (Ten Brummelhuis & Bakker, 2012). Further research into moderators that impact management of one's resources (e.g., self-regulation, polychronicity, mindfulness, or mental health conditions; cf. Halbesleben et al., 2013) may help to enhance positive outcomes associated with engagement.

Beyond individual-level moderators, there is a need to further explore moderators that organizations can manage to influence the relationship between engagement and outcomes. For example, the conscientiousness of the employee in managing their time can really only impact work–family conflict to the extent that the employee has the ability to make such changes to their schedule. Flexible work and schedule control have been explored as factors associated with higher levels of engagement (e.g., Rudolph & Baltes, 2017; Swanberg et al., 2011), but they also may enhance the ability of employees to invest the excess resources associated with engagement in ways that enhance outcomes.

Various forms of support in the workplace (e.g., supervisor, coworker, organizational) have been widely studied as resources that are associated with higher levels of engagement (e.g., Xanthopoulou et al., 2009) and as moderators that facilitate the relationship between resources and engagement (e.g., Shin et al., 2020). However, support may also play a role in moderating the impact of engagement on outcomes. For example, the relationship between engagement and job crafting may be moderated by the supervisor's or organization's level of support for job crafting. Of particular interest in this case may be to understand how that support might shift over time in light of the previously discussed notion that engagement and job crafting may lead to resource gain cycle. Such a cycle could potentially lead employees to craft their jobs in ways that increase resources, but may not be what the organization truly needs (see Halbesleben, 2011; Sonnentag et al., this volume). Whereas a supervisor may have supported job crafting initially, the cycle may reach a point where that support is reduced to focus the employee on what the organization needs.

A final potential boundary condition to the investment process in need of additional research is the specific nature of the excess resources associated with engagement. I noted above the need to further examine the differentiation between general employee engagement and more specific forms of engagement (see also Saks, this volume). In addition to highlighting situations where different foci of engagement could compete (general engagement leading to workarounds of safety protocols), additional work is needed on whether "excess" resources can always be invested in ways that lead to positive outcomes. Early in the chapter, I noted that COR defines resources in terms of their relevance. If those efforts to increase engagement do not provide additional resources that are relevant to the outcome, presumably they will not lead to the intended outcome. Additional research that differentiates between the impact of general and specific forms of engagement on outcomes could help guide interventions or other efforts by the organization to improve outcomes by increasing specifically-focused as well as general engagement.

Conclusion

The goal of this chapter was to review individual-level outcomes of engagement, with a particular focus on outcomes that have received recent attention by researchers. While a number of important research questions remain unanswered, recent research has suggested that engagement can lead to a variety of positive – and occasionally negative – outcomes for employees.

References

Agarwal, U. A., and Gupta, V. (2018). Relationships between job characteristics, work engagement, conscientiousness and managers' turnover intentions: A moderated-mediation analysis. *Personnel Review, 47*(2), 353–377.

Albrecht, S., Breidahl, E., and Marty, A. (2018). Organizational resources, organizational engagement climate, and employee engagement. *Career Development International, 23*(1), 67–85.

Asif, M., Qing, M., Hwang, J., and Shi, H. (2019). Ethical leadership, affective commitment, work engagement, and creativity: Testing a multiple mediation approach. *Sustainability, 11*(16), 4489–4504.

Baethge, A., Vahle-Hinz, T., Schulte-Braucks, J., and van Dick, R. (2018). A matter of time? Challenging and hindering effects of time pressure on work engagement. *Work & Stress, 32*(3), 228–247.

Bailey, C., Madden, A., Alfes, K., and Fletcher, L. (2017). The meaning, antecedents and outcomes of employee engagement: A narrative synthesis. *International Journal of Management Reviews, 19*(1), 31–53.

Bakker, A. B., Albrecht, S. L., and Leiter, M. P. (2011). Key questions regarding work engagement. *European Journal of Work and Organizational Psychology, 20*(1), 4–28.

Bakker, A. B., and Hakanen, J. J. (2019). Engaging aging: A model of proactive work behavior and engagement with increasing age. In T. Taris, M. Peeters, and H. De Witte (Eds), *The Fun and Frustration of Modern Working Life: Contributions from an Occupational Health Psychology Perspective* (pp. 153–163). Antwerp: Pelckmans Pro.

Bakker, A. B., Tims, M., and Derks, D. (2012). Proactive personality and job performance: The role of job crafting and work engagement. *Human Relations, 65,* 1359–1378.

Boswell, W. R., and Olson-Buchanan, J. B. (2007). The use of communication technologies after hours: The role of work attitudes and work–life conflict. *Journal of Management, 33*(4), 592–610.

Christian, M. S., Garza, A. S., and Slaughter, J. E. (2011). Work engagement: A quantitative review and test of its relations with task and contextual performance. *Personnel Psychology, 64*(1), 89–136.

Dalal, R. S., Baysinger, M., Brummel, B. J., and LeBreton, J. M. (2012). The relative importance of employee engagement, other job attitudes, and trait affect as predictors of job performance. *Journal of Applied Social Psychology, 42,* E295–E325.

Derks, D., van Duin, D., Tims, M., and Bakker, A. B. (2015). Smartphone use and work–home interference: The moderating role of social norms and employee work engagement. *Journal of Occupational and Organizational Psychology, 88*(1), 155–177.

Dubbelt, L., Demerouti, E., and Rispens, S. (2019). The value of job crafting for work engagement, task performance, and career satisfaction: Longitudinal and quasi-experimental evidence. *European Journal of Work and Organizational Psychology, 28*(3), 300–314.

Ford, M. T., Matthews, R. A., Wooldridge, J. D., Mishra, V., Kakar, U. M., and Strahan, S. R. (2014). How do occupational stressor-strain effects vary with time? A review and meta-analysis of the relevance of time lags in longitudinal studies. *Work & Stress, 28*(1), 9–30.

Frins, W., van Ruysseveldt, J., van Dam, K., and van den Bossche, S. N. (2016). Older employees' desired retirement age: A JD-R perspective. *Journal of Managerial Psychology, 31*(1), 34–49.

Gawke, J. C., Gorgievski, M. J., and Bakker, A. B. (2017). Employee intrapreneurship and work engagement: A latent change score approach. *Journal of Vocational Behavior, 100,* 88–100.

Gorgievski, M. J., and Hobfoll, S. E. (2008). Work can burn us out or fire us up: Conservation of resources in burnout and engagement. In J. R. B. Halbesleben (Ed.), *Handbook of Stress and Burnout in Health Care* (pp. 7–22). Hauppauge, NY: Nova Science Publishers.

Gustomo, A., Febriansyah, H., Ginting, H., and Santoso, I. M. (2019). Understanding narrative effects: The impact of direct storytelling intervention on increasing employee engagement among the employees of state-owned enterprise in West Java, Indonesia. *Journal of Workplace Learning, 31*(2), 166–191.

Hakanen, J., and Peeters, M. (2015). How do work engagement, workaholism, and the work-to-family interface affect each other? A 7-year follow-up study. *Journal of Occupational and Environmental Medicine, 57*(6), 601–609.

Hakanen, J. J., Perhomeini, L., and Toppinen-Tanner, S. (2008). Positive gain spirals at work: From job resources to work engagement, personal initiative and work-unit innovativeness. *Journal of Vocational Behavior*, *73*, 78–91.

Halbesleben, J. R. (2011). The consequences of engagement: The good, the bad, and the ugly. *European Journal of Work and Organizational Psychology*, *20*(1), 68–73.

Halbesleben, J. R. B., and Bellairs, T. (2015). Employee well-being and safety behaviors: The mediating role of safety workarounds. In T. Probst, S. Clarke, F. Guldenmund, and J. Passmore (Eds), *Wiley-Blackwell Handbook of the Psychology of Occupational Safety and Workplace Health* (pp. 251–271). Hoboken, NJ: Wiley-Blackwell.

Halbesleben, J. R. B., Harvey, J. B., and Bolino, M. C. (2009). Too engaged? A conservation of resources view of the relationship between work engagement and work interference with family. *Journal of Applied Psychology*, *94*, 1452–1465.

Halbesleben, J. R., Neveu, J. P., Paustian-Underdahl, S. C., and Westman, M. (2014). Getting to the "COR" understanding the role of resources in conservation of resources theory. *Journal of Management*, *40*(5), 1334–1364.

Halbesleben, J. R., Wakefield, D. S., and Wakefield, B. J. (2008). Work-arounds in health care settings: Literature review and research agenda. *Health Care Management Review*, *33*, 2–12.

Halbesleben, J. R., and Wheeler, A. R. (2008). The relative roles of engagement and embeddedness in predicting job performance and intention to leave. *Work and Stress*, *22*, 242–256.

Halbesleben, J. R., Wheeler, A. R., and Shanine, K. K. (2013). The moderating role of attention-deficit/hyperactivity disorder in the work engagement–performance process. *Journal of Occupational Health Psychology*, *18*(2), 132–143.

Hamm, J. M., Heckhausen, J., Shane, J., Infurna, F. J., and Lachman, M. E. (2019). Engagement with six major life domains during the transition to retirement: Stability and change for better or worse. *Psychology and Aging*, *34*(3), 441–456.

Harter, J. K., Schmidt, F. L., and Hayes, T. L. (2002). Business-unit-level relationship between employee satisfaction, employee engagement, and business outcomes: A meta-analysis. *Journal of Applied Psychology*, *87*, 268–279.

Henker, N., Sonnentag, S., and Unger, D. (2015). Transformational leadership and employee creativity: The mediating role of promotion focus and creative process engagement. *Journal of Business and Psychology*, *30*(2), 235–247.

Hobfoll, S. E. (1988). *The Ecology of Stress*. New York, NY: Hemisphere.

Hobfoll, S. E. (1989). Conservation of resources: A new attempt at conceptualizing stress. *American Psychologist*, *44*, 513–524.

Hobfoll, S. E. (2001). The influence of culture, community, and the nested self in the stress process: Advancing conservation of resources theory. *Applied Psychology: An International Review*, *50*, 337–370.

Hobfoll, S. E., Halbesleben, J., Neveu, J. P., and Westman, M. (2018). Conservation of resources in the organizational context: The reality of resources and their consequences. *Annual Review of Organizational Psychology and Organizational Behavior*, *5*, 103–128.

Houlfort, N., Fernet, C., Vallerand, R. J., Laframboise, A., Guay, F., and Koestner, R. (2015). The role of passion for work and need satisfaction in psychological adjustment to retirement. *Journal of Vocational Behavior*, *88*, 84–94.

Hyvonen, K., Feldt, T., Salmela-Aro, K., Kinnunen, U., and Mäkikangas, A. (2009). Young managers' drive to thrive: A personal work goal approach to burnout and work engagement. *Journal of Vocational Behavior*, *75*, 183–196.

Iqbal, I., Zia-ud-Din, M., Arif, A., Raza, M., and Ishtiaq, Z. (2017). Impact of employee engagement on work life balance with the moderating role of employee cynicism. *International Journal of Academic Research in Business and Social Sciences*, *7*(6), 1088–1101.

Kahn, W. A. (1990). Psychological conditions of personal engagement and disengagement at work. *Academy of Management Journal*, *33*(4), 692–724.

Kim, W., and Park, J. (2017). Examining structural relationships between work engagement, organizational procedural justice, knowledge sharing, and innovative work behavior for sustainable organizations. *Sustainability*, *9*(2), 205.

Knight, C., Patterson, M., and Dawson, J. (2017). Building work engagement: A systematic review and meta-analysis investigating the effectiveness of work engagement interventions. *Journal of Organizational Behavior*, *38*(6), 792–812.

Kooij, D. T. A. M, Tims, M., and Akkermans, J. (2017) The influence of future time perspective on work engagement and job performance: The role of job crafting. *European Journal of Work and Organizational Psychology*, *26*, 4–15.

Laguna, M., Razmus, W., and Żaliński, A. (2017). Dynamic relationships between personal resources and work engagement in entrepreneurs. *Journal of Occupational and Organizational Psychology*, *90*(2), 248–269.

Lee, M. C. C., Idris, M. A., and Tuckey, M. (2019). Supervisory coaching and performance feedback as mediators of the relationships between leadership styles, work engagement, and turnover intention. *Human Resource Development International*, *22*(3), 257–282.

Leijten, F. R., Hoekstra, T., Geuskens, G. A., and Burdorf, A. (2017). "Mental retirement?" Trajectories of work engagement preceding retirement among older workers. *Scandinavian Journal of Work, Environment & Health*, *43*(1), 34–41.

Macey, W. H., and Schneider, B. (2008). The meaning of employee engagement. *Industrial and Organizational Psychology*, *1*, 3–30.

Mäkikangas, A., Aunola, K., Seppälä, P., and Hakanen, J. (2016). Work engagement–team performance relationship: Shared job crafting as a moderator. *Journal of Occupational and Organizational Psychology*, *89*, 772–790.

Markos, S., and Sridevi, M. S. (2010). Employee engagement: The key to improving performance. *International Journal of Business and Management*, *5*(12), 89–96.

Matthews, R. A., Wayne, J. H., and Ford, M. T. (2014). A work–family conflict/subjective well-being process model: A test of competing theories of longitudinal effects. *Journal of Applied Psychology*, *99*(6), 1173–1187.

McCaughey, D., McGhan, G. E., Walsh, E., Rathert, C., and Belue, R. (2014). The relationship of positive work environments and workplace injury: Evidence from the National Nursing Assistant Survey. *Health Care Management Review*, *39*(1), 75–88.

Meyer, J. P., and Gagné, M. (2008). Employee engagement from a self-determination theory perspective. *Industrial and Organizational Psychology*, *1*(1), 60–62.

Meyer, J. P., Gagné, M., and Parfyonova, N. M. (2010). Toward an evidence-based model of engagement: What we can learn from motivation and commitment research. In S. L. Albrecht (Ed.), *New Horizons in Management: Handbook of Employee Engagement – Perspectives, Issues, Research and Practice* (p. 62–73). Cheltenham, UK, and Northampton, MA: Edward Elgar Publishing.

Mueller, M. (2019). Show me the money: Toward an economic model for a cost-benefit analysis of employee engagement interventions. *International Journal of Organization Theory & Behavior*, *22*(1), 43–64.

Mullins, R. (2018). Measuring employee engagement: Are engaged employees less likely to sustain a workplace injury? (Master's Thesis). Retrieved from https://encompass .eku.edu/etd/545/.

Nahrgang, J. D., Morgeson, F. P., and Hofmann, D. A. (2011). Safety at work: A meta-analytic investigation of the link between job demands, job resources, burnout, engagement, and safety outcomes. *Journal of Applied Psychology*, *96*, 71–94.

Park, Y. K., Song, J. H., Yoon, S. W., and Kim, J. (2014). Learning organization and innovative behavior: The mediating effect of work engagement. *European Journal of Training and Development*, *38*, 75–94.

Radic, A. (2019). Occupational and health safety on cruise ships: Dimensions of injuries among crew members. *Australian Journal of Maritime & Ocean Affairs*, *11*(1), 51–60.

Rafiq, M., Wu, W., Chin, T., and Nasir, M. (2019). The psychological mechanism linking employee work engagement and turnover intention: A moderated mediation study. *Work*, *62*(4), 615–628.

Rich, B. L., LePine, J. A., and Crawford, E. R. (2010). Job engagement: Antecedents and effects on performance. *Academy of Management Journal*, *53*, 617–635.

Rudolph, C. W., and Baltes, B. B. (2017). Age and health jointly moderate the influence of flexible work arrangements on work engagement: Evidence from two empirical studies. *Journal of Occupational Health Psychology*, *22*, 40–58.

Russell, E., Woods, S. A., and Banks, A. P. (2017). Examining conscientiousness as a key resource in resisting email interruptions: Implications for volatile resources and goal achievement. *Journal of Occupational and Organizational Psychology*, *90*(3), 407–435.

Seppälä, P., Hakanen, J. J., Tolvanen, A., and Demerouti, E. (2018). A job resources-based intervention to boost work engagement and team innovativeness during organizational restructuring: For whom does it work? *Journal of Organizational Change Management*, *31*(7), 1419–1437.

Shin, Y., Hur, W. M., and Choi, W. H. (2020). Coworker support as a double-edged sword: A moderated mediation model of job crafting, work engagement, and job performance. *International Journal of Human Resource Management*, *31*(11), 1417–1438.

Shipp, A. J., and Cole, M. S. (2015). Time in individual-level organizational studies: What is it, how is it used, and why isn't it exploited more often? *Annual Review of Organizational Psychology and Organizational Behavior*, *2*, 237–260.

Sundaray, B. K. (2011). Employee engagement: A driver of organizational effectiveness. *European Journal of Business and Management*, *3*(8), 53–59.

Swanberg, J. E., McKechnie, S. P., Ojha, M. U., and James, J. B. (2011). Schedule control, supervisor support and work engagement: A winning combination for workers in hourly jobs? *Journal of Vocational Behavior*, *79*(3), 613–624.

Ten Brummelhuis, L. L., and Bakker, A. B. (2012). A resource perspective on the work–home interface: The work–home resources model. *American Psychologist*, *67*(7), 545–556.

Tims, M., Bakker, A. B., and Derks, D. (2012). Development and validation of the job crafting scale. *Journal of Vocational Behavior*, *80*, 173–186.

Wachter, J. K., and Yorio, P. L. (2014). A system of safety management practices and worker engagement for reducing and preventing accidents: An empirical and theoretical investigation. *Accident Analysis & Prevention*, *68*, 117–130.

Whiteoak, J. W., and Mohamed, S. (2016). Employee engagement, boredom and frontline construction workers feeling safe in their workplace. *Accident Analysis & Prevention*, *93*, 291–298.

Wingerden, J. V., Bakker, A. B., and Derks, D. (2016). A test of a job demands-resources intervention. *Journal of Managerial Psychology*, *31*(3), 686–701.

Wrzesniewski, A., and Dutton, J. E. (2001). Crafting a job: Revisioning employees as active crafters of their work. *Academy of Management Review*, *26*(2), 179–201.

Xanthopoulou, D., Bakker, A. B., Demerouti, E., and Schaufeli, W. B. (2009). Work engagement and financial returns: A diary study on the role of job and personal resources. *Journal of Occupational and Organizational Psychology*, *82*, 183–200.

Zhang, X., and Bartol, K. M. (2010). The influence of creative process engagement on employee creative performance and overall job performance: A curvilinear assessment. *Journal of Applied Psychology*, *95*, 862–873.

PART II

Conceptualizing engagement in the changing world of work

7. Contracting, engagement, and the "gig" economy

Peter Cappelli and Liat Eldor

Engagement and the employment construct

Managers agree that the employee–organization relationship is challenging for organizations in the contemporary competitive organizational setting. The pressure to achieve more with less requires employees who are fully engaged in their work. The question is this: Can the management literature apply the concept of work engagement as both a measure and a mechanism for securing desired behaviors, especially with respect to discretionary effort, to the "gig" economy?

At its core, work engagement refers to involvement, passion, enthusiasm, and energy (Eldor, 2016; Macey & Schneider, 2008). Kahn (1990) originally defined engagement as "the harnessing of organization members' selves to their work roles, by which they employ and express themselves physically, cognitively, and emotionally during role performance" (p. 694). Engagement is therefore an ideal employee–organization relationship for the organization (Eldor & Harpaz, 2016; Kahn, 1990, 1992) through which employees invest their "hands, head, and heart" (Ashforth & Humphrey, 1995, p. 110) into their organization's objectives.

The definition of work engagement and the human capital practices that cultivate it are established on the foundations of a relatively traditional conceptualization and perception of employment. Mainly they draw on the theoretical perspective of social exchange theory (Blau, 1964), the norm of reciprocity (Gouldner, 1960), and the inducements–contributions model (March & Simon, 1958). These conceptual foundations represent important elements in the theoretical and empirical frameworks of the employee–organization relationship in general, and engagement in particular. Current engagement theory assumes a shared organizational vision and common interests between the organization and its employees (Kahn, 1990; Macey & Schneider, 2008). It also implicitly assumes "standard employment" based on a daily, fixed schedule, at the employer's physical location, continued employment, and a long-term orientation (Broschak & Davis-Blake, 2006).

The contemporary challenge is that work does not always fit that mode (Boudreau, this volume). As Cappelli and Keller (2013) outlined, there are now many forms of work that do not fit any of the above assumptions. Thus, the conceptualization we have for understanding the work engagement of standard employees does not apply to the many forms of alternative work arrangements in the gig economy, such as contractors. To illustrate, given that contractors are outsiders to the organization, they do not have a common interest with their client (i.e., the other side of the contract that hires them). The fact that they may work for many clients at the same time makes it next to impossible to maintain a shared vision. Their relationships with the client are defined by contract, which makes social exchange difficult, and of course they cannot be supervised, which is the source through which leader–member exchange and other relationships that engage individuals with their work operate.

The rise of contracting work

Anyone working for pay who is not an employee – those in the "gig" economy managed by electronic platforms or independent contractors – is governed in all Anglo-American countries and in most civil law countries by contract law, not employment law. The reason this matters for management research is, as noted above, that our most important management frameworks, including work engagement, do not apply to a contractor arrangement. Given that 14 percent of US workers may be working under a contractor arrangement, they cannot be "managed" using any of the practices that are typical for employees.[1] In the European Union, more than 15 percent of workers are independent contractors (OECD, 2017).

Information technology platforms function as brokers arranging contracts between contractors and clients. Ride-sharing at Uber and Lyft, complex information technology work via the Upwork platform (the consolidation of oDesk and Elance), Amazon's Mechanical Turk for simple online tasks, and TaskRabbit for household-related tasks are all examples. Despite the enormous attention given to the gig economy in the business press, the number of individuals working in these online contracting arrangements is still small. Most contract work is of a more traditional form, mainly traditional independent contractors.

Nevertheless, interest in contractors has been explosive in part because their use has spread to new contexts. While we have long had contractors driving cabs, the explosive growth of Uber, Lyft, and other shared car services changed that industry enormously. Companies like Microsoft and Google have tens of thousands of contractors doing programming work that is not unlike the tasks performed by their regular employees (Barley & Kunda, 2006; Bidwell, 2009). In our world, college teaching is increasingly done by instructors who are contractors – adjuncts, lecturers, and so forth.

How contracting is different

The distinction between what defines an employee versus a contractor varies somewhat across US statutes (e.g., for purposes of payroll taxes vs coverage by wage and hour laws), but they are all rooted in the "common law employment test" based on how the "client" or "employer" treats the worker. (See Social Security Administration, 2018, for a simple description of the test and how it applies in this case to social security coverage.) While the totality of factors ultimately determines whether a relationship is employment and not contracting, the important factors include whether the work is central to the business itself (as it is for gig work like drivers at Uber), whether the relationship is expected to continue, whether the worker is dependent on the client/employer for their income (e.g., they do not work elsewhere for pay), and whether the client/employer can dictate how the work is performed (see Carlson, 2001, for an overview).

Employers have the right to "direct" employees – tell them what to do and, importantly, how to do it – and can change all those directions at a moment's notice. Employees have a "duty of loyalty" to employers that includes not disparaging the employer, not doing anything to compete with the employer's interest, and generally looking after those interests. They also have duties of fidelity and a broad duty of care, which relates to being a good steward of the employer's resources. These are legal obligations that give the employer the opportunity to influence the work engagement of employees.

Contracting is quite different. It is not an open-ended relationship. The expectation is that the relationship ends unless the parties act to renegotiate a new agreement, which limits the scope for any social exchange. Most importantly, contractors and clients do not have any of the obligations to each other associated with employment. "Clients" cannot manage the work of their contractors: They cannot change the goals without renegotiating the contract, and they cannot tell contractors how to perform their work. They can only specify the outcomes and broad inputs. Not only do contractors have no common law obligations to their clients, some of the behaviors we associate with work engagement, such as discretionary effort, might even violate their contractual obligations – for example, taking actions that the contractor believes might be in the client's interest without getting approval – by going beyond what the contract requires.

While organizations employ contractors to increase flexibility and reduce costs, doing so imposes managerial challenges because the process of managing strictly by contract is difficult. If we think about the aphorism about disengaged employees – "not in my job description" as their response to anything new – we can see the problem in working with contractors for whom their "job description" literally is the limit of their legal requirements. Anticipating every issue and putting down in writing how it should be handled is virtually impossible.

The principal challenge can be described as relating to their *work* engagement. Consider this in the context of work such as Uber drivers, who are not employees (at least in most jurisdictions) yet they are the face of the company and are providing its core service. How do we get them to execute their tasks in effective, consistent ways that represent accurately the company's brand? In the absence of supervision, how do we engage them with customer service in a manner that appropriately represents the company's brand?

Many of the mechanisms that we believe create work engagement among employees cannot or do not seem to apply to contractors. For example, clients are not allowed to train contractors or to engage them in social activities and events for employees without turning those contractors into employees (see Internal Revenue Service, 2016, for such guidance). Moreover, what is "the organization" in the mechanism of organizational support if you do work brokered through Upwork? Is Upwork per se the client, and if it is the client and you never see it, what does the perception of support mean? If you are a sole contractor working for a single client, for example, and you negotiated up front for the kind of support you needed along with your fee, would you see the client as responsible for good support? Or consider leader–member exchange: The client has no formal authority over the contractor, so who is the leader in that case?

Engagement and contracting

Although we might expect that contract workers do not feel like they are a part of their client organizations and should be less likely to be engaged to the extent that employees are, actual findings on the differences in engagement and identification between permanent and contract workers have been mixed (Harrison et al., 2006; McDonald & Makin, 2000). This may partially be because of construct-validity concerns relating to the applicability of the conceptualization and measurement of work engagement in a contracting relationship. From a conceptual perspective, defining engagement with such components as full dedication and profound identification that are not expected in contract arrangements by either side (whether contractors or clients) points to the problematic issue of using a traditional definition of work engagement. Measuring engagement by items such as "I find the work that I do for the organization full of meaning and purpose," or "When I am working, I forget everything else around me" (see Utrecht Work Engagement Scale, www.wilmarschaufeli.nl/) does not represent the working reality of many contractors.

Moreover, the reality of engagement's aspects like "going the extra-mile or above and beyond" (Macey & Schneider, 2008) has very different financial implications for contractors than for employees. Employees may expect that, in the longer run, the organization will reward and support them for doing so. For contractors, going above and beyond represents an opportunity cost because they otherwise could be using that time and effort for a new client who is paying for their time. Their contract with the client has both formal and normative power over their behavior: If it says "I will be paid $100 for every hour I work," we should not expect contractors to work extra hours without pay to help the client out, which is typically routine for employees.[2] Further, what does it mean to be "fully there" (Kahn, 1990) for gig workers who typically have more than one client and need to be hunting for new ones?

What can we expect the equivalent of work engagement to mean in the context of contractors; that they will behave in the spirit of the contract as opposed to the letter of the contract? That is, where they are not otherwise directed by the contract, will they, at the margin, act to help the client: If they know something that is not covered by their contract with the client, will they nevertheless convey it to them? If they are acting as a consultant, in the hours for which they are billing will they bring their full efforts to bear on the project and their best ideas? Or will they withhold them in hope of being able to use them later in a new contract with the client?

At present, to the extent that clients attempt to "manage" their contractors, they do so by elaborating their legal contracts to cover more behavior. Franchise agreements between the franchisor (client) and the franchisee (contractor) run to hundreds of pages, detailing how even simple tasks should be performed. A common arrangement in organizations is for the point of a contact for contractors to be a separate "vendor management" office rather than the group for whom the contractor is working, extending the arms-length nature of the relationship. Vendor management typically negotiates and manages all outside contracts for the organization, from purchasing to equipment to workers. Their expertise is in contracts and negotiations. An Aberdeen Group (2015) survey reports that the primary concern of vendor management offices is cost reduction and savings (92 percent reported). This way of dealing with contractors is simply an attempt to make behaviors associated with work engagement explicit and contractual. The drawback is that work engagement is useful precisely where we cannot specify in advance and monitor behaviors that are important for outcomes.

We might expect the effect of these practices to *reduce* contractor engagement: The more requirements we specify explicitly, the less we can expect implicitly as we shift compliance further from intrinsic to extrinsic motivations (see Gagné et al., this volume).

An obvious solution is just to treat contractors more like employees, but aside from violating the law, that approach contradicts policy justification for ensuring that clients do not treat contractors as employees. Contractors, other things being equal, have fewer protections and benefits than do employees. Clients do not pay payroll taxes for contractors nor provide them with the various legal benefits (e.g., worker compensation and unemployment insurance) that employees have. Allowing clients to have the advantages of employees with all the cheaper costs of contractors simply undercuts the protections that employees have.

Engaging contractors in social exchange is possible under the current framework: Nothing prevents giving them gifts that might make them feel the need to reciprocate by engaging more profoundly and qualitatively in their work. Yet if the contractor perceives that the "gifts" were really due to their negotiating skill or conditions in the market (e.g., the client had no other options), then no social exchange takes place. Whether it is possible to create the perception of a gift that motivates social exchange in a transactional relationship is an issue we consider below.

Cultivating engagement in contractors

We recognize that there are many other practices that could improve contractor engagement that also apply to employees. Giving them tasks that are more interesting may likely increase their engagement. When we focus on issues of particular importance to contractors, we identify two sets of needs characterizing contractors through which engagement might be cultivated: market-oriented needs, which focus on creating future employability opportunities and competitive professional advantage; and identity-based needs, which focus on cultivating social ties and psychological prosperity. We propose that by meeting these two needs, something close to engagement can be cultivated in contractors.

Market-oriented mechanisms

The essence of these mechanisms lies in a rational approach to self-interest.

Prestige and attractiveness

Contractors are likely to be more engaged with work that is performed for organizations that have positive external prestige and attractiveness relative to parallel organizations. Association with organizations viewed as attractive and desirable could be "contagious" in the sense that it provides contractors with some "reflected glory" that makes them seem more desirable. This may boost their market value and increase their future employability chances and opportunities. This may be particularly so because contract work is inherently insecure and uncertain (Dex et al., 2000; O'Mahony & Bechky, 2006; Storey et al., 2005). Anything that helps them become more attractive to other clients is useful in that context (Brown & Sessions, 2005; Kreiner & Ashforth, 2004; Reade, 2001). In other words, it is in their self-interest to perform well and manifest the behaviors of work engagement when working for prestigious clients.

Ethical behavior

The apparent ethics of the client may also affect the contractor's engagement. We can define its ethical behavior as compliance with legal and professional codes of conduct, and an emphasis on strict adherence to ethical norms, as well as an authentic concern and caring for its workers' well-being (Victor

& Cullen, 1988). More engaging relationships are increasingly likely to occur when a client organization behaves ethically toward its contractors. Late payments and even non-payment are common experiences in contract work. Interviewing contractors, qualitative studies have revealed increasingly unethical behavior, such as lying, cheating, violating the spirit of a contract, and deliberately inducing a contract breach (Osnowitz, 2010). In this sense, the ethical behavior of the client rebounds to the self-interest of the contractor: We are reluctant to put in extra effort for a client who might cheat us. It is not surprising that Liden et al. (2003) have found that contingent workers rated fairness and ethics as the most important factor in evaluating the level of organizational support received from clients.

The contractor's reputation

Because contractors are almost always searching for new business, how they are perceived in the broader community matters greatly to them. The need to sustain a strong personal and professional reputation is crucial currency to help contractors secure future business, and that reputation is driven at least in part by what clients think and say about them. Van Slyke (2007) reported that public organizations use contractors' reputation as a sanction and reward mechanism to control contractor behavior. They also found that contractors whose reputations are enhanced tend to be given better opportunities for future projects by other organizations as well (Van Slyke, 2007). Recommendations and word-of-mouth praise that result from engaged contractors can be a form of social exchange between clients and contractors.

We also consider what appears to be the evolving model of managing contractors, at least in gig work moderated by electronic platforms. In order to keep the workers in contractor status, companies are trying to avoid "supervising" them directly, and instead do it through these platforms. Uber is perhaps the best-known for this effort, but a wide array of platform firms, from Deliveroo to Task Rabbit to Upwork, use similar approaches (Mazmanian et al., 2013; Sewell & Taskin, 2015).

Their processes typically begin with monitoring the contractor to generate measures of performance. Upwork, for example, generates measures of the amount of time contractors spend on projects and shares it with the clients, essentially helping clients monitor contractors. The incentive is that the client might not engage them again if the monitoring suggests some sort of malfeasance or a negative review will be posted, damaging the contractor's ability to get further work. Uber, Lyft, and the delivery companies do the reverse and ask clients to monitor and report driver quality to them. Here the platform companies may drop the contractor if the clients report that the work is poor.

Conflict management skills

Arguably the opposite extreme from having contractors who are engaged in tasks for their clients is having contractors who "work to rule" and appeal to the written contract whenever client needs do not neatly fit that written document. How different expectations and apparent conflicts in them get adjudicated without going to court is an important issue that has been examined in other contexts. On construction sites, for example, work is performed by skilled trade workers like carpenters who have a contractual relationship with general contractors, who in turn have a contractual relationship with the client. Conflicts can arise daily on these sites as unforeseen challenges appear that clash with one or more overlapping contractual arrangements. Successful construction sites have contractors and clients who learn how to negotiate these conflicts away quickly.

Much the same skill should apply in white-collar and other workplaces. We can think of these as informal side deals and other one-off arrangements that essentially rewrite the contract on the fly. Rather than expecting the contractor to pitch in and help the client with last-minute work not defined in the contract because they are engaged, as an employee might be, the client may agree to give them something in return, such as swapping those additional hours now for time off in the future. These work-arounds happen in employment relations, too (Rousseau et al., 2006), but there are exceptions there.

Identity-based mechanisms

The need to belong

Working as a contractor is often accompanied by a sense of fragmentation and discontinuity (Brocklehurst, 2001; Kallinikos, 2003). This is because of the nature of contracts that keeps them moving from job to job, sometimes in different cities. Thus, their inner need for relatedness would likely not be met. Given that contractors usually work alone and remotely, feelings of loneliness and isolation are typically experienced (Baines, 2002; Baruch, 2001; Cooper & Kurland, 2002; Golden, 2006; Kurland & Bailey, 1999). The related construct of belongingness – a profound need to be connected and psychologically attached to a group (Baumeister & Leary, 1995) – provides individuals with a degree of security and affects their identity (Deci & Ryan, 2000) and is likely to be unmet for contractors.

The need to have a purpose

Employers can arguably engage contractors in feeling as though they are part of the mission of a project or the activity of which they are a part even if they cannot make them part of the employee workplace. That could be done by sharing information about the mission, about progress on it, and about the contractor's role and contribution to it, much as we should be doing with employees (Eldor, 2020). Drawing on the job characteristics model (Hackman & Oldham, 1976) and the self-determination theory (Deci & Ryan, 2000; Ryan & Deci, 2000) that link the fulfillment of the need of being competent and significant to engagement (see also Gagné et al., this volume), it is therefore reasonable to believe that a sense of purpose can serve as a mechanism for contractors to engage with their work.

Social ties

Connections and social ties between standard employees and contractors can engage contractors in their work. Contractors often feel disconnected from other individuals/employees (Barley & Kunda, 2006; Bolino & Feldman, 2000; Turkle, 2011). Barley and Kunda (2006) note how brokers who bring IT consultants together with clients do maintain professional relationships with their contractor consultants, often over long periods of time. The complication is that involving contractors in social activities organized by the workplace contributes to a violation of the common law employment test, but informal social relationships are possible.

Nothing prevents clients from engaging contractors in actual work activities. Even where contractors perform their tasks elsewhere, clients can bring them into the workplace for meetings, rather than telecommuting. Studies have pointed to the importance of relationships with standard employees in making contractor workers feel less socially isolated (George & Chattopadhyay, 2005; Kunda et al., 2002). The sense of exclusion that contractors feel may make them keenly attuned to how they are treated by others, and social ties and positive treatment are particularly appreciated (Bartel et al., 2007; George & Chattopadhyay, 2005). Such relationships need not be long-standing to have positive and engaging effects. Sometimes it is enough for people simply to connect (Broschak & Davis-Blake, 2006; Dutton & Ragins, 2007). The small acts of positive connecting with contractors that simply signal inclusion can cultivate the contractors' sense of engagement at work by attaching them to the social fabric of the organization.

It may be impossible and undesirable for the contractor to develop ties and commitment to the client per se given that their formal relationship is likely to be with "vendor management" departments. But it is easier and quite likely desirable for them to have ties and feel engagement to the people with whom they work. Engagement with a team of people working on a project may serve essentially the same purpose as engagement with work.

A related aspect of social ties has to do with an adaptation of the leader–member exchange concept (Graen & Uhl-Bien, 1995). The client is not the supervisor of a contractor, and in most contexts, the point-person for contractors is the vendor management office with whom they otherwise have no interaction. This situation seems like a mistake. It would be much more helpful all around for the project leader or person who most directly receives the work from the contractor to be more of a point of contact with contractors. In part, this is simply to facilitate communication concerning the work, but also to build social ties and some kind of social exchange that could facilitate smoother operations and engaged contractor outcomes.

With the project leader in direct contact, it may be possible to engage in meaningful social exchange with contractors. Anyone who has ever bought coffee for their house painter understands the simple things that can be done to build social exchange relationships. These can easily become richer than the basic exchange of engagement for references noted above.

Guidance for future research

As contracting work continues to evolve, we need more theorizing on how it affects the kind of work and the way work is done, how contractors feel about their work, and more generally how it differs from employment and employees. In our review, we found almost no recent management or organizational psychology research published on work engagement of contractors. This is a critical direction for future research, particularly, because the number of contractors is increasing globally.

Perhaps the most basic questions are simply how contract work and contract workers differ from employment and how work engagement is uniquely manifested in contract work and contract workers. Qualitative studies examining questions such as what gives contractors fulfillment at work or frustration, how is their professional identity shaped, and how do contractors visualize career development are obvious to explore (see Macey, this volume, for a more detailed discussion of qualitative methods). The topic of temp work was examined in some depth a decade or more ago, but that research often conflated employee temps (on-call workers) with agency temps and with leased employees (employees of agencies) and with independent contractors. We also need research on the recruiting and selecting processes of contractors examining beneficial ways to do that for contractors and clients and whether personality characteristics can be used in these gig-oriented hiring processes (see Hough and Oswald, this volume).

More novel approaches include "nudging" the contractors with psychological and symbolic rewards to set goals for themselves or change the actual rewards to secure different behavior, as in "surge pricing" to encourage greater performance. We can think of these algorithmic approaches as the equivalent of automating side deals with the contractors.

As a matter of practice, of course, what clients want from contractors, especially those working independently on short engagements, may well not be the same as what they want from employees. What clients want is someone who will do the tasks in the contract exactly as specified. They also want a good deal – low price, high output. Clients no doubt do not care if contractors are engaged as long as they do what is specified in the contract. Where contractors have little discretion, concepts like work engagement may not matter much.

This point about client interest is also a way of noting that how we conceptualize issues like work engagement for contractors depends greatly on the work they are doing. The discussions above implicitly think of contractors doing tasks that are similar to what white-collar employees do, especially creative work where there is discretion. They are much less relevant if we are thinking about bringing in a painter to repaint an office. We recognize that the arguments above are fundamentally about how clients can get more from their contractors. It is difficult to argue that these efforts should come at the expense of the contractors. The legal restraints on how clients must deal with contractors and the policy principles behind them are so frequently violated, with contractors treated as employees, that many of our academic colleagues are surprised to discover that they exist at all. Efforts at the state level in the US are underway to rewrite relationships with contractors and narrow the circumstances under which they can be used.

Contractors have the equivalent interest in getting more out of their clients, just as employees do in securing more from their employers. Whether some of the mechanisms we describe above are symmetrical in the sense that they would work equally well if contractors used them with clients is an interesting question for future studies. Typically, the power dynamics work in favor of clients, however, as the supply of potential contractors typically exceeds the supply of available clients.

Beyond that, understanding the blended workplace structure, where permanent employees and contractors work side by side, is the next step in the research agenda. It may also help us rethink what is truly unique about employment in the process.

Notes

1. There is considerable debate in the US as to what the actual figures are as two possible sources of information give two different answers. The Bureau of Labor Statistics Contingent Worker Survey shows that independent contracting has actually declined in the last 20 years, to about 7 percent, but the percentage of people filing 1099 income tax returns for income from non-employment work has risen to about 11 percent. See Abraham et al. (2018). A different survey by Katz and Krueger (2016) put the figure at 14 percent.
2. Whether there is such a thing as a psychological contract for contractors when they already are governed by an explicit, legal contract is an interesting question. We think of the former as representing their beliefs and expectations of a reciprocal exchange between employees and their employer (Rousseau, 1989). The psychological contract of contractors has been considered by Rousseau (1990) and De Cuyper et al. (2008) as being transactional, which is the definition of the legal contract.

References

Aberdeen Group (2015). The value of strategic supplier data management. www.aberdeen.com.

Abraham, K. G., Haltiwanger, J. C., Sandusky, K., and Spletzer, J. R. (2018). *Measuring the Gig Economy: Current Knowledge and Open Issues*. NBER Working Paper No. 24950. National Bureau of Economic Research.

Ashforth, B. E., and Humphrey, R. H. (1995) Emotion in the workplace: A reappraisal. *Human Relations, 48*, 97–124. doi:10.1177/001872679504800201.

Baines, S. (2002). New technologies and old ways of working in the home of the self-employed teleworker. *New Technology, Work, and Employment, 17*, 89–101. doi:10.1111/1468-005x.00096.

Barley, S. R., and Kunda, G. (2006). Contracting: A new form of professional practice. *Academy of Management Perspectives, 20*(1), 45–66. doi:10.5465/amp.2006.19873409.

Bartel, C. A., Wrzesniewski, A., and Wiesenfeld, B. (2007). Identifying from afar: Communicating organizational membership in remote contexts. In C. A. Bartel, S. Blader, and A. Wrzesniewski (Eds), *Identity and the Modern Organization.* Lawrence Erlbaum.

Baruch, Y. (2001). The status of research on teleworking and an agenda for future research. *International Journal of Management Reviews, 3,* 113–129. doi:10.1111/1468-2370.00058.

Baumeister, R. F., and Leary, M. R. (1995). The need to belong: Desire for interpersonal attachments as a fundamental human motivation. *Psychological Bulletin, 117,* 497–529. doi:10.1037/0033-2909.117.3.497.

Bidwell, M. J. (2009). Do peripheral workers do peripheral work? Comparing the use of highly skilled contractors and regular employees. *ILR Review, 62,* 200–225. doi:10.1177/001979390906200204.

Blau, P. M. (1964). Justice in social exchange. *Sociological Inquiry, 34,* 193–206.

Bolino, M. C., and Feldman, D. C. (2000). The antecedents and consequences of underemployment among expatriates. *Journal of Organizational Behavior, 21,* 889–911. doi:10.1002/1099-1379(200012)21:8[889::AID-JOB60]3.0.CO.

Brocklehurst, M. (2001). Power, identity and new technology homework: Implications for "new forms" of organizing. *Organization Studies, 22,* 445–466. doi:10.1177/0170840601223003.

Broschak, J. P., and Davis-Blake, A. (2006). Mixing standard work and nonstandard deals: The consequences of heterogeneity in employment arrangements. *Academy of Management Journal, 49,* 371–393. doi:10.5465/AMJ.2006.20786085.

Brown, S., and Sessions, J. G. (2005). Employee attitudes, earnings and fixed-term contracts: International evidence. *Review of World Economics, 141,* 296–317. doi:10.1007/s10290-005-0029-5.

Cappelli, P., and Keller, J. (2013). Classifying work in the new economy. *Academy of Management Review, 38,* 575–596. doi:10.5465/amr.2011.0302.

Carlson, R. R. (2001). Why the law can't tell an employee when it sees one and how it ought to stop trying. *Berkeley Law Journal, 22,* 295–368.

Cooper, C. D., and Kurland, N. B. (2002). Telecommuting, professional isolation, and employee development in public and private organizations. *Journal of Organizational Behavior, 23,* 511–532. doi:10.1002/job.145.

De Cuyper, N., De Jong, J. P., De Witte, H., Isaksson, K., Rigotti, T., Schalk, R. (2008). Literature review of theory and research on the psychological impact of temporary employment: Towards a conceptual model. *International Journal of Management Reviews, 10,* 25–51. doi:10.1111/j.1468-2370.2007.00221.x.

Deci, E. L., and Ryan, R. M. (2000). The "what" and "why" of goal pursuits: Human needs and the self-determination of behavior. *Psychological Inquiry, 11,* 227–268.

Dex, S., Willis, J., Paterson, R., and Sheppard, E. (2000). Freelance workers and contract uncertainty: The effects of contractual changes in the television industry. *Work, Employment & Society, 14,* 283–305. doi:10.1177/09500170022118419.

Dutton, J. E., and Ragins, B. R. (2007). *Exploring Positive Relationships at Work: Building a Theoretical and Research Foundation.* LEA.

Eldor, L. (2016). Work engagement: Toward a general theoretical enriching model. *Human Resource Development Review, 15,* 317–339.

Eldor, L. (2020). How collective engagement creates competitive advantage for organizations: A business-level model of shared vision, competitive intensity, and service performance: Collective engagement creates competitive advantage for organizations. *Journal of Management Studies*, *57*, 177–209. doi:10.1111/joms.12438.

Eldor, L., and Harpaz, I. (2016). A process model of employee engagement: The learning climate and its relationship with extra-role performance behaviors. *Journal of Organizational Behavior*, *37*, 213–235.

George, E., and Chattopadhyay, P. (2005). One foot in each camp: The dual identification of contract workers. *Administrative Science Quarterly*, *50*, 68–99.

Golden, T. D. (2006). The role of relationships in understanding telecommuter satisfaction. *Journal of Organizational Behavior*, *27*, 319–340. doi:10.1002/job.369.

Gouldner, A. W. (1960). The norm of reciprocity: A preliminary statement. *American Sociological Review*, *25*, 161–178.

Graen, G. B., and Uhl-Bien, M. (1995). Relationship based approach to leadership: Development of leader–member exchange (LMX) theory of leadership over 25 years: Applying a multi-level multi-domain perspective. *Leadership Quarterly*, *6*, 219–247. doi:10.1016/1048–9843(95)90036–5.

Hackman, J. R., and Oldham, G. R. (1976). Motivation through the design of work: Test of a theory. *Organizational Behavior and Human Performance*, *16*, 250–279.

Harrison, D. A., Newman, D. A., and Roth, P. L. (2006). How important are job attitudes? Meta-analytic comparisons of integrative behavioral outcomes and time sequences. *Academy of Management Journal*, *49*, 305–325. doi:10.5465/amj.2006.20786077.

Internal Revenue Service (IRS). (2016). Small business/self-employed topics: Behavioral control. www.irs.gov/businesses-self-employer/behavioral-control.html.

Kahn, W. A. (1990). Psychological conditions of personal engagement and disengagement at work. *Academy of Management Journal*, *33*, 692–724. doi:10.2307/256287.

Kahn, W. A. (1992). To be fully there: Psychological presence at work. *Human Relations*, *45*, 321–349.

Kallinikos, J. (2003). Work, human agency and organizational forms: An anatomy of fragmentation. *Organization Studies*, *24*, 595–618. doi:10.1177/0170840603024004005.

Katz, L. F., and Krueger, A. B. (2016). *The Rise and Nature of Alternative Work Arrangements in the United States, 1995–2015*. Princeton University Industrial Relations Section Working Paper.

Kreiner, G. E., and Ashforth, B. E. (2004). Evidence toward an expanded model of organizational identification. *Journal of Organizational Behavior*, *25*, 1–27. doi:10.1002/job.234.

Kunda, G., Barley, S. R., and Evans, J. A. (2002). Why do contractors contract? The experience of highly skilled technical professionals in a contingent labor market. *Industrial and Labor Relations Review*, *55*, 234–261.

Kurland, N. B., and Bailey, D. E. (1999). Telework: The advantages and challenges of working here, there, anywhere, and anytime. *Organizational Dynamics*, *28*(2), 53–67.

Liden, R. C., Wayne, S. J., Kraimer, M. L., and Sparrowe, R. T. (2003). The dual commitments of contingent workers: An examination of contingents' commitment to the agency and the organization. *Journal of Organizational Behavior*, *24*, 609–625. doi:10.1002/job.208.

Macey, W. H., and Schneider, B. (2008). The meaning of employee engagement. *Industrial & Organizational Psychology: Perspectives on Science and Practice*, *1*, 3–30. doi:10.1111/j.1754-9434.2007.0002.x.

March, J. G., and Simon, H. A. (1958). *Organizations*. John Wiley & Sons.

Mazmanian, M., Orlikowski, W. J., and Yates, J. (2013). The autonomy paradox: The implications of mobile email devices for knowledge professionals. *Organization Science, 24,* 1137–1357.

McDonald, D. J., and Makin, P. J. (2000). The psychological contract, organizational commitment and job satisfaction of temporary staff. *Leadership & Organization Development Journal, 21,* 84–91. doi:10.1108/01437730010318174.

OECD (Organization of Economic Cooperation and Development). (2017). Temporary employment. https://data.oecd.org/emp/temporary-employment.htm.

O'Mahony, S., and Bechky, B. A. (2006). Stretch work: Managing the career progression paradox in external labor markets. *Academy of Management Journal, 49,* 918–941.

Osnowitz, D. (2010). *Freelancing Expertise: Contract Professionals in the New Economy.* Cornell University Press.

Reade, C. (2001). Dual identification in multinational corporations: Local managers and their psychological attachment to the subsidiary versus the global organization. *International Journal of Human Resource Management, 12,* 405–424. doi:10.1080/713769627.

Rousseau, D. M. (1989). Psychological and implied contracts in organizations. *Employee Responsibilities and Rights Journal, 2,* 121–139.

Rousseau, D. M. (1990). New hire perceptions of their own and their employer's obligations: A study of psychological contracts. *Journal of Organizational Behavior, 11,* 389–400.

Rousseau, D. M., Ho, V. T., and Greenberg, J. (2006). I-deals: Idiosyncratic terms in employment relationships. *Academy of Management Review, 31,* 977–994. doi:10.5465/AMR.2006.22527470.

Ryan, R. M., and Deci, E. L. (2000). Self-determination theory and the facilitation of intrinsic motivation, social development, and well-being. *American Psychologist, 55,* 68–78.

Sewell, G., and Taskin, L. (2015). Out of sight, out of mind in a new world of work? Autonomy, control, and spatiotemporal scaling in telework. *Organization Studies, 36,* 1507–1529.

Social Security Administration (2018). How to apply the common law control test in determining an employer/employee relationship. www.ssa.gov/section218training/advanced_course_10.htm#5.

Storey, J., Salaman, G., and Platman, K. (2005). Living with enterprise in an enterprise economy: Freelance and contract workers in the media. *Human Relations, 58,* 1033–1054. doi:10.1177/0018726705058502.

Turkle, S. (2011). *Alone Together: Why We Expect More from Technology and Less from Each Other.* Basic Books.

Van Slyke, D. M. (2007). Agents or stewards: Using theory to understand the government-nonprofit social service contracting relationship. *Journal of Public Administration Research and Theory, 17,* 157–187. doi:10.1093/jopart/mul012.

Victor, B., and Cullen, J. B. (1988). The organizational bases of ethical work climates. *Administrative Science Quarterly, 33,* 101–125. doi:10.2307/2392857.

8. Engagement with perpetually deconstructed and reinvented work

John W. Boudreau

The concept of "job" engagement can be usefully extended to encompass engagement with deconstructed job elements (e.g., tasks, activities, projects). By considering engagement with these deconstructed elements, future engagement research can better examine and inform emerging systems in which job elements are perpetually deconstructed and reconstructed to reinvent work. Such work reinvention will be increasingly necessary as organizations face accelerated changes due to uncertainty, automation and new work arrangements. As rapid change increasingly requires a future work ecosystem to more fluidly deconstruct and reconstruct jobs, the individual work elements become the key work unit, not the job (see Saks, this volume). Thus, engagement with the work *elements* is vital to understanding how workers will engage with perpetually reinvented jobs and work. This extension from job engagement to work-element engagement enables future research to better inform workers and leaders about how to optimize work reinvention, and to measure and inform better decisions about the future of work, workers and organizations.

The chapter begins with an illustrative example using the job of bank teller to show why deconstructing and reconstructing the individual work elements that make up traditional jobs is necessary for organizations to adapt rapidly to work automation. That bank teller example also illustrates how workers might differentially engage with individual work elements.

Then, the chapter shows how work-element engagement can clarify important distinctions from prior engagement research, and how prominent job-engagement theories can be applied to work-element engagement. The chapter shows how work-element engagement can be an important addition to research on work automation and alternative work arrangements. Then, the chapter turns to the *process* of perpetual work deconstruction and reinvention, noting how engagement theory and measures can be used to better understand how workers and leaders engage with the process of work crafting. The chapter concludes with suggestions for an enhanced engagement research agenda.

Future work challenges transcend employment and jobs

Here is a brainteaser: You are given a candle, a box of tacks and a book of matches. How do you attach the candle to a wall so that it can be lit without dripping wax onto the floor below? The solution to the "candle problem" (Duncker, 1945) is to deconstruct the box of tacks into its parts (box, tacks), attach the box to the wall with the tacks and attach the candle to the bottom of the box. In experiments, people who get the tacks inside the box cannot solve the problem, but those given a pile of tacks beside the box solve it easily.

Typically, work is "constructed" into job descriptions similar to the box of tacks. Jobs are the repository for work requirements. Job holders are the repository for worker capabilities. This obscures powerful opportunities to optimize the work and the workforce, enhancing productivity, alignment and engagement. Those opportunities require perpetual work "reinvention," based not on jobs and jobholders, but on their deconstructed elements. In the dynamic work environments of the future, work-related research and practice should address dilemmas that resemble the candle puzzle. It is time to take the tacks out of the box.

Understanding and optimally responding to the future of work will increasingly require deconstructing jobs into their elements. It is at the work-elements level that we find the key building blocks to understanding and optimizing trends such as automation and alternative work arrangements. For example, work automation only rarely involves substituting a robot, chatbot or artificial intelligence (AI) for the human worker in a particular "job." Rather, the vast majority of work automation effects will reinvent the job, requiring that humans and automation work together, as some of the tasks formerly done by the human worker are now done by automation, but many of the formerly human tasks will still be done by the human worker (Jesuthasan & Boudreau, 2018; World Economic Forum, 2018). Similarly, "alternative work arrangements" that offer options to regular full-time employment (such as contractors, freelancers and volunteers) seldom fully substitute a non-employee for an employee. Rather, some of the tasks in a "job" formerly done by a regular employee "jobholder" might be done by a contractor or freelancer, but many of the remaining job tasks would still be done by a regular employee (Boudreau, Jesuthasan & Creelman, 2015; Capelli & Eldor, this volume).

Of course, this shift toward defining work in terms of job elements instead of jobs will not affect all work immediately, and in many work arenas the traditional focus on jobs and jobholders will be adequate. However, evidence shows that a significant and growing portion of work will require deconstruction and reinvention.

Similarly, engagement has typically been defined with a focus on *employees* who hold *jobs* within a single *organization*. Saks and Gruman (2014, p. 156) note that "some argue that it should be called *employee engagement*, while others suggest it should be called *job engagement* (Rich, LePine & Crawford, 2010) or *work engagement* (Shaufeli & Salanova, 2011)." Bakker (2017, p. 67) introduces his review of "work engagement" by stating that "organizations increasingly rely on the strengths and talents of their employees." He notes that modern organizations' competitiveness relies on "engaged employees."

The concept of engagement applied to intact jobs and job holders (regular full-time employees) in an organization is certainly valuable, but if future work is a fluid set of elements that are constantly being reinvented, then engagement research is severely limited by the implicit assumption that work is contained exclusively in a "job" performed by a job holder. This is increasingly true as work and workers evolve more rapidly than job titles, whether due to automation, changing skills, work arrangements that go beyond regular full-time employment, and so on. The good news is that worker engagement is still a vital and valuable concept when applied to the "deconstructed" work elements, and those elements are the currency for understanding perpetually reinvented work. This is "work engagement deconstructed" or "work engagement reinvented."

Debate about this focus has long characterized engagement research. Indeed, Kahn's (1990) original concept of engagement as placing one's complete self into the role essentially requires considering work as deconstructed elements that can be reinvented to create new roles. A fundamental question at the heart of work engagement is how the total set of worker attributes changes in any given role as it is deconstructed and reinvented, and how worker engagement, burnout and demand–resource relationships might vary across the distinct role elements (e.g., tasks, projects; see Saks and McLarnon, Morin & Litalien, this volume).

Thus, we might suggest that the term "work engagement" is the high-level concept that can include engagement with work at any level, including tasks, projects and the more traditional jobs. We might suggest that the term "task engagement" captures engagement with deconstructed work elements (Newton et al., 2020; Saks, this volume).

Human bank tellers and ATMs

On June 27, 1967, Barclays Bank installed in London a machine that allowed cash withdrawals using paper vouchers. The British press called it the "robot cashier." London bank tellers so feared losing their jobs that they sneaked out and covered the keyboards with honey (Segarra, 2017).

Work automation is often framed in simple terms – how many jobs will new technology replace? For example, on June 14, 2011, U.S. President Barack Obama stated that ATMs allowed businesses to "become much more efficient with a lot fewer workers." Actually, the number of teller jobs *increased* with the number of ATMs. In 1985, the U.S. had 60,000 ATMs and 485,000 bank tellers. In 2002, there were 352,000 ATMs and 527,000 bank tellers (Fishman, 2004).

James Bessen (2015) explains why more ATMs spawned more teller jobs. The average bank branch employed 20 workers before ATMs. The use of ATMs reduced the number to about 13, making it cheaper for banks to open branches. Meanwhile, the number of banking transactions soared, and banks began to compete by promising better customer service: more bank employees, at more branches, handling more complex tasks than tellers in the past. More recently, personal devices and cloud-based financial transactions are further changing the work of banks. While more than 8,000 U.S. bank branches have closed over the past decade (an average of more than 150 per U.S. state) and more than 90 percent of transactions now take place online, the number of U.S. bank employees has remained relatively stable at more than two million (Heath, 2017). Bank branches remain a brick-and-mortar presence, where modern tellers may help customers with a smartphone or tablet in hand. Or, many customers may now find a teller online. It's a role exemplified in Bank of America's new experiment with hybrid banking, small unstaffed mini-branches that offer a direct link to tellers via video conference (Murakami-Fester, 2017).

The ATM story offers an important parable for leaders, workers and policy makers. It vividly shows why simplistic ideas like "technology replaces human jobs" are both so enticing and so misleading. Solving the organizational, social and strategic challenges of work automation demands a pivotal future capability – optimizing the constantly-evolving options that combine human and automated work. Work engagement can be an important component of such solutions and optimization, but it requires extending the engagement construct to work elements, which are key to understanding and predicting work evolution.

Deconstructing and reinventing bank teller work and work engagement

The bank teller job evolution offers instructive lessons for work deconstruction and the future of work engagement measurement and research. These lessons have been alluded to in early discussions of "strategic job analysis" (Schneider & Konz, 1989) that encouraged analysis of changing "job" requirements at the task and skill level, and in frameworks to optimize alternative work arrangements (Boudreau et al., 2015) and work automation (Jesuthasan & Boudreau, 2018). Leading labor economists and automation futurists have also endorsed the notion of work deconstruction. For example, Frank et al. (2019, p. 6533) noted that "Increasing a labor model's specificity into workplace tasks and skills might further resolve labor trends and improve predictions of automation from AI."

This fact has long been recognized by scholars and other professionals who study the evolution of work and automation. For example, the seminal work by Frey and Osborne (2013) examined the probability jobs would be lost to automation by calculating the likelihood of automation replacing tasks within jobs. This was an extension of the "task model" introduced by Autor, Levy and Murnane (2003) and extended by Brynjolfsson and McAfee (2011). For example, Frey and Osborne (Table 1, p. 31) show that certain tasks from the O*Net library (Perception/Manipulation; Creative Intelligence; and Social Intelligence) represent "bottlenecks to computerization" (p. 30). Muro, Maxim and Whiton (2019), in a Brookings Institution study, estimated the "automation potential" of occupation groups by examining the "share of tasks that are susceptible to automation" (p. 54).

Similarly, websites that calculate the probability that a job can be automated, such as replacedbyrobot.info, base their calculations on the tasks within the job. For example, if you search the job "bank teller" at this site (www .replacedbyrobot.info/66207/bank-teller), you find an estimate of a 98 percent chance of job automation. Then, the site lists the tasks for the bank teller job, based on O*Net and the U.S. Bureau of Labor Statistics. Table 8.1 shows the work activities listed by O*Net for the job of bank teller.

Table 8.1   Work activities of a bank teller listed by O*Net

Performing for or working directly with the public
Interacting with computers
Establishing and maintaining interpersonal relationships
Communicating with supervisors, peers, or subordinates
Evaluating information to determine compliance with standards
Getting information
Processing information
Making decisions and solving problems
Resolving conflicts and negotiating with others
Updating and using relevant knowledge
Identifying objects, actions, and events
Analyzing data or information
Selling or influencing others
Documenting/recording information
Monitoring processes, materials, or surroundings
Judging the qualities of things, services, or people
Organizing, planning, and prioritizing work
Assisting and caring for others
Interpreting the meaning of information for others
Communicating with persons outside the organization
Scheduling work and activities
Estimating the quantifiable characteristics of products, events, or information
Inspecting equipment, structures, or material

Source: O*Net, www.onetonline.org/link/summary/43-3071.00.

Some of these tasks are indeed highly susceptible to automation that might *replace* the human worker, such as "documenting/recording information" and "interacting with computers." Others are unlikely to be substituted by automation but might be *augmented* by improved information or algorithmic decision rules, such as "assisting and caring for others," "resolving conflicts and negotiating with others," and "interpreting the meaning of information for others." Still other tasks will likely be *reinvented* by the combination of humans and automation, such as "making decisions and solving problems," where the automated databases and decision rules would improve the knowledge and judgment of humans in ways not possible without automation. As we saw in the earlier section, the end result is an evolving "job" of bank teller that today contains few of the traditional repetitive tasks, but that now includes remote human tellers whose work is systematically enhanced by a collaboration with automation.

We can also imagine how work arrangements beyond traditional full-time employment might affect the future role of bank teller. As the work can be done more remotely, it is possible to envision enlisting workers as contractors, who might work from home on particular tasks such as analyzing customer data for patterns to improve products or services. Workers can enlist through a freelance platform for specific projects such as testing a new work system to enhance its functionality or user interface. As with work automation, these options mean that the work that was formerly contained in the "job" of bank teller, and was done by a regular full-time employee, will now be partly done by human workers through alternative arrangements.

There is some controversy about how fast these alternative work arrangements have grown, particularly the question of whether such alternative arrange-ments produce comparable value to regular full-time employment (e.g., Cappelli & Eldor, this volume; Collins et al., 2019; Federal Reserve, 2019; Irwin, 2019). Even if such arrangements are unlikely to provide full-time work that replaces a regular job, there is evidence that such platforms are used by millions of workers globally, often as a side-gig, to supplement their income (Manyika et al., 2016). There is also evidence (Boudreau et al., 2015) that organizations such as IBM employ internal "freelance" platforms with their regular full-time employees, to offer those employees project-based assignments as a means to achieve flexibility and greater worker engagement. Platforms like Snag.Work (https://snag.work/) offer the opportunity for businesses to post their available shift work, and workers to pick up those shifts. The shift is a deconstructed part of the full-time job, which makes it particularly attractive for a freelance model, either limited to regular employees or extended beyond the organiza-tion boundary to capture a much broader available workforce willing to engage on a shift-by-shift basis (Coletta, 2018). The platform Wonolo (www.wonolo .com/) provides this service for workers and companies, for shifts in work such as warehouse operations, general labor, delivering, food production, event staffing, and merchandizing, among others.

In light of such changes, how should we define "engagement" with the bank teller "job"? For example, if a bank teller jobholder feels deeply engaged with tasks such as counting money and verifying accounts – where automation will *replace* humans – that suggests imminent engagement problems as their most engaging work is replaced by automation. Conversely, if a bank teller jobholder is deeply engaged with tasks that will be *augmented* by automation, or tasks where automation will *reinvent* the work to make the human more valuable, then they are well positioned to be engaged with the new job as it evolves to become a combination of automated and human work.

Or, suppose a bank teller is very engaged with the shift-based work of being physically on site and working directly with customers, but not very engaged with sitting at one branch for eight hours a day, five days a week. Now, the most engaging work arrangement may not be a full-time job, but rather the opportunity to work through a freelance platform, offering banking shifts across many different banking companies, in greater quantity and with greater scheduling flexibility.

When engagement is examined at the work-shift level in this instance, it reveals that the "organization" is actually an ecosystem of banking shifts, across different companies, suggesting new levels of analysis (see González-Romá, this volume). These distinctions can only be seen if we consider the work-element level (tasks, shifts, projects, etc.), and not exclusively the "job" level. Engagement measures and theories that focus on the "job" will overlook this more granular pattern of engagement, and likely overlook insights and opportunities to enhance both research and practice.

Engagement research can better reflect perpetual work evolution

Schneider et al. (2017) noted that engagement measures originally focused on "work" engagement (e.g., the Utrecht Work Engagement Scale, or UWES). More recent measures, particularly those developed by polling or consulting companies, such as Gallup, have incorporated additional issues such as turnover intentions and commitment, focusing more on a measure that predicts individual, team and ultimately organizational financial outcomes. The vast majority of studies and applications of "work engagement" focus on organizational members defined as holding traditional regular full-time employment, with the "work" being embedded in their "job." Indeed, Bakker (2017) reviews engagement research through the perspective of the "Job Demands–Resources" theory, with work engagement as a function of the "job demands and resources provided by the organization" (p. 68). Saks and Gruman (2014) title their article "What Do We Really Know About Employee Engagement?" Clearly, even writers who acknowledge that the focus of engagement may vary still often revert to an assumption that "work" is a traditional full-time job in a traditional organization.

Yet, Bakker (2017) also points out that when William Kahn coined the term "engagement" in 1990, it referred to "the simultaneous employment and expression of a person's 'preferred self' in task behaviors that promote connections to work and to others" (p. 67). Bakker further notes that academic research defines and measures engagement "as a positive, fulfilling work-related state of mind that is characterized by vigor, dedication, and absorption" (p. 67). Thus, while the focus of both research and practice in work engagement has been on traditional jobs, there is certainly nothing in the fundamental concept or definition that limits the idea only to jobs, employment and single-organizational membership. Indeed, as illustrated by the bank teller example, one can easily imagine measuring concepts such as vigor, dedication and absorption focused on the deconstructed tasks that make up a job, or the specific projects that make up a short-term work connection for a freelance worker, or the work elements that are specifically included in an agreement with a contractor (Saks, this volume).

Three theories of work engagement noted by Saks and Gruman (2014) include "psychological meaningfulness" (Kahn, 1990), "job burnout" (Maslach, Schaufeli & Leiter, 2001) and "job demands and resources" (Bakker & Demerouti, 2007). These need not be attached to a "job" and "organization" to maintain their value and relevance. They apply equally to the distinct work elements of traditional jobs, and to the process of perpetual deconstruction and reinvention of those work elements that characterize much future work. Engagement occurs at multiple levels (see González-Romá and Xanthopoulou & Bakker, this volume), and promising insights may be revealed by extending engagement research to the level of the work elements or tasks. The concept of "multiple targets" (Saks, this volume) is also relevant here.

Next, this chapter will explore implications of "perpetually reinvented work," and the untapped potential for engagement research to contribute insights that enhance the future of work for workers, organizations and society.

How is overall job engagement related to configurations of job-element engagement?

Future engagement research should measure work engagement at the granular level, such as tasks or projects. Such research could be easily built upon current engagement measures. The theories of engagement causes, consequences and covariates could as easily apply to tasks/projects. Even in work arenas where the "job" is likely to contain the work, we may learn a great deal by understanding how engagement varies across the tasks within that job. Overall job engagement may show interesting patterns at the task or project level, driven by varying configurations of engagement with different job elements. For some jobs, overall engagement might be simply the sum of job-element engagement, with job elements combining in a compensatory way. For other jobs, overall engagement might be a function of engagement with one or two pivotal elements, while other job elements are irrelevant. For still other jobs, overall engagement may be a configuration, where the elements interact with each other, such that engagement in one element predicts overall engagement only in the presence of a sufficient level of another element or elements (see McLarnon et al., this volume, for a discussion of person-centered analytic strategies that can be used to investigate engagement configurations).

This can be extended to the concept of engagement with reinvented work, as in the bank teller example. Once researchers measure engagement with work elements (tasks, projects, etc.), then when those elements are reconstructed or "reinvented" into new jobs, the element-level data about engagement, burnout, resources–demands, and so on can be used to predict likely engagement with the newly reconstructed job, or with the newly-created projects. This is key to empirically addressing the dynamics of engagement (see Sonnentag, Wiegelmann & Czink, this volume), as those dynamics will often occur at the work element level, as jobs are deconstructed and reinvented.

What are the causes, consequences and covariates of engagement of workers with non-standard work arrangements?

In addition to marketplaces that are internal to organizations, engagement research can provide important insights into the engagement of those who work through freelance platforms and other alternative arrangements, often described as the "gig" economy (see Cappelli & Eldor, this volume). What is engagement among those who work primarily through deconstructed tasks or projects?

In 2019, California passed Assembly Bill 5 (Myers, Bhuiyan & Roosevelt, 2019), which joined many legislative attempts to more precisely classify work as either employment or freelance, and to protect workers from perceived abuses by platform companies like Uber, Lyft and Postmates. There is much debate about whether, and under what conditions, freelance workers are eager for the protections of employment, or prefer to work through a platform. The specific case of freelance journalism has shown the complexity of such legislation (Cowan, 2019), with some types of workers more protected, while others face greater work challenges, producing often-arbitrary decisions necessary to reconcile the costs and benefits of employment requirements that are needed to complete the legislation.

Cascio and Boudreau (2017) noted that while much research on nonstandard workers proceeds from the presumption that they are less engaged, satisfied and committed, and that they desire permanent employment, the evidence is actually mixed. Clinton et al. (2011) surveyed 1,169 temporary workers in Europe. They found that prior experience as a temporary worker associated positively with individual performance, but was not associated with job insecurity, job satisfaction or organizational commitment. Guest's (2004) review reached a similar conclusion, noting that workers on flexible contracts are not invariably disadvantaged, and that knowledge workers pursuing boundaryless careers are especially likely to report positive outcomes. Allan and Sienko (1997) administered the Job Diagnostic Survey (JDS) of Hackman and Oldham (1980) to 149 permanent and 48 contingent workers doing the same types of jobs in six U.S. locations of a large unit of a telecommunications company. Results showed contingent workers to have higher motivating potential scores, due to higher Task Identity and Feedback scores. Contingents also scored higher on Knowledge of Results and Growth Need Strength, while permanent employees were higher in Satisfaction with Job Security. Bardasi and Francesconi (2004) examined subjective indicators of mental health, general health status, life satisfaction and job satisfaction. They compared workers with temporary contracts, part-time workers and full-time workers, using a panel of 7,000 workers from the first 10 waves of the British Household Panel Survey, 1991–2000. They found "Controlling for background characteristics, atypical employment does not appear to be associated with adverse health consequences for either men or women" (p. 1671).

Notably, much of the existing research on these alternative arrangements has not focused specifically on worker engagement. Yet, engagement theories and measures have much to offer in better understanding and resolving important questions about the causes, consequences and covariates of engagement among non-standard workers. Again, consider the insights that could be produced by applying the theoretical framework suggested by Bakker (2017) and Meyer (2017), including vigor–dedication–absorption and job demands–resources, to workers in nonstandard arrangements. Issues such as job demands and resources, as well as outcomes such as burnout, could be usefully illuminated with existing engagement frameworks and measures, now applied to non-standard workers.

What are the causes, consequences and covariates of engagement with work automation?

This chapter began with the example of the bank teller, which is a particular case of work deconstruction driven significantly by automation. It is beyond the scope of this chapter to examine the broad topic of work automation (see Brynjolfsson & McAfee, 2011, and Jesuthasan & Boudreau, 2018, for more extensive treatments), but job deconstruction and reinvention is pivotal to work automation, and the vast majority of work automation will produce work where humans and automation work together, likely in evolving relationships. Thus, because human workers will be integral to future work automation, the construct, theories, findings and research on engagement should play an important role in understanding, predicting and optimizing work automation outcomes for various stakeholders.

Research suggests that engagement with work automation may be quite low, driven by a general impression that automation replaces human workers, rather than the more likely outcome that humans and automation will work together. A Pew Research Center survey (Smith & Anderson, 2017, p. 5) showed that 85 percent of U.S. adults favored a policy that would limit machines to "doing dangerous or unhealthy jobs," and 58 percent agreed that in the event that robots are capable of doing human jobs, there "should be limits on the number of jobs businesses can replace with machines, even if they are better and cheaper than humans." Also, 72 percent of U.S. adults were "worried" about a "future where robots and computers can do many human jobs" (p. 3).

The constructs and theories of work engagement have much to tell us about what underpins the widespread distrust and worry about work automation, and perhaps how to enhance work automation engagement. Yet, the greatest attention today is on worker skills (Oswald, Behrend & Foster, 2019), and upskilling to meet new work requirements. Attention to comprehensive worker skills (rather than simply their qualifications for a particular job) is important and consistent with a more granular focus on deconstructed work, but while worker *capability* is necessary, it is hardly sufficient. Worker attributes such as trust, alignment and *motivation* to support work automation are also pivotal, and fall squarely in the domain of future engagement research. Clearly, engagement with the process and outcomes of work automation will be key to its success and social value.

Measuring engagement at the work-element level could distinguish engagement with work elements that are differentially susceptible to automation, and then apply theories such as resources–demands across the spectrum of automation-susceptible work elements, to inform the causes and consequences of worker engagement with work automation.

What are the causes, consequences and covariates of engagement in the *process* of work deconstruction and reinvention?

As we have seen, engagement "deconstructed" rests on the capability, opportunity and motivation of workers, leaders and organization systems to define work in more granular terms, and to deconstruct and reinvent jobs to reflect and optimize against work changes such as automation and new work arrangements. To this point, this chapter has focused on engagement with the deconstructed work elements, and the perpetually reinvented jobs that are constructed from those work elements. It is also important to consider and study how leaders and workers are "engaged" and motivated by the *process* of continually deconstructing and reinventing work. Thus far, this chapter has treated work reinvention as the province of the organizations that enlist or employ workers. This is the traditional and common perspective in most research on work and engagement – that organizations design work, and then workers react to those work designs. Yet, the process of work deconstruction and reinvention is carried out not only by the organization, but also by the workers themselves. Freelance workers, independent contractors and even consultants employed by firms often have discretion in how they design their work, with the freedom to choose what projects they undertake, how to form project teams and (in the case of freelancers or contractors) even what organizations to work with.

Gagné et al. (this volume) discuss the motivational processes likely to be affected by job re-design. They describe how SMART design features (stimulating, mastery-oriented, agentic, relational and tolerable) can contribute to need satisfaction and engagement. Wrzesniewski and Dutton (2001) coined the term "job crafting," noting that even with fixed jobs, workers may have some discretion in their work tasks and relationships and the meaning they attach to their work tasks. Bakker and Demorouti (2016, p. 276) noted that through job crafting, workers can reduce work strain, increase work challenges and thus increase their work engagement. Lazazzara, Tims and de Gennaro (2020) synthesized quantitative and qualitative job crafting research, suggesting that workers may be proactive (to reach desirable goals or improve performance) or reactive (coping with organizational change and pressure), and involve either approach (improving work and interpreting work stressors positively) or avoidance (reducing or eliminating negative job elements). Notably, all these approaches to job crafting rely on deconstructed elements of a job to understand and define both the content and the process.

If we shift the focus from jobs to work elements, then the concept of "work crafting" will be even more relevant as job deconstruction and reconstruction becomes more prevalent. As organizations increasingly deconstruct and reconstruct work, those doing the work will gain greater insight into the perpetual reinvention process, and will likely influence and even explicitly shape their own work deconstruction and reinvention. Both workers and the organizations that employ them will be important parties to job deconstruction and reinvention, so both workers and leaders will experience engagement with the process itself. Lazazzara et al. (2020) noted that job crafting can result in both positive (meaningfulness, recognition, job satisfaction) and negative (regrets, overload, stress, health problems) outcomes. These outcomes resemble and include common elements of work engagement.

Future engagement research can contribute by analyzing the causes, consequences and covariates of engagement with the work deconstruction and reinvention process. For example, we know virtually nothing about whether workers and leaders are engaged or resistant to:

1. Discovering tasks within their jobs that can be better done by automation or alternatively-engaged human workers;
2. Continually reconstructing their work through new combinations of tasks and projects; and
3. Taking on projects outside their regular job, either as external "side gigs" or as internal projects on a talent marketplace.

Unilever is a global consumer products organization that is testing a management system called FLEX (Bersin, 2019; WebWire, 2019) that begins by asking employees to write "purpose statements," and to share their existing and desired skills and work tasks in an online platform, with the goal of using AI to match work with worker capability, optimizing both the needed capabilities but also the capabilities workers desire to develop. Such experiments are becoming more common (Boudreau et al., 2015), and present an opportunity for engagement researchers to apply decades of evidence-based knowledge about engagement with "jobs" to this new work ecosystem of projects, tasks and boundary-less reconfiguration. It is striking that Unilever and others emphasize how such systems can contribute to overall employee engagement and "purpose," by "democratizing" the workplace (Boudreau, 2016). Such goals seem not only compatible with engagement measures and theories, but also are likely to require the application of "engagement deconstructed" to fully understand and optimize these new systems, with insights into the cognitive and behavioral processes that underlie them.

Conclusions and a research agenda

Engagement "deconstructed" and "reinvented" is an opportunity to extend the relevance and applicability of an important construct that has largely been confined by the assumption that work exists in "jobs" being done by "employees." Future engagement researchers, and practicing managers, will no doubt find value in this traditional focus of engagement, because much work will still be done on traditional jobs and with employees of organizations.

However, increasingly work is being redefined through deconstruction and reinvention at the level of job elements. Extending engagement definitions, measures, theories and research to this emerging concept of work will keep the engagement concept relevant to some of the most exciting and important future developments. This offers engagement scholars and practitioners important and exciting new avenues for research that will help uncover insights and relationships that might be overlooked with an exclusive focus on "jobs." Engagement research should:

- Develop new engagement measures focused on the work-element level of analysis, by drawing on emerging task-based work taxonomies such as O*Net, and the research of scholars examining automation at the work-element level, as well as the task- and project-based work taxonomies that are evolving in talent marketplaces such as internal and external free-lance platforms.

- Develop new engagement theories that focus on this work-element level of analysis, drawing on existing engagement causes, consequences and covariates, including existing research on work involvement, burnout and demands–resources relationships.
- Develop and test theories about how engagement at the work-element level may aggregate to inform engagement at the job level, and what configural rules define that aggregation (see McLarnon et al., this volume).
- Apply engagement measures and theories more fully to emerging issues such as non-standard work arrangements and work automation, to offer unique insights that are currently overlooked by research and practice in these areas.
- Examine how the construct of engagement itself may be applied and inform worker attitudes, reactions and behaviors in areas such as work deconstruction, non-standard work arrangements and work automation.
- Explore the antecedents of engagement in various job elements rather than assuming that different job elements all have the same antecedents.

References

Allan, P., and Sienko, S. (1997). A comparison of contingent and core workers' perceptions of their jobs' characteristics and motivational properties. *SAM Advanced Management Journal, 62*(3), 4–9.

Autor, D., Levy, F., and Murnane, R. J. (2003). The skill content of recent technological change: An empirical exploration. *Quarterly Journal of Economics, 118*(4), 1279–1333.

Bakker, A. (2017). Strategic and proactive approaches to work engagement. *Organizational Dynamics, 46*, 67–75.

Bakker, A., and Demerouti, E. (2016). Job demands–resources theory: Taking stock and looking forward. *Journal of Occupational Health Psychology, 22*(3), 273–285.

Bakker, A. B., and Demerouti, E. (2007). The job demands-resources model: State of the art. *Journal of Managerial Psychology, 22*(3), 309–328.

Bardasi, E., and Francesconi, M. (2004). The impact of atypical employment on individual wellbeing: Evidence from a panel of British workers. *Social Science & Medicine, 58*, 1671–1688.

Bersin, J. (2019, July). The company as a talent marketplace: Unilever and Schneider Electric show the way. Josh Bersin: Insights on Corporate Talent, Learning, and HR Technology. https://joshbersin.com/2019/07/the-company-as-a-talent-network-unilever-and-schneider-electric-show-the-way/.

Bessen, J. (2015). *Learning by Doing*. New Haven, CT: Yale University Press.

Boudreau, J. W. (2016). HR at the tipping point: The paradoxical future of our profession. *People + Strategy, 38*(4), 46–54.

Boudreau, J. W., Jesuthasan, R., and Creelman, D. (2015). *Lead the Work*. Hoboken, NJ: John Wiley & Sons.

Brynjolfsson, E., and McAfee, A. (2011). *Race Against the Machine: How the Digital Revolution Is Accelerating Innovation, Driving Productivity, and Irreversibly Transforming Employment and the Economy*. Lexington, MA: Digital Frontier Press.

Cascio, W. F., and Boudreau, J. W. (2017). Talent management of nonstandard employees. In D. G. Collings, K. Mellahi, and W. F. Cascio (Eds), *The Oxford Handbook of Talent Management* (pp. 494–520). Oxford, UK: Oxford University Press.

Clinton, M., Bernhard-Oetell, C., Rigotti, T., and de Jong, J. (2011). Expanding the temporal context of research on non-permanent work. *Career Development International*, 16(2), 114–139.

Coletta, J. (2018, September 11). Shifting for the gig economy. *Human Resource Executive*. https://hrexecutive.com/shifting-for-the-gig-economy/.

Collins, B., Garin, A., Jackson, E., Koustas, D., and Payne, M. (2019). Is gig work replacing traditional employment? Evidence from two decades of tax returns. Unpublished paper, IRS SOI Joint Statistical Research Program. www.irs.gov/pub/irs-soi/19rpgigworkreplacingtraditionalemployment.pdf.

Cowan, J. (2019, September 12). Why newspapers are fighting California's landmark labor bill. *New York Times*. www.nytimes.com/2019/09/12/us/newspapers-gig-economy-bill-california.html.

Duncker, K. (1945). On problem-solving. *Psychological Monographs*, 58(5), i–113. https://doi.org/10.1037/h0093599.

Federal Reserve. (2019). *Report on the Economic Well-Being of US Households in 2018, May 2019*. Board of Governors of the Federal Reserve System, Washington, DC. www.federalreserve.gov/publications/files/2018-report-economic-well-being-us-households-201905.pdf.

Fishman, C. (2004). The toll of a new machine. *Fast Company*, May 1.

Frank, M. R., Autor, D., Bessen, M. E., Brynjolfsson, E., Cebrian, M., Deming, D. J., Feldman, M., Groh, M., Logo, J., Moro, E., Wang, D., Youn, H., and Rahwan, I. (2019). Toward understanding the impact of artificial intelligence on labor. *Proceedings of the National Academy of Science*, 116(14), 6531–6539.

Frey, C. B., and Osborne, M. A. (2013). *The Future of Employment: How Susceptible Are Jobs to Computerization?* Oxford, UK: University of Oxford. www.oxfordmartin.ox.ac.uk/downloads/academic/The_Future_of_Employment.pdf.

Guest, D. (2004). Flexible employment contracts, the psychological contract and employee outcomes: An analysis and review of the evidence. *International Journal of Management Reviews*, 5(1), 1–19.

Hackman, J. R., and Oldham, G. R. (1980). *Work Redesign*. Reading, MA: Addison-Wesley.

Heath, T. (2017, February 8). Bank tellers are the next blacksmiths. *Washington Post*. www.washingtonpost.com/business/economy/bank-tellers-are-the-next-blacksmiths/2017/02/08/fdf78618-ee1c-11e6-9662-6eedf1627882_story.html.

Irwin, N. (2019, September 15). Maybe we're not all going to be gig economy workers after all. *New York Times*. www.nytimes.com/2019/09/15/upshot/gig-economy-limits-labor-market-uber-california.html.

Jesuthasan, R., and Boudreau, J. W. (2018). *Reinventing Jobs: A Four-Step Approach for Applying Automation to Work*. Boston, MA: Harvard Business Review Press.

Kahn, W. A. (1990). Psychological conditions of personal engagement and disengagement at work. *Academy of Management Journal*, 33(4), 692–724.

Lazazzara, A., Tims, M., and de Gennaro, D. (2020). The process of reinventing a job: A meta-synthesis of qualitative job crafting research. *Journal of Vocational Behavior, 116*, 103267.

Manyika, J., Lund, S., Bughin, J., Robinson, K., Jischke, J., and Mahajan, D. (2016). *Independent Work: Choice, Necessity, and the Gig Economy*. New York, NY: McKinsey Global Institute.

Maslach, C., Schaufeli, W. B., and Leiter, M. P. (2001). Job burnout. *Annual Review of Psychology, 52*(1), 397–422.

Meyer, J. P. (2017). Has engagement had its day: What's next and does it matter? *Organization Dynamics, 46*, 87–95.

Murikami-Fester, A. (2017, March 27). Why bank tellers won't become extinct any time soon. *USA Today*. www.usatoday.com/story/money/personalfinance/2017/03/27/why-bank-tellers-wont-become-extinct-any-time-soon/99320674/.

Muro, M., Maxim, R., and Whiton, J. (2019). *Automation and Artificial Intelligence: How Machines Are Affecting People and Places*. Washington, DC.: Brookings Institution. www.brookings.edu/wp-content/uploads/2019/01/2019.01_BrookingsMetro_Automation-AI_Report_Muro-Maxim-Whiton-FINAL-version.pdf.

Myers, J., Bhuiyah, J., and Roosevelt, M. (2019, September 18). Newsom signs bill rewriting California employment law, limiting use of independent contractors. *Los Angeles Times*. www.latimes.com/california/story/2019–09–18/gavin-newsom-signs-ab5-employees0independent-contractors-california.

Newton, D. W., LePine, J. A., Kim, J. K., Wellman, N., and Bush, J. T. (2020). Taking engagement to task: The nature and functioning of task engagement across transitions. *Journal of Applied Psychology, 105*(1), 1–18.

Oswald, F., Behrend, T. S., and Foster, L. (Eds) (2019). *Workforce Readiness and the Future of Work*. New York, NY: Routledge.

Rich, B. L., LePine, J. A., and Crawford, E. R. (2010). Job engagement: Antecedents and effects of job performance. *Academy of Management Journal, 53*(3), 617–635.

Saks, A. M., and Gruman, J. A. (2014). What do we really know about employee engagement? *Human Resource Development Quarterly, 25*(2), 155–182.

Schaufeli, W., and Salanova, M. (2011). Work engagement: On how to better catch a slippery concept. *European Journal of Work and Organizational Psychology, 20*(1), 39–46.

Schneider, B., and Konz, A. M. (1989). Strategic job analysis. *Human Resource Management, 28*(1), 51–63.

Schneider, B., Yost, A. B., Dropp, A., Kind, C., and Lam, H. (2017). Workforce engagement: What it is, what drives it, and why it matters for organizational performance. *Journal of Organizational Behavior, 39*(4), 462–480.

Segarra, M. (2017). Happy birthday, ATMs. *Marketplace*. June 27. www.marketplace.org/2017/06/27/business/happy-birthday-atms/.

Smith, A., and Anderson, M. (2017, October 4). Automation in everyday life. Washington, DC.: Pew Research Center. www.pewinternet.org/2017/10/04/automation-in-everyday-life/.

WebWire (2019, June 28). Unilever announces new AI-powered talent marketplace. www.webwire.com/ViewPressRel.asp?aId=242981.

World Economic Forum (2018, December). *The Future of Jobs Report 2018*. London: Centre for the New Economy and Society.

Wrzesniewski, A., and Dutton, J. E. (2001). Crafting a job: Revisioning employees as active crafters of their work. *Academy of Management Review, 26*(2), 179–201.

9. How does future work need to be designed for optimal engagement?

Marylène Gagné, Sharon K. Parker, and Mark A. Griffin

What is the future of work?

Both jobs and the workforce are transforming. Automation and artificial intelligence are changing what we do and how we do it, information we have access to, and how we connect. Changing skill requirements and whether we will have a job at all in this future is the focus of much popular discussion on the topic. Importantly, we also need to think about how to embed technology into our jobs and organizations. We need to ensure that technology is designed alongside human aspects to help achieve organizational goals more effectively, and ensure humans have work that is positive, engaging, and healthy (see Boudreau, this volume, and Salanova, this volume).

For this purpose, we combine three frameworks to help us understand how to optimize employee engagement in future work. First, we use a work performance framework that explains performance requirements in an increasingly uncertain and interconnected future. Second, we use self-determination theory (SDT; Deci & Ryan, 1985; Gagné & Deci, 2005) to frame requirements for employee engagement in the light of this context. Third, we use the SMART work design framework (Parker & Knight, in preparation) to guide the creation of engaging future work. The integration of these frameworks (see Figure 9.1) allows us to make theoretically-driven predictions about how changes in work will influence engagement through the lens of work design, and conversely how we can influence these changes to ensure engagement is not negatively impacted. We elaborate on a research agenda that would use this integrated model to drive the design of new work or redesign of existing work considering changes in technology, uncertainty, and interconnectedness.

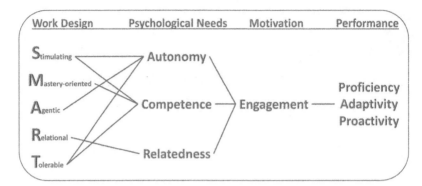

Figure 9.1   How work design influences performance through
engagement

An expanded view of work performance

The creation of future work is happening in an increasingly uncertain and
interconnected world (Howard, 1995). Uncertainty is created when we lack
information (or it is changing too rapidly) to estimate the probability of future
events. Work-related uncertainty is influenced by rapidly evolving technology,
an unclear political and economic landscape, and crises, such as the recent
pandemic. Our increasing use of technology to get work done and communicate with others (and with the technology itself) not only changes what we do
at work, but also requires us to communicate and coordinate work with others
(and with technology) more frequently and quickly.

The resulting transformation of work is bringing about changes in how we
need to conceptualize and assess work performance. Griffin et al. (2007)
suggest a move away from an emphasis on the performance of "highly specified jobs" for which the focus is on *proficiency* (doing one's predicted tasks
to a high standard), considering instead how work must increasingly be performed in a world that is interconnected and uncertain. Uncertainty generates
the need for more *adaptive* (i.e., being cognitively and behaviorally flexible in
the face of change) and more *proactive* (i.e., taking self-directed action to insti-
gate change) employee behavior. Carpini et al. (2017) showed that 97 different
performance constructs could be categorized into the Griffin and colleagues'
model of *work role performance*, which considers proficient, adaptive, and
proactive behaviors across the individual, team, and organizational levels.

Uncertainty involves dealing with unpredictable inputs, processes, and outputs of work systems (Wall et al., 2002), and consequently influences the extent to which roles can or should be formalized, and brings into question whether the mere mastery of job requirements is sufficient for high work role performance. Uncertainty both prompts and requires the emergence of more adaptive and proactive behaviors to become part of work roles. In a nutshell, employees need not just do their core and predicted tasks well, they need to be able to adapt to changing requirements in their tasks (adaptivity) and they need to be able to self-initiate changes in requirements through leading change and introducing new ideas (proactivity).

Interconnectedness is often reflected in levels of interdependence in a work context, which describes the social system in which work gets done and the need for individuals to coordinate their work to achieve shared goals. An inter-dependent context requires behaviors that maintain and build the social aspect of work (Griffin et al., 2007; Morgeson & Humphrey, 2006), such as commu-nication, social monitoring, the coordination of work behaviors, supporting the organization, and conflict management, all of which ensure organizational goals are realized (Cummings & Blumberg, 1987; Marks et al., 2001). From the interdependence perspective, therefore, effective work performance includes not only being proficient, adaptive, and proactive in relation to the core aspects of one's individual role (individual behavior), but also being proficient, adap-tive, and proactive in terms of one's contributions to the team (team-member behavior) and the organization (organization-member behavior).

The degree of uncertainty and interdependence, coupled with rapidly evolving technology, changes the relative importance of proficiency, adaptivity and proactivity, with the latter two increasingly becoming more crucial aspects of work roles. Promoting the enactment of such behaviors requires the right type of motivation or engagement. To understand how uncertainty and inter-dependence are likely to influence engagement, we use SDT, which not only offers insights into the nature and importance of engagement for work role performance, but can also serve to guide and evaluate the impact of interven-tions aimed at fostering more adaptive and proactive workplace behaviors.

Self-determination theory

SDT offers a multidimensional conceptualization of motivation that distin-guishes intrinsic motivation (doing something for its inherent pleasure) from extrinsic motivation (doing something for an instrumental reason). Through the idea that people can come to internalize externally imposed demands by valuing their importance (Ryan, 1995), extrinsic motivation can be further divided into three types. External regulation is a non-internalized form of motivation that represents doing something to obtain a reward or avoid a punishment. Introjected regulation is a partially internalized form of motivation that represents doing something out of ego-involvement (i.e., to feel worthy or to avoid feeling shame). Identified regulation is a fully internalized form of motivation that represents doing something because of its perceived value or importance. Over 40 years of research shows that the last form of extrinsic motivation, identified regulation, along with intrinsic motivation, yield more optimal functioning than the other two forms of extrinsic motivation (Ryan & Deci, 2017). Optimal functioning is defined through indicators of intra- and inter-personal growth and development, including well-being, attitudes, and behavior (Van den Broeck et al., 2019). At work, these would include things such as positive emotions, vitality, performance, proactivity, and collaboration, whereas burnout, stress, negative emotions, and avoiding responsibilities would indicate lower functioning.

Identified and intrinsic motivation are often described together as representing a person's autonomous motivation, which has been argued to be an indicator of "state engagement" (Meyer & Gagné, 2008), represented by feelings of energy, satisfaction, involvement, commitment, and empowerment (Macey & Schneider, 2008). Though there is apparent overlap between these indicators, SDT separates them into antecedents and outcomes of one another. For example, psychological empowerment is often described using four psychological states, consisting of competence, autonomy, meaning, and impact (Spreitzer, 1996). SDT defines many of these components of empowerment as antecedents of autonomous motivation that represent the satisfaction of psychological needs, as will be described below (Gagné et al., 1997). In addition, psychological engagement has often been conceptualized as the experience of vigor, absorption, and dedication at work (Schaufeli et al., 2002). SDT research often portrays these engagement indicators as outcomes or consequences of autonomous motivation (Li et al., 2015). Standing at the center of this engagement process, autonomous motivation can be operationalized by reasons for engaging in a behavior (e.g., work task) that reflect meaning and enjoyment.

In short, SDT offers the view that not all motivation can necessarily be equated with engagement. Only autonomous forms of motivation would. This becomes particularly relevant when considering that future work will demand more adaptivity and proactivity. Macey and Schneider (2008) argued that both adaptivity and proactivity are indicators of behavioral engagement, whereas they did not portray proficient work performance as indicative of engagement.

They also regarded "role expansion" as another indicator of behavioral engagement, a concept close to a flexible role orientation and also close to job crafting (Xanthopoulou & Bakker, this volume).

Research has shown that autonomous motivation is more strongly associated with deeper conceptual information processing (Vansteenkiste et al., 2004), performance on cognitively demanding tasks (Boggiano et al., 1993), behaving flexibly (Koestner & Zuckerman, 1994; McGraw & McCullers, 1979), and is consequently considered necessary to proactivity. Indeed, indicators of autonomous motivation, such as a flexible role orientation, predict proactive behaviors like innovation (e.g., Parker et al., 2006). This evidence aligns well with Meyer et al.'s (2010) argument that engagement "manifests itself in proactive value-directed behavior" (p. 64). We therefore argue that in a world where uncertainty will demand more cognitive, emotional, and behavioral flexibility (e.g., vigilance, openness, adjustment), where interdependence and connectivity will increase, and where cognitive demands will increase as technology replaces menial work, autonomous motivation will become a greater requirement than ever before because it is the type of motivation associated with optimal functioning.

The next question is what promotes autonomous motivation (or engagement) at work? SDT proposes that if basic psychological needs for autonomy, competence, and relatedness are satisfied, autonomous motivation is more likely to develop (Deci & Ryan, 2000; Meyer et al., 2010), something that has been supported through meta-analytic evidence in the work domain (Van den Broeck et al., 2016). Autonomy refers to feeling agentic and self-directed, competence refers to feeling masterful and self-efficacious, and relatedness refers to feeling connected to others and caring/being cared for.

Support for a sequence from satisfying these three psychological needs, to promoting autonomous motivation, to fostering adaptivity and proactivity, comes from various sources. The organizational change literature is useful to understand factors that lead to adaptivity. Many of the psychological states that relate to resistance to change and readiness to change revolve around feeling prepared and competent to handle change, feeling a sense of ownership and agency towards the change, and not feeling uprooted or isolated through the change process (Oreg et al., 2011). This stream of research concurs with research showing that feeling agentic is at the heart of flexible role orientations (Parker et al., 1997). Similarly, research on proactive work behavior demonstrates that feelings of efficacy and having a flexible role orientation are key to promoting proactivity at work (e.g., Parker et al., 2010).

This sequence from psychological needs to work role performance via engagement indicates that we must pay attention to the design of future work. Technology will certainly change what work we will do and how we will do it in the future, but now is the time to influence how this technology is designed to optimize employee engagement and performance. Uncertainty requires that future work be designed in a way that will promote adaptivity and proactivity to deal with it. Interdependence requires that future work be designed with social and coordination aspects in mind, to optimize team and organizational performance.

Future work design

We use a comprehensive model of work design, SMART work design, to lead the discussion of how future work needs to be designed for optimal work role performance. This framework identifies five superordinate categories of work characteristics that each have clear links to wider organization design decisions, such as how organizations divide tasks and coordinate efforts, and that have psychological significance in terms of engagement, strain, and learning.

Stimulating work design refers to the degree of mental complexity and variety as a result of the nature and organization of one's work tasks, responsibilities, and relationships, as indicated by, for example, task variety, skill variety, and problem-solving demands. *Mastery-oriented work design* refers to the degree to which one understands what one's tasks, activities, relationships, and responsibilities are, how they "fit" in the wider system, and how well they are being executed. Mastery-oriented work design includes work characteristics such as job feedback, feedback from others, and role clarity. *Agentic work design* refers to the degree of autonomy, control, and influence one has over one's work tasks, activities, relationships, and responsibilities. *Relational work design* captures the degree to which, as a result of the nature and organization of one's tasks and activities, one experiences support, connection, and an opportunity to positively impact others, and includes task significance, beneficiary contact, and social support. Finally, *tolerable work design* is the degree to which one's level of work demands are not overly taxing or impairing of one's ability to carry out non-work roles, reflected by indicators such as reasonable workloads and time pressure.

This new SMART work design framework yields interesting research questions, particularly around how the higher-order dimensions affect the satisfaction of psychological needs, engagement, and performance. Three of the categories of work characteristics map on very well to the three psychological needs proposed by SDT, namely mastery-oriented work design (competence), agentic work design (autonomy), and relational work design (relatedness). Stimulating work design would also affect autonomous motivation by providing novelty and challenge, thereby increasing enjoyment and meaning (i.e., autonomous motivation). Tolerable work design means that work is not overwhelming and draining, which should affect both autonomy and competence need fulfilment.

Beyond these simple relations, it is useful to hypothesize about how changes to future work are likely to impact these work characteristics and experiment with what could be done about it (see Parker & Grote, 2019, for more details). Below, we consider how changes in technology, uncertainty, and interconnectedness might transform these work characteristics. In the subsequent section, we discuss how these changes might impact need satisfaction, engagement, and the promotion of the three work performance aspects; how we could conduct research to test these hypotheses; and the sort of concerns organizations should keep in mind when designing or redesigning future work.

Technology

Technological advances can enhance the complexity and challenge of the work we do (that is, the extent to which it is "stimulating") because the more routine and replicable aspects of the work are readily automated (see Boudreau, this volume). For example, complexity was enhanced amongst tax accountants whose work has been increasingly digitized, and similar observations were made for robot operators and bank tellers (Gostautaite et al., 2019; Hummert et al., 2019; Jacoby, 2015). Conversely, evidence shows that technology sometimes reduces task variety and skill usage (Parker & Grote, 2019). Technology can be used, for example, to increase specialization and standardization in operator work (Delbridge, 2005; Parker, 2003). With respect to "mastery", there are similar mixed effects. On the one hand, technology can enable job feedback and thereby foster mastery and learning, such as a call center agent receiving feedback on his or her empathic tone when talking to customers. On the other hand, as shown by decades of study in aviation, the reliance on autopilot impairs feedback and has contributed to a situation in which pilots "forget how to fly" (Parker & Grote, 2019). Recent studies in robotic surgery similarly show negative effects for learning (Beane, 2018).

With respect to "agency" work characteristics, increases in cognitive complexity require paying attention to the degree of agency or autonomy people have in their work, because autonomous motivation has been shown to be particularly important for tasks that involve heuristics, or that require problem-solving or creativity (Boggiano et al., 1993; Koestner et al., 1984; Vansteenkiste et al., 2004). Moreover, autonomy has also been shown to enhance both adaptivity and proactivity needed for future work (Hornung & Rousseau, 2007; Parker et al., 1997; Parker et al., 2006). Although technologies can augment and enhance human decision making, they also have the potential to remove choice (e.g., algorithmic management; Rosenblat & Stark, 2016) and to excessively monitor human behavior (Enzle & Anderson, 1993), thereby decreasing autonomy. In addition, some technologies, as they get more complex, become opaque to operators' understanding of them. For example, Parker and Grote (2019) argue that the use of machine learning creates major challenges for keeping developers and operators accountable for these systems as they understand and control them less and less over time.

Consequently, research is needed to understand the full implications of machine learning for human agency. For example, a study demonstrated that human workers react in the same way to the fairness of task allocation decisions made by a computer versus a human manager, showing the importance of fairness no matter the source of decisions (Otting & Maier, 2018). Yet giving workers control of technologies can help enhance their feelings of autonomy; for example, by allowing them to solve technological issues themselves (e.g., Wall et al., 1990), by giving workers discretion to use or not use the technology (e.g., Stanton & Barnes-Farrell, 1996), or even allowing workers to participate in its design (DeTienne & Abbott, 1993). This control should be considered in the design of technology and future work and is addressed in a recent charter of ethical guidelines for the design of autonomous systems (IEEE, 2019).

Relational aspects of work are also affected by technology. As illustrated through numerous popular memes of groups of adults and children interacting through screens when they are next to each other, we relate differently with others because of technology, which enables almost unlimited communication through distance and time, creating unprecedented networks that continually influence businesses and economies. We further elaborate on the implications of technology-driven communication in the section on connectedness. In addition, we must now also consider what humans make of their interactions with robots. Anecdotal evidence suggests that humans prefer to interact with robots that have human-like appearances, and that human operators often attribute intentions and emotions to their robots and even bond with them (Gostautaite et al., 2019; Orso et al., 2019). This concurs with the idea that we will not only adopt technology, but that we will "collaborate" with it (Boudreau et al., 2017), creating new "relational" aspects to our work. For example, there is mounting evidence that we are increasingly applying relationship-related constructs, such as trust, to technology, when we are really referring to its reliability and transparency (Bailey et al., 2012). It will be important for future research to examine how technology influences relational work design.

Finally, "tolerable" aspects of work are also affected by technology. Workers have reported their workload, especially work pace, increasing to levels they find difficult to sustain because of the intensification enabled by surveillance systems (Parker & Grote, 2019). On the other hand, physical demands can be reduced with technology as heavy manual work is replaced by automation.

In addition to considering work design, the Principles of Positive Technologies (Peters et al., 2018), based on SDT, can inform technology design by helping us understand the psychological mechanisms involved in human–computer interactions. Focused on creating technologies that trigger "quality" affect, engagement, growth, and connectedness, they stress the importance of the need for technologies to fulfil needs for autonomy, competence, and relatedness in order to foster an engaging experience. The authors propose that this can happen across multiple spheres of experience with the technology, including its adoption (choosing it), interface (interacting with it), technology-enabled tasks (task engagement), technology-enabled behavior (behavior change and support), in a person's overall life (individual well-being), and in society (societal functioning and well-being). This model could also be used to conduct research into the effects of technological design on engagement and performance.

Uncertainty

Organizations have traditionally tried to reduce uncertainty through man-agement control (Otley, 1980) meant to "engineer" organizational behavior through monitoring, evaluating, and incentivizing. Not only have these tech-niques been related to decreased autonomous motivation (see Ryan & Deci, 2017, for a review), they are also not likely to be conducive to adaptive and proactive work behaviors. Management control is therefore unlikely to be an appropriate solution for contemporary and future workplaces in which it will not be possible to "manage out" uncertainty. Instead, uncertainty needs to be leveraged and regulated, which requires adaptive and proactive approaches (Griffin & Grote, 2020).

In terms of how uncertainty might change the design of work, it is likely to make work more stimulating by increasing problem-solving demands. On the other hand, it could decrease mastery characteristics by reducing role clarity, and decrease the tolerability of job demands by increasing time pressure and role conflict. We argue that the agentic and relational characteristics of work are particularly important under uncertainty. For example, by giving workers power to make decisions about different aspects of their work (agentic work design), they can more quickly and proactively be effective under uncertainty. Agency gives individuals the latitude to deal directly with uncertainties, which not only fosters faster responses to problems, but also increases worker learning (Wall & Jackson, 1995). Additionally, social support (an aspect of relational work design) may help workers cope with the more uncontrollable aspects of uncertainty (Carver et al., 1989). These hypotheses could be tested using natural or quasi-experiments in work organizations in which uncertainty occurs suddenly (e.g., a pandemic or an economic crisis).

Interconnectedness

In addition to our consideration of relational aspects of work design in the above section, our use of communication technologies is increasing the overall frequency of our communications with others but also with machines. Some describe this new reality as being "hyperconnected", which on the one hand points to the need for workers to develop new skills around effective virtual communication and time management. On the other hand, interconnectedness might change the design of work by pushing for more frequent communication, using new media, simultaneously with a greater number of people, and even with machines (e.g., bots). It might also change how we coordinate our work activities, often virtually and across different locations and time zones, which might be creating more team-based work that effectively changes how tasks and roles are distributed. The Covid-19 pandemic has illustrated these issues quite eloquently with many organizations and workers forced to quickly learn to coordinate virtual work through communication technologies previously underexploited. Finally, communication with machines also forces workers to adjust their work rhythms to achieve coordination with the machines.

When analyzing future work through the SMART work design framework (see Wang et al., 2020, for a review), naturally an important characteristic we consider is "relational". Changes in the way we communicate and with whom will likely modify social networks and connections we have with colleagues and other organizational stakeholders (e.g., suppliers, beneficiaries). Though technology can enable social networks, it can also make it challenging to connect at a deeper level with colleagues and beneficiaries, or coordinate work (Cramton & Webber, 2005; Cummings & Turner, 2009; Kiesler & Cummings, 2002).

Other work design characteristics are likely to be impacted by communication technologies. The fact that we are now connected 24/7 might increase the risk of having intolerable workloads and unmanageable demands. Depending on how communication demands are appraised by employees, they might feel either more agentic by being able to choose when and where to communicate or may feel pressured into communicating instantly to incoming demands. Finally, the way people's tasks and roles get redesigned and coordinated with other people and machines could influence the amount of variety, identity, and cognitive complexity in either direction (either taken away or increased). This may depend on how the communication technologies are set up and how they are being exploited by organizations.

Conscious choices can be made in this regard to ensure work is redesigned to be engaging. The monitoring capabilities of communication technologies could also influence how controlled people feel, though feedback created through monitoring could also enhance feelings of mastery. Thus, as communication technologies are developed and adopted, it will be important to keep these issues in mind and conduct research to test them out.

A work design research agenda for future work engagement

We argue that work design research should prioritize the examination of how technology, uncertainty, and interconnectedness transform work. The model presented in Figure 9.1 can serve as a framework to guide research on the effects of work design and redesign on employee engagement and optimal functioning as work is transformed through technology, uncertainty, and interconnectedness. As illustrated in the previous section, the SMART work design model is a useful framework to guide the comparison between current and future work design and guide the development of work redesign initiatives. The SDT and work role performance frameworks enhance the SMART framework by offering guiding principles to yield optimal engagement and performance.

The model can be used to design research using different methodological approaches. For example, natural "experiments" arising from crises that create uncertainty and force organizations to adjust work design, such as economic downturns, disasters, political unrest, and pandemics, can be tracked and investigated. During such events, organizations often scramble to adjust work, as we have witnessed during the Covid-19 pandemic. Preliminary results from an ongoing study of employees working from home conducted during Australian restrictions in April and May 2020 provides good initial support for our model when examining cross-sectional correlations between SMART work design, need satisfaction, and the three types of work performance (Parker et al., 2020). Results also revealed that the move to working from home created more psychological distress when people felt their managers did not trust them and when they were highly monitored. Organizations have had to rely on employee adaptivity and proactivity during the pandemic to remain effective, but anecdotal evidence from various media during the pandemic suggests that the amount of agency employees have had when working from home varied greatly. Therefore, it would be useful to examine how employees' authority to engage in proactivity via, for example, job crafting helps to enable them to engage with their work and perform effectively (particularly in terms of their adaptive and proactive performance) during extreme levels of uncertainty.

It would also be interesting to extend findings on how decision-makers design work in situations where they are asked to *re*design work in a crisis context. In normal circumstances, people tend to design good work (i.e., SMART work) if they have knowledge about enriched work design, if they tend to hold open rather than conservation values (Schwartz et al., 2012), and if they have well-designed work themselves (Parker et al., 2019). The question is whether educating decision-makers, promoting certain values (e.g., valuing enjoyment at work), or relying on individuals' mimicking their own work designs will help when managers need to redesign work during a crisis. It might be, for example, that the extreme level of uncertainty during a crisis engenders greater rigidity in work design decision-making, and especially lower levels of agency, consistent with threat rigidity theory (Staw et al., 1981). On the other hand, extreme uncertainty and the ensuing losses faced by some businesses might, according to prospect theory (Kahneman and Tversky, 1979), cause work designers to engage in more risky behaviour by allowing employees greater agency than traditionally they might. In other words, we know little about how broader levels of uncertainty in the wider context will shape work design choices and their implications for engagement. Simulations could help answer these questions by asking people to redesign existing work under different crises conditions and levels of uncertainty.

Pre/post simulation and field study designs could be used when new technologies are introduced into specific jobs to assess how the technology influences work design, engagement, and performance. Research on how technology developers decide on technology design, and whether they have knowledge and awareness of good work design would be useful to ensure technologies are designed using human-centered principles that might be more likely to satisfy psychological needs and foster engagement. Importantly, there is no pre-determined effect of technology on work design, with the effects depending on various higher-level factors (e.g., the level of skill in the occupation; institutional regimes; management ideologies) as well as individual factors (Parker & Grote, 2019). To support such sociotechnical and human-centered approaches, the four-step approach developed by Boudreau and colleagues is helpful (e.g., Jesuthasan & Boudreau, 2018). This approach involves:

1. Deconstructing jobs into their core task components that then are analyzed in terms of how repetitive versus variable, independent versus interactive, and physical versus mental they are;
2. Re-aligning work tasks with strategic goals;
3. On the basis of decisions made in steps 1 and 2, deciding which tasks can be automated and what sort of automation would be desirable (e.g., robotic process automation versus artificial intelligence); and
4. Reconstructing jobs for humans around the introduced automation with the strategic goals in mind.

As Boudreau (this volume) points out, implications for employee engagement could be another key consideration at each step in the process.

To conclude, we proposed that when adjusting work design because of the introduction of new technology or to deal with a crisis, it is crucial to consider the SMART work design model to redesign work in a way that is more psychologically informed in order to ensure workers remain engaged and perform effectively. Considering the three psychological needs proposed by SDT and the model of work performance that takes into account uncertainty and interconnectedness helps inform what work design principles must be followed to ensure employees thrive in the future of work.

References

Bailey, D. E., Leonardi, P. M., and Barley, S. R. (2012). The lure of the virtual. *Organization Science*, *23*(5), 1485–1504.

Beane, M. (2018). Shadow learning: Building robotic surgical skill when approved means fail. *Administrative Science Quarterly*, *64*(1), 87–123.

Boggiano, A. K., Flink, C., Shields, A., Seelbach, A., and Barrett, M. (1993). Use of techniques for promoting students' self-determination: Effects on students' analytic problem-solving skills. *Motivation and Emotion*, *17*, 319–336.

Boudreau, J., Ziskin, I., and Rearick, C. (2017). *Black Hole and White Spaces: Reimagining the Future of Work and HR with the CHREATE Project*. Alexandria, VA: HR People + Strategy.

Carpini, J. A., Parker, S. K., and Griffin, M. A. (2017). A look back and a leap forward: A review and synthesis of the individual work performance literature. *Academy of Management Annals, 11*(2), 825–885.

Carver, C. S., Scheier, M. F., and Weintraub, J. K. (1989). Assessing coping strategies: A theoretically based approach. *Journal of Personality and Social Psychology, 56,* 267–283.

Cramton, C. D., and Webber, S. S. (2005). Relationships among geographic dispersion, team processes, and effectiveness in software development work teams. *Journal of Business Research, 58*(6), 758–765.

Cummings, T., and Blumberg, M. (1987). Advanced manufacturing technology and work design. In T. Wall, C. Clegg, and N. Kemp (Eds), *The Human Side of Advanced Manufacturing Technology* (pp. 37–60). Chichester: Wiley.

Cummings, E., and Turner, P. (2009). Patient self-management and chronic illness: Evaluating outcomes and impacts of information technology. *Studies in Health Technology and Informatics, 143,* 229–234.

DeTienne, K. B., and Abbott, N. T. (1993). Developing an employee-centered electronic monitoring system. *Journal of Systems Management, 44,* 12–12.

Deci, E. L., and Ryan, R. M. (1985). *Intrinsic Motivation and Self-Determination in Human Behavior.* New York, NY: Plenum Press.

Deci, E. L., and Ryan, R. M. (2000). The "what" and "why" of goal pursuits. *Psychological Inquiry, 11,* 37–41.

Delbridge, R. (2005). Workers under lean manufacturing. In D. Holman, T. D. Wall, C. W. Clegg, P. Sparrow, and A. Howard (Eds), *The Essentials of the New Workplace: A Guide to the Human Impact of Modern Working Practices* (pp. 15–32). Chichester: Wiley.

Enzle, M. E., and Anderson, S. C. (1993). Surveillant intentions and intrinsic motivation. *Journal of Personality and Social Psychology, 64*(2), 257–266.

Gagné, M., and Deci, E. L. (2005). Self-determination theory and work motivation. *Journal of Organizational Behavior, 26,* 331–362.

Gagné, M., Senécal, C. and Koestner, R. (1997). Proximal job characteristics, feelings of empowerment, and intrinsic motivation: A multidimensional model. *Journal of Applied Social Psychology, 27,* 1222–1240.

Gostautaite, B., Liuberte, I., Buciuniene, I., Stankeviciute, Z., Staniskiene, E., Reay, T., and Moniz, A. (2019, May). Robots at work: How human-robot interaction changes work design. Presentation at the European Association of Work and Organizational Psychology conference, Turin, Italy.

Griffin, M. A., and Grote, G. (2020). When is more uncertainty better? A model of uncertainty regulation and effectiveness. *Academy of Management Reviews.* Advanced online publication.

Griffin, M. A., Neal, A., and Parker, S. K. (2007). A new model of work role performance: Positive behavior in uncertain and interdependent contexts. *Academy of Management Journal, 50*(2), 327–347.

Hornung, S., and Rousseau, D. M. (2007). Active on the job-proactive in change: How autonomy at work contributes to employee support for organizational change. *Journal of Applied Behavioral Science, 43*(4), 401–426.

Howard, A. (1995). *The Changing Nature of Work.* San Francisco: Jossey-Bass.

Hummert, H., Traum, A., Goers, P. K., and Nerdinger, F. W. (2019, May). Impact of digitization on job satisfaction, stress, and organizational commitment in service companies. Presentation at the European Association of Work and Organizational Psychology conference, Turin, Italy.

IEEE (2019). *The IEEE Global Initiative on Ethics of Autonomous and Intelligent Systems: Ethically Aligned Design – A Vision for Prioritizing Human Well-being with Autonomous and Intelligent Systems.* Retrieved from: https://standards.ieee.org/content/ieee-standards/en/industry-connections/ec/autonomous-systems.html.

Jacoby, T. (2015). Technology isn't a job killer. *Wall Street Journal*, May 20. www.wsj.com/articles/technology-isnt-a-job-killer-1432161213.

Jesuthasan, R., and Boudreau, J. W. (2018). *Reinventing Jobs: A 4-Step Approach for Applying Automation to Work.* Boston, MA: Harvard Business Review Press.

Kahneman, D., and Tversky, A. (1979). Prospect theory: An analysis of decision under risk. *Econometrica, 47*, 263–291.

Kiesler, S., and Cummings, J. N. (2002). What do we know about proximity and distance in work groups? A legacy of research. In P. J. Hinds and S. Kiesler (Eds), *Distributed Work* (pp. 57–80). Cambridge: MIT Press.

Koestner, R., Ryan, R. M., Bernieri, F., and Holt, K. (1984). Setting limits on children's behavior: The differential effects of controlling versus informational styles on children's intrinsic motivation and creativity. *Journal of Personality, 54*, 233–248.

Koestner, R., and Zuckerman, M. (1994). Causality orientations, failure, and achievement. *Journal of Personality, 62*(3), 321–346.

Li, M., Wang, Z., You, X., and Gao, J. Y. (2015). Value congruence and teachers' work engagement: The mediating role of autonomous and controlled motivation. *Personality and Individual Differences, 80*, 113–118.

Macey, W. H., and Schneider, B. (2008). The meaning of employee engagement. *Industrial and Organizational Psychology: Perspectives on Science and Practice, 1*, 3–30.

Marks, M. A., Mathieu, J. E., and Zaccaro, S. J. 2001. A temporally based framework and taxonomy of team processes. *Academy of Management Review, 26*, 356–376.

McGraw, K. O., and McCullers, J. C. (1979). Evidence of a detrimental effect of extrinsic incentives on breaking a mental set. *Journal of Experimental Social Psychology, 15*(3), 285–294.

Meyer, J. P., and Gagné, M. (2008). Employee engagement from a self-determination theory perspective. *Industrial and Organizational Psychology: Perspectives on Science and Practice, 1*, 60–62.

Meyer, J. P., Gagné, M., and Parfyonova, N. M. (2010). Toward an evidence-based model of engagement: What we can learn from motivation and commitment research. In S. Albrecht (Ed.), *Handbook of Employee Engagement* (pp. 62–73). Cheltenham, UK, and Northampton, MA: Edward Elgar Publishing.

Morgeson, F. P., and Humphrey, S. E. (2006). The Work Design Questionnaire (WDQ): Developing and validating a comprehensive measure for assessing job design and the nature of work. *Journal of Applied Psychology, 91*(6), 1321–1339.

Oreg, S., Vakola, M., and Armenakis, A. (2011). Change recipients' reactions to organizational change: A 60-year review of quantitative studies. *Journal of Applied Behavioral Science, 47*(4), 461–524.

Orso, V., Pittaro, E., and Gamberini, L. (2019, May). Robot as workmates: Are we ready? A systematic literature review on robot acceptance in the work environment. Presentation at the European Association of Work and Organizational Psychology conference, Turin, Italy.

Otley, D. T. (1980). The contingency theory of management accounting: Achievements and prognosis. *Accounting, Organizations and Society, 5*(4), 413–428.

Otting, S. K., and Maier, G. W. (2018). The importance of procedural justice in human-machine interactions: Intelligent systems as new decision agents in organizations. *Computers in Human Behavior, 89,* 27–39.

Parker, S. K. (2003). Longitudinal effects of lean production on employee outcomes and the mediating role of work characteristics. *Journal of Applied Psychology, 8*(4), 620–634.

Parker, S. K., Andrei, D. M., and Van den Broeck, A. (2019). Poor work design begets poor work design: Capacity and willingness antecedents of individual work design behavior. *Journal of Applied Psychology, 104*(7), 907–928.

Parker, S. K., Bindl, U., and Strauss, K. (2010). Making things happen: A model of proactive motivation. *Journal of Management, 36*(4), 827–856.

Parker, S. K., and Grote, G. (2019). Automation, algorithms and beyond: Why work design matters more than ever in a digital world. *Applied Psychology: An International Review.* Advanced online publication. doi: 10.1111/apps.12241.

Parker, S. K., and Knight, C. (in preparation). *Structuring Work Design: A Higher-Order Analysis of Work Characteristics.* Bentley: Curtin University.

Parker, S. K., Knight, C., and Keller, A. (2020). Remote managers are having trust issues. *Harvard Business Review* (online). https://hbr.org/2020/07/remote-managers -are-having-trust-issues.

Parker, S. K., Wall, T. D., and Jackson, P. R. (1997). "That's not my job": Developing flexible employee work orientations. *Academy of Management Journal, 40*(4), 899–929.

Parker, S. K., Williams, H. M., and Turner, N. (2006). Modeling the antecedents of proactive behavior at work. *Journal of Applied Psychology, 91*(3), 636–652.

Peters, D., Calvo, R. A., and Ryan, R. M. (2018). Designing for motivation, engagement and wellbeing in digital experience. *Frontiers in Psychology, 9,* 1–15.

Rosenblat, A., and Stark, L. (2016). Algorithmic labor and information asymmetries: A case study of Uber's drivers. *International Journal of Communication, 10,* 3758–3784.

Ryan, R. M. (1995). Psychological needs and the facilitation of integrative processes. *Journal of Personality, 63*(3), 397–427.

Ryan, R. M., and Deci, E. L. (2017). *Self-Determination Theory: Basic Psychological Needs in Motivation, Development, and Wellness.* New York, NY: Guilford.

Schaufeli, W. B., Salanova, M., González-Romá, V., and Bakker, A. B. (2002). The measurement of engagement and burnout: A two-sample confirmatory factor analytic approach. *Journal of Happiness Studies, 3,* 71–92.

Schwartz, S. H., Cieciuch, J., Vecchione, M., Davidov, E., Fischer, R., Beierlein, C., … and Konty, M. (2012). Refining the theory of basic individual values. *Journal of Personality and Social Psychology, 103,* 663–688.

Spreitzer, G. M. (1996). Social structural characteristics of psychological empowerment. *Academy of Management Journal, 39*(2), 483–504.

Stanton, J. M., and Barnes-Farrell, J. L. (1996). Effects of electronic performance monitoring on personal control, task satisfaction, and task performance. *Journal of Applied Psychology, 81,* 738–745.

Staw, B. M., Sandelands, L. E., and Dutton, J. E. (1981). Threat rigidity effects in organizational behavior: A multilevel analysis. *Administrative Science Quarterly, 26*(4), 501–524.

Van den Broeck, A., Carpini, J., and Diefendorff, J. (2019). Work motivation: Where do the different perspectives lead us? In R. M. Ryan (Ed.), *Oxford Handbook of Human Motivation* (2nd Ed.). New York, NY: Oxford University Press.

Van den Broeck, A., Ferris, D. L., Chang, C.-H., and Rosen, C. C. (2016). A review of self-determination theory's basic psychological needs at work. *Journal of Management, 42*, 1195–1229.

Vansteenkiste, M., Simons, J., Lens, W., and Sheldon, K. M. (2004) Motivating learning, performance, and persistence: The synergistic role of intrinsic goals and autonomy-support. *Journal of Personality and Social Psychology, 87*, 246–260.

Wall, T. D., Corbett, J. M., Martin, R., Clegg, C. W., and Jackson, P. R. (1990). Advanced manufacturing technology, work design, and performance: A change study. *Journal of Applied Psychology, 75*, 691–697.

Wall, T. D., and Jackson, P. R. (1995). New manufacturing initiatives and shopfloor work design. In A. Howard (Ed.), *The changing nature of work* (pp. 139–174). San Francisco, CA: Jossey-Bass.

Wall, T. D., Cordery, J. L., and Clegg, C. W. (2002). Empowerment, performance, and operational uncertainty. *Applied Psychology: An International Review, 51*, 146–169.

Wang, B., Liu, Y., and Parker, S. K. (2020). How does the use of information communication technology affect individuals? A work design perspective. *Academy of Management Annals*. Advance online publication.

10. Employee engagement and engagement in change: a research agenda

Simon L. Albrecht

Employee engagement and organizational change

Employee engagement has remained a "hot topic" (Macey & Schneider, 2008) over the past twenty-five years because enthusiastic, motivated and involved employees have been recognized as a critical source of competitive advantage (Albrecht et al., 2015; Schneider et al., 2017). Engaged employees feel positive, are involved in their work and are willing to work toward the achievement of work role and organizational goals (Albrecht et al., 2015; Macey et al., 2009). Despite more than thirty years of research and organizational focus on employee engagement, practitioners and researchers continue to report that a very large percentage of workers are not engaged (e.g., Saks, 2017). Some of that percentage has been attributed to an uneven commitment by senior leaders to a strategic focus on engagement (Albrecht et al., 2015), to non-conducive organizational climates (Iverson et al., 1998), and to the sub-optimal management of ongoing organizational change (Thundiyil et al., 2015).

Organizational change is also a hot topic because change is widely recognized as a constant in contemporary organizational contexts (Tsaousis & Vakola, 2018). As a consequence of the challenges associated with volatile, uncertain, ambiguous and complex environments (Bennett & Lemoine, 2014), organizations and researchers continue to focus on understanding how best to manage ongoing organizational change. Despite organizational change being "the new normal", researchers and organizations often report that change does not achieve anticipated benefits (e.g., Burnes, 2011). Much of the success or failure of organizational change has been attributed to the extent that employees are open to proposed organizational changes (e.g., Oreg et al., 2011). Senior leadership support, organizational climate and employee engagement have also been identified as important to the success or failure of change initiatives through their influence on employee attitudes to change (e.g., Armenakis & Bedeian, 1999; Rafferty et al., 2013).

To a large extent, the employee engagement and organizational change literatures have run on separate paths, with very little cross-fertilization. However, given that employee engagement and employee attitudes to change are increasingly recognized as critical to organizational competitiveness and success (Straatmann et al., 2016), it is important to understand how the constructs and their key antecedents inter-relate. This is because organizations that have well-developed and well-integrated engagement and change strategies and resources are recognized to be better equipped to face the challenges and opportunities presented by ongoing needs for organizational change (e.g., Collins & Hansen, 2012).

There are also theoretical grounds for examining the relationships between engagement and change. For example, employee engagement and positive employee attitudes to change can both be characterized as high-arousal and high-valence constructs within well-established circumplex models of job-related affect (Albrecht, 2010; Oreg et al., 2018; Russell, 2003). Constructs that are characterized by activated positive affect are likely to influence employee action readiness (Frijda, 1986) – their readiness to invest energy and involvement, their willingness to adopt and promote organizational change, and their willingness to engage in adaptive and proactive behavior (Griffin et al., 2007). Therefore, an examination of how the two constructs and their antecedents inter-relate may help advance theoretical and practical understanding of key employee-related organizational success factors in contemporary organizational contexts. More broadly, Thundiyil et al. (2015), in their meta-analysis of the antecedents and outcomes of change cynicism, called for additional research on the relationship between change cynicism and engagement. Albrecht et al. (2018) called for additional examination of the relationship between employee engagement and employee attitudes to change.

Drawing from existing models of employee engagement and organizational change, this chapter adds to the engagement literature and the change literature by identifying domain-specific antecedents of employee engagement and positive employee attitudes to change. As shown as Figure 10.1, the chapter offers a framework that conceptually connects employee perceptions of senior leader engagement, senior leader change leadership, engagement climate, change climate, employee engagement and employee change engagement. As such, the framework depicts how key domain-specific organizational context factors influence key employee psychological states that are likely to deliver organizations ongoing competitive advantage in the face of ongoing change. The solid, dashed and dotted lines, respectively, suggest that all proposed relationships in the model can be direct, indirect and reciprocal.

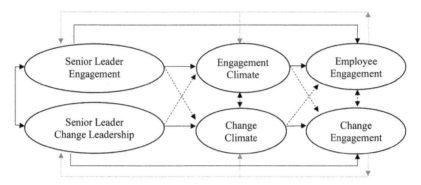

Figure 10.1   Domain-specific leadership, climates, change engagement, and engagement

Note: Items, error terms, and potential multi-level effects not modeled for ease of representation; dashed arrows represent proposed cross-construct associations that have less strong effects than solid arrows; grey dotted arrows represent reciprocal relationships; double-headed arrows represent correlations between constructs.

In terms of how the chapter is structured, firstly, the distinction between organizational climate and domain-specific climates is briefly overviewed. Then the constructs of engagement climate and change climate are introduced. Next, the influence that employee perceptions of senior leader engagement and change leadership can have on engagement climate and change climate is examined. Then, the influence that an engagement climate and a change-focused climate can have on employee engagement and change engagement is described. Future research opportunities and practical implications are then addressed. Given the focus on organizational resources and their influence on employee engagement and change, the chapter will not include a review of how job and personal resources (e.g., autonomy, self-efficacy) and job-level and personal change resources (e.g., involvement in change, change-related self-efficacy) might also influence employee engagement or change engagement.

Organizational climate

Organizational climate is widely recognized as an important determinant of attitude-, behavior- and performance-related outcomes (Beus et al., 2020). Although there is no universal consensus about how to define and measure the construct, organizational climate is commonly understood in terms of shared perceptions and "the meaning employees attach to their experience, and the behaviors they observe getting rewarded, supported and expected" (Schneider & Barbera, 2014a, p. 10).

Despite some advances in theory, research and practice (e.g., Albrecht, 2014; Schneider et al., 2017), the links between organizational climate and employee engagement have not been clearly drawn. Although meta-analytic evidence (Crawford, et al., 2010; Halbesleben, 2010) shows that organizational climate has links with engagement, the evidence is based on a limited number of studies that use differing generic measures of organizational climate. Similarly, there has been very little empirical research linking organizational climate and employee attitudes to change.

Domain-specific climates

Schneider (1975) suggested that, rather than conceptualizing climate as a generic and global construct, it is better conceptualized as a domain- or facet-specific construct. Schneider's (1975) early research, for example, focused on a "climate for service". Subsequently, researchers have focused on climates for innovation (Brown & Leigh, 1996), safety (Zohar, 1980) and fairness (Colquitt et al., 2002). Albrecht (2014) argued in support of an engagement climate.

Engagement climate

A number of researchers have suggested that, beyond individual-level employee engagement, engagement can be conceptualized as an organizational-level construct (e.g., Barrick et al., 2015; Schneider et al., 2017). Barrick et al. defined collective organizational engagement as "the shared perceptions of organizational members that members of the organization are, as a whole, physically, cognitively, and emotionally invested in their work" (p. 113). Barrick et al. measured collective engagement with items such as "I find nearly everyone devotes a lot of effort and energy to our work" and "Nearly everyone at work feels passionate and enthusiastic about our jobs." These items address individual perceptions about the extent to which people in the collective invest energy, effort and enthusiasm in their work. Along similar lines, and extrapolating from previously published definitions of individual-level employee engagement, Albrecht (2014) defined organizational engagement climate as shared perceptions about the energy and involvement willingly focused by employees toward the achievement of organizational goals.

Albrecht (2014) argued that incorporating core elements that have previously been used to define engagement at the individual level of analysis might provide for a more face-valid and internally-consistent definition of engagement climate. The focus on goal-directed energy and involvement is broadly in line with definitions of climate that refer to collective and stable perceptions of psychologically-important elements of an organizational environment (e.g., Ashforth, 1985; Edwards et al., 2009). However, the proposed definition contrasts with definitions of climate that include more encompassing considerations of "shared perceptions of and the meaning attached to the policies, practices, and procedures employees experience and the behaviors they observe getting rewarded, and that are supported and expected" (Schneider et al., 2013, p. 361).

Consistent with "levels of analysis" and "referent shift" arguments (see Chan, 2014), Albrecht et al. (2018) measured organizational engagement climate with items such as "People in this organization are enthusiastic about their work", "People here are fully involved in their work" and "Overall, people in this organization strive to perform at the best of their ability." In contrast to alternative conceptualizations and measurements of organizational-level engagement (e.g., Saks, 2019; Schneider et al., 2017), the referent for Albrecht's survey items "shifted" from perceptions and experiences related to self, to perceptions and experiences about the organization as a whole. Albrecht et al. (2018) reported confirmatory factor analytic evidence in support of the convergent and discriminant validity and the reliability of their measure (e.g., a = 0.93), and showed that the construct, as expected, had a positive association with employee engagement, also measured at the individual level of analysis.

Change climate

Schneider et al. (1996) noted that, "what people in an organization experience as the climate and believe is the culture ultimately determines whether sustained change is accomplished" (p. 18). For present purposes, and parallel to the definition proposed for engagement climate, *change climate* here refers to shared perceptions about employee energy and involvement willingly focused toward the adoption, support and promotion of organizational change. The construct could be measured with items such as "In this organization, nearly everyone devotes a lot of effort and energy to organizational change" and "People strive to make organizational change as successful as possible." Again, the proposed definition focuses less on perceptions about policies, practices, procedures and expected behaviors regarding change and more on shared perceptions about the pervasiveness of employee enthusiasm for and involvement in change. Perceptions about human resource policies, practices and procedures might alternatively be conceptualized as antecedent "conditions" (Macey & Schneider, 2008) or "embedding mechanisms" (Schein, 2010) for domain-specific climates (Albrecht et al., 2018; Barrick et al., 2015; Ehrhart & Raver, 2014). As per the modeling in Figure 10.1, when employees experience a pervasive and coherent change-focused climate, embedded (at least in part) by messaging, modeling and directives from senior leadership (Schein, 2010; Shea et al., 2014), individual employees will likely feel a genuine enthusiasm and willingness to support, adopt and promote organizational change.

Domain-specific senior leadership

The senior leadership of an organization is typically composed of the CEO, vice-presidents, divisional heads, functional heads and others who directly contribute to an organization's key strategic and business priorities and decisions (Albrecht & Travaglione, 2003). Senior leaders "symbolise the values of the organization, determine the flow of the organizational resources, and model employees' ways of thinking, feeling, and reacting to important events" (Leiter & Bakker, 2010, p. 5). The senior leadership group is recognized within the practitioner and research literature as playing an important role in setting the "tone at the top" and influencing the formation and maintenance of organizational climate (Deloitte, 2015; Schneider & Barbera, 2014b). Although numerous additional factors have been identified as influencing organizational climate (e.g., Albrecht et al., 2018), the primary focus for this chapter is on the influence of senior leadership. In support of this focus, Barrick et al. (2015) showed that transformational senior leadership had a significantly stronger influence on collective organizational engagement than did motivating work design or human resource management practices, and Schneider et al. (2017) reported a similar finding such that senior leadership had a significantly stronger impact on work engagement than did work characteristics themselves.

Beyond leadership styles such as transformational, empowering or authentic leadership, researchers have proposed that more specific forms of leadership, such as innovation leadership (Kremmer et al., 2019), change leadership (Herold et al., 2008) and engagement leadership (Schaufeli, 2015), are also worthy of research attention. In support of this argument, Yukl et al. (2019) argued that faster "progress would be made in learning about effective leadership behavior if more studies examined a wide range of specific behaviors rather than only focusing on … broadly defined behaviors" (p. 775).

Senior leader engagement and engagement climate

Alimo-Metcalfe et al. (2008) argued that, in contrast to more "heroicised" styles of leadership (e.g., charismatic leadership), "we are now living in … an era that is characterized by a much more inclusive, 'engaging' style of leadership" (p. 587). According to Alimo-Metcalfe et al., engaging leadership manifests as "respect for others and concern for their development and wellbeing; in the ability to unite different groups of stakeholders in developing a joint vision; in supporting a developmental culture; and in delegation of a kind that empowers and develops individuals' potential" (p. 587). Along slightly different lines, Schaufeli (2015) proposed "engaging" leadership as a particular style or type of leadership that promotes employee engagement. However, as with many other leadership researchers, Schaufeli's referent for engaging leadership was focused more at employee perceptions of line-managers, team leaders or supervisors, rather than at the level of senior leaders. In contrast, and consistent with the qualities widely used to define employee engagement (e.g., vigor, energy, involvement, dedication, striving), Albrecht et al. (2018) focused on and measured employee perceptions of senior leader engagement with items such as "Senior leaders in this organization strive to perform to the best of their ability", "Senior leaders in this organization are very positive about meeting organizational goals" and "Senior leaders in this organization are willing to do their best to achieve the best possible outcomes for the organization."

With respect to empirical support for the proposed relationship between senior leader engagement and engagement climate (see Figure 10.1), Albrecht et al. (2018) showed that employee perceptions of senior leaders' engagement exerted a stronger influence on organizational engagement climate than alternative organizational resources such as human resource management (HRM) support, clarity of organizational goals, strategic alignment, organizational autonomy and organizational adaptivity. Also in support of Figure 10.1, Albrecht et al. reported a significant correlation between perceptions of senior leader engagement and employee engagement ($r = 0.46$) and showed, using structural equation modeling, that senior leader engagement had a significant indirect effect through engagement climate on engagement. These results suggest that when employees perceive senior leaders to be energetically striving for the successful achievement of organizational goals, employees will, collectively and individually, likely feel a genuine enthusiasm for their work and strive toward the achievement of individual, group and organizational goals, and as such be engaged.

Senior leader change leadership and change climate

Senior leadership's active support of change is widely recognized as fundamental to the success of any particular change initiative, and for successful ongoing change (e.g., Armenakis & Bedeian, 1999; Kotter, 1990). Senior leaders need to promote, communicate and reinforce the need for ongoing change, and develop and nurture organizational climates that support adaptability and responsiveness as core organizational values (Johnson, 2016). In recent years, an increasing amount of practitioner and research attention has been devoted to defining the importance, characteristics and dimensions of effective change leadership (e.g., Bendixen et al., 2017; Hughes, 2016).

Change leadership has been defined as an "ability to influence and enthuse others, through personal advocacy, vision and drive, and to access resources to build a solid platform for change" (Higgs & Rowland, 2000, p. 124). Ekvall (1991) proposed that change-centered leadership is associated with creating vision and setting direction, being open to ideas, making quick decisions, encouraging communication and cooperation, encouraging achievement, and being committed, flexible and dynamic. Yukl et al. (2019) conceptualized and measured change leadership in terms of advocating change, encouraging innovation and envisioning change.

As proposed in Figure 10.1, research evidence shows that senior-level change leaders who initiate and implement new directions within organizations will likely foster an organizational climate that promotes innovation and embraces organizational readiness for change (Choi & Ruona, 2011). With respect to the proposed association between change leadership and change engagement (see below), Oreg and Berson's (2019) integrative model of leadership and organizational change showed change leadership being positively associated with employee attitudes to change and change effectiveness. More generally, Burke (2014) argued that the relationship between top management support for change and employee attitudes to change is a "truth" that has been established across many empirical studies.

Change engagement

Employee attitudes to change have consistently been shown to have a significant effect on the success of change initiatives. Beyond merely being open and receptive toward change (Miller et al., 1994), employees need to be willing to positively and actively engage in change processes. Ongoing successful change requires employees who feel energized by change, who are willing to experiment with change, and who actively support and adopt proposed new initiatives through changes in their attitudes and behavior (Choi, 2011; Oreg et al., 2011). Analogous to employee engagement as an affectively-activated and high-arousal construct (e.g., Albrecht, 2010; Inceoglu & Fleck, 2010), "change engagement" potentially provides a more agentic, high-arousal and motivational extension of previously researched attitudes to change such as acceptance of change (Iverson, 1996), openness to change (Wanberg & Banas, 2000), change readiness (Holt et al., 2007) and affective commitment to change (Herscovitch & Meyer, 2002). Change engagement, as described below, shares more in common with constructs such as change proactivity (Oreg et al., 2018) and intentional readiness for change (Bouckenooghe et al., 2009).

A limited number of practitioners and researchers have indirectly referred to the notion of employee engagement in change (e.g., Dhensa-Kahlon & Coyle-Shapiro, 2013; Straatmann et al., 2016). However, to date, a conceptualization of "change engagement", as an analogue of employee engagement, has not been explicitly defined within the change literature. Extrapolating from existing definitions of engagement, change engagement is here defined as an enduring and positive work-related psychological state characterized by a genuine enthusiasm for and willingness to support, adopt and promote organizational change. The definition captures the essential qualities of positive energy, involvement and focused effort that characterize work engagement (González-Romá et al., 2006; Macey et al., 2009); however, it applies them to the context of change. Measures of change engagement might include items such as "I am enthusiastic about change in this organization", "I feel energized when we are going through change", "I am willing to invest my time and energy to the implementation of organizational change" and "I am willing to convince colleagues of the benefits of ongoing change."

Cross-level and reciprocal effects

The dashed arrows in Figure 10.1 represent cross-construct relationships (e.g., senior leader engagement–change climate) that are proposed to be less strong than construct-specific associations (e.g., senior leader engagement–engagement climate). The modeling is consistent with reviews and research (e.g., Beus et al., 2020; Kuenzi & Schminke, 2009) showing the relatively stronger influence of facet-specific constructs (e.g., safety climate), versus generic constructs (e.g., organizational climate), on directly related facet-specific outcomes (e.g., safety outcomes such as accident rates). Nevertheless, it is here proposed that the energizing and involving character of senior leader change leadership will, for example, also likely have a positive spillover influence on engagement climate and employee engagement. Similarly, the energizing and involving character of senior leadership engagement will have a positive spillover influence on change climate and employee change engagement.

The dotted arrows in Figure 10.1 represent reciprocal relationships between the constructs. It is proposed, drawing from a broaden-and-build perspective (Fredrickson, 2001), that an increased pervasiveness of employee engagement will, over time, result in an upstream increase of engagement experienced at the climate level and more positive employee perceptions about senior leadership engagement. Similarly, over time, an increase in individual change engagement is likely to influence shared perceptions about change and senior leaders' support of change. Although Kuenzi and Schminke (2009) acknowledged that the idea of reciprocal relationships is not new in the climate literature, they could only find "one study that explored this type of relationship" (p. 707). More research is needed to address this issue.

Future research

Given the conceptual nature of the proposed model, empirical research is needed to test and elaborate the constructs and relationships proposed. A number of research questions can usefully be advanced to further integrate the leadership, change and engagement literatures.

Firstly, additional research is needed to establish the construct validity of the measures suggested in the chapter. For example, and as previously mentioned, empirical research is needed to establish that items such as "I feel energized when we are going through change" constitute a change engagement scale that is meaningfully different from constructs such as openness to change, readiness for change, willingness to change and commitment to change. Similarly, measures of employee perceptions of senior leadership engagement, senior leader change leadership, engagement climate and change climate also need to be validated. Although the proposed measures are, in the main, domain-specific adaptations of existing constructs, and despite some preliminary evidence of validity and reliability (e.g., Albrecht, 2014; Albrecht et al., 2018), their psychometrics need to be more fully established.

A second line of research could usefully look at examining relationships between the engagement- and change-related constructs represented in the model. For example, research could focus on determining whether the relationship between engagement climate and change climate is of sufficient strength to warrant conceptualizing both constructs as sub-dimensions of a higher-order motivational climate construct. Additionally, Kuenzi and Schminke (2009) argued that it is important to empirically examine how facet-specific climates "relate to one another and whether certain [domain-specific] climates exert greater relative impacts on outcomes than others" (p. 705). Similarly, Schulte et al. (2009) suggested that more research be conducted to establish the joint and interactive effects of domain-specific climates across a range of outcomes in a broad range of organizational contexts. The use of latent profile analyses might help determine the influence of different configurations of domain-specific climates (see McLarnon, Morin & Litalien, this volume).

Research determining the spatial configuration of domain-specific climates with reference to theoretically-defined models could also be usefully extended. Although Albrecht (2014) and Beus et al. (2020) conceptualized the location of a number of domain-specific climates with reference to the Competing Values Framework (CVF; Quinn & Rohrbaugh, 1983), multi-dimensional scaling techniques could be used to empirically locate existing and additional domain-specific climates in theoretical space. A conceptual framework, such as the CVF, that helps organize research on organizational climates "may prove useful not only as an organizational tool but also as a way to identify gaps that can be addressed in future climate research" (Schneider et al., 2011, p. 383).

Parallel research to that outlined above can also be applied to the relationships between employee perceptions of senior leadership engagement and senior leader change leadership, and between employee engagement and change engagement. That is, research could usefully establish if they are best conceptualized as independent first-order constructs, or as facets of a higher-order construct. With respect to leadership, and as previously noted, only a limited amount of research has focused on engagement or change-focused leadership, and additional research is needed to establish how such domain-specific leadership styles relate to each other and to alternative and more established styles.

A third line of ongoing research involves testing the proposed structural relationships between the constructs shown in Figure 10.1. That is, the statistical significance of the parameters modeled in Figure 10.1 will need to be established. The direct effects, the implicit indirect effects and the reciprocal relationships all need to be established using large-sample longitudinal research. As previously noted, the relative strength of the cross-construct structural relationships modeled could also usefully be investigated. The generalizability of any such results will need to be established across multiple organizations and different industry sectors.

A fourth line of research might usefully involve testing the multi-level relationships implicit within the model. Although not all data lends itself to multi-level modeling (e.g., Albrecht et al., 2018; Rafferty et al., 2013), senior leadership engagement and change leadership, and engagement climate and change climate will often be appropriately represented as organizational-level constructs. Employee engagement and change engagement will often be appropriately represented as individual-level constructs. As such, and consistent with Xanthopoulou and Bakker (this volume), a number of the solid-line arrows in Figure 10.1 can represent cross-level processes, with organizational-level constructs directly and indirectly influencing conceptually compatible individual-level constructs. In terms consistent with González-Romá and Hernández (2017), such relationships represent a form of 2–2–1 multi-level model, whereby the numbers indicate the level of the predictor, mediator, and outcome variables. Future research is needed to test such multi-level modeling after first establishing prerequisite levels of non-independence in nested data (see González-Romá, this volume).

A fifth line of research might usefully involve elaborating the proposed model to include additional organizational resources, job resources, personal resources and outcome variables. As previously noted, this chapter does not include a review of how job and personal resources (e.g., autonomy, self-efficacy) and job-level and personal change-related resources (e.g., involvement in change, change-related self-efficacy) might also influence employee engagement or change engagement. The elaboration of the relationships shown in Figure10.1 to accommodate a more comprehensive set of causal relationships is clearly an area for further conceptualization and research. Importantly, an elaboration of the proposed model should help identify important mediating or moderating mechanisms that explain the influence of domain-specific senior leadership and domain-specific climates on attitudes, behaviors and outcomes. Albrecht et al. (2015) proposed a comprehensive strategic engagement model that included HRM practices focused on engagement, an organizational climate focused on engagement, job resources (e.g., autonomy, supervisor support), personal resources (e.g., meaningful work, psychological safety) and a range of attitudinal, behavioral and performance outcomes. Such a model could be elaborated to include parallel change-related resources that can potentially influence employee engagement and employee engagement in change. More generally, the positive high-arousal character of both employee engagement and change engagement suggests research could usefully be conducted on their individual and joint influence on individual, team and organizational adaptive and proactive performance.

Practical implications

In practical terms, the proposed model can potentially be used to help organizations develop an easily-communicated common language around organizational resources as drivers of employee engagement and attitudes to change. Furthermore, the model can serve to underpin the development of a practically useful diagnostic for organizations wanting to understand what they can do to optimize employee engagement and engagement in change. Interventions based on survey results, using measures suggested in the chapter, can be aimed at developing senior leadership support of engagement and change, and change- and engagement-focused organizational climates.

Conclusion

This chapter has attempted an initial integration of domain-specific leadership, climate and engagement constructs into a practically useful model. Engagement remains an important source of competitive advantage (Albrecht et al., 2015) and the influence of "upstream" organizational resources such as senior leader engagement and engagement climate need to be further understood. Additionally, and considering the increasing prevalence and pace of organizational change, it is essential that researchers and practitioners further develop an understanding of the factors that drive positive employee attitudes toward change. This is because the extent to which employees adopt or resist change has a clear impact on the implementation effort, cost and success of ongoing organizational change. In this chapter it was proposed that the domain-specific constructs of senior leadership engagement, senior leader change leadership, organizational engagement climate and change climate have an important influence on employee engagement and change engagement. In line with domain-specific strategic approaches to HRM, and as previously noted, organizations that have well-developed and integrated engagement and change strategies, resources and capabilities will likely be better equipped to face the challenges and opportunities associated with ongoing organizational change. The model proposed provides a potentially useful framework within which to advance the research.

References

Albrecht, S., Breidahl, E., and Marty, A. (2018). Organizational resources, organizational engagement climate, and employee engagement. *Career Development International*, 23(1), 67–85.

Albrecht, S., and Travaglione, A. (2003). Trust in public-sector senior management. *International Journal of Human Resource Management*, 14(1), 76–92.

Albrecht, S. L. (2010). Employee engagement: 10 key questions for research and practice. In S. L. Albrecht (Ed.), *Handbook of Employee Engagement: Perspectives, Issues, Research and Practice* (pp. 3–19). Edward Elgar Publishing.

Albrecht, S. L. (2014). A climate for engagement: Some theory, models, measures, research and practical applications. In B. Schneider and K. Barbera (Eds), *The Handbook of Organizational Climate and Culture: Antecedents, Consequences, and Practice* (pp. 400–414). Oxford University Press.

Albrecht, S. L., Bakker, A. Gruman, J., Macey, W., and Saks, A. (2015). Employee engagement, human resource management practices and competitive advantage. *Journal of Organizational Effectiveness: People and Performance*, 2(1), 7–35.

Alimo-Metcalfe, B., Alban-Metcalf, J., Bradley, M., Mariathasan, J., and Samele, C. (2008). The impact of engaging leadership on performance, attitudes to work and wellbeing at work: A longitudinal study. *Journal of Health Organization and Management*, 22(6), 586–598.

Armenakis, A. A., and Bedeian, A. (1999). Organizational change: A review of theory and research in the 1990s. *Journal of Management*, 25(3), 293–315.

Ashforth, B. (1985). Climate formation: Issues and extensions. *Academy of Management Review*, 10, 837–847.

Barrick, M. R., Thurgood, G., Smith, T., and Courtright, S. (2015). Collective organizational engagement: Linking motivational antecedents, strategic implementation, and firm performance. *Academy of Management Journal*, 58(1), 111–135.

Bendixen, S. M., Campbell, M., Criswell, C. and Smith, R. (2017). Change-capable leadership: The real power propelling successful change. www.ccl.org/wp-content/uploads/2016/04/Change-Capable-Leadership.pdf.

Bennett, N., and Lemoine, G. (2014). What VUCA really means for you. *Harvard Business Review*, Jan/Feb. https://hbr.org/2014/01/what-vuca-really-means-for-you.

Beus, J. M., Solomon, S., Taylor, E., and Esken, C. (2020). Making sense of climate: A meta-analytic extension of the competing values framework. *Organizational Psychology Review*, *10*(3–4), 136–168.

Bouckenooghe, D., Devos, G., and Van den Broeck, H. (2009). Organizational change questionnaire: Climate of change, processes, and readiness – Development of a new instrument. *Journal of Psychology*, *143*(6), 559–599.

Brown, S. P., and Leigh, T. (1996). A new look at psychological climate and its relationship to job involvement, effort, and performance. *Journal of Applied Psychology*, *81*(4), 358–368.

Burke, W. W. (2014). Organizational change. In B. Schneider and K. Barbera (Eds), *The Handbook of Organizational Climate and Culture: Antecedents, Consequences, and Practice* (pp. 457–483). Oxford University Press.

Burnes, B. (2011). Introduction: Why does change fail and what we can do about it? *Journal of Change Management*, *11*, 445–450.

Chan, D. (2014). Multilevel and aggregation issues in climate and culture research. In B. Schneider and K. Barbera (Eds), *The Handbook of Organizational Climate and Culture: Antecedents, Consequences, and Practice* (pp. 484–495). Oxford University Press.

Choi, M. (2011). Employees' attitudes toward organizational change: A literature review. *Human Resource Management*, *50*, 479–500.

Choi, M., and Ruona, W. A. (2011). Individual readiness for organizational change and its implications for human resource and organization development. *Human Resource Development Review*, *10* (1), 46–73.

Collins, J., and Hansen, M. (2012). *Great by Choice: Uncertainty, Chaos, and Luck – Why Some Thrive Despite Them All*. Harper Books.

Colquitt, J. A., Noe, R., and Jackson, C. (2002). Justice in teams: Antecedents and consequences of procedural justice climate. *Personnel Psychology*, *55*(1), 83–109.

Crawford, E. R., LePine, J., and Rich, B. (2010). Linking job demands and resources to employee engagement and burnout: A theoretical extension and meta-analytic test. *Journal of Applied Psychology*, *95*, 834–848.

Deloitte (2015). Tone at the top: The first ingredient in a world-class ethics and compliance program. www2.deloitte.com/content/dam/Deloitte/us/Documents/risk/us-aers-tone-at-the-top-sept-2014.pdf.

Dhensa-Kahlon, R., and Coyle-Shapiro, J. (2013). Anticipatory (in)justice and organizational change: Understanding employee reactions to change. In S. Oreg, A. Michel and R. By (Eds), *The Psychology of Organizational Change: Viewing Change from the Employee's Perspective* (pp. 173–194). Cambridge University Press.

Edwards, M., Ashkanasy, N. M., and Gardner, J. (2009). Deciding to speak up or to remain silent following observed wrongdoing: The role of discrete emotions and climate of silence. In J. Greenberg and M. Edwards (Eds), *Voice and Silence in Organizations* (pp. 83–109). Emerald Group.

Ehrhart, M., and Raver, J. (2014). The effects of organizational climate and culture on productive and counterproductive behavior. In B. Schneider and K. Barbera (Eds), *The Handbook of Organizational Climate and Culture: Antecedents, Consequences, and Practice* (pp. 153–176). Oxford University Press.

Ekvall, G. (1991). Change-centred leaders: Empirical evidence of a third dimension of leadership. *Leadership and Organization Development Journal*, *12*, 18–23.

Fredrickson, B. (2001). The role of positive emotions in positive psychology: The broaden and build theory of positive emotions. *American Psychologist*, *56*(3), 218–226.

Frijda, N. H. (1986). *The Emotions.* Cambridge University Press.

González-Romá, V., and Hernández, A. (2017). Multilevel modeling: Research-based lessons for substantive researchers. *Annual Review of Organizational Psychology and Organizational Behavior, 4,* 183–210.

González-Romá, V., Schaufeli, W., Bakker, A., and Lloret, S. (2006). Burnout and work engagement: Independent factors or opposite poles? *Journal of Vocational Behavior, 68*(1), 165–174.

Griffin, M. A., Neal, A., and Parker, S. K. (2007). A new model of work role performance: Positive behavior in uncertain and interdependent contexts. *Academy of Management Journal, 50,* 327–347.

Halbesleben, J. R. B. (2010). A meta-analysis of work engagement: Relationships with burnout, demands, resources and consequences. In A. Bakker and M. Leiter (Eds), *Work Engagement: A Handbook of Essential Theory and Research* (pp. 102–117). Psychology Press.

Herold, D. M., Fedor, D., Caldwell, S., and Liu, Y. (2008) The effects of transformational and change leadership on employees' commitment to a change: A multilevel study. *Journal of Applied Psychology, 93*(2), 346–357.

Herscovitch, L., and Meyer, J. P. (2002). Commitment to organizational change: Extension of a three-component model. *Journal of Applied Psychology, 87*(3), 474–487.

Higgs, M., and Rowland, D. (2000). Building change leadership capability: "The quest for change competence". *Journal of Change Management, 1*(2), 116–130.

Holt, D. T., Armenakis, A., Feild, H., and Harris, S. (2007). Readiness for organizational change: The systematic development of a scale. *Journal of Applied Behavioral Science, 43*(2), 232–255.

Hughes, M. (2016). *The Leadership of Organizational Change.* Routledge.

Inceoglu, I., and Fleck, S. (2010). Engagement as a motivational construct. In S. L. Albrecht (Ed.), *Handbook of Employee Engagement: Perspectives, Issues, Research and Practice* (pp. 74–86). Edward Elgar.

Iverson, R. (1996). Employee acceptance of organizational change: The role of organizational commitment. *International Journal of Human Resource Management, 7*(1), 122–149.

Iverson, R., Olekalns, M., and Erwin, P. (1998). Affectivity, organizational stressors, and absenteeism: A causal model of burnout and its consequences. *Journal of Vocational Behavior, 52,* 1–23.

Johnson, K. J. (2016). The dimensions and effects of excessive change. *Journal of Organizational Change Management, 29*(3), 445–459.

Kotter, J. P. (1990). How leadership differs from management. *Free Press, 240,* 59–68.

Kremmer, H., Villamor, I., and Aguinis, H. (2019). Innovation leadership: Best-practice recommendations for promoting employee creativity, voice, and knowledge sharing. *Business Horizons, 62*(1), 65–74.

Kuenzi, M., and Schminke, M. (2009). Assembling fragments into a lens: A review, critique, and proposed research agenda for the organizational climate literature. *Journal of Management, 35*(3), 634–717.

Leiter, M. P., and Bakker, A. (2010). Work engagement: Introduction. In A. B. Bakker and M. P. Leiter (Eds), *Work Engagement: A Handbook of Essential Theory and Research* (pp. 1–9). Psychology Press.

Macey, W. H., and Schneider, B. (2008). The meaning of employee engagement. *Industrial and Organizational Psychology: Perspectives on Science and Practice, 1,* 3–30.

Macey, W. H., Schneider, B., Barbera, K., and Young, S. (2009). *Employee Engagement: Tools for Analysis, Practice, and Competitive Advantage.* Wiley.

Miller, V. D., Johnson, J., and Grau, J. (1994). Antecedents to willingness to participate in planned organizational change. *Journal of Applied Communication Research, 22,* 59–80.

Oreg, S., Bartunek, J., Lee, G., and Do, B. (2018). An affect-based model of recipients' responses to organizational change events. *Academy of Management Review, 43*(1), 65–86.

Oreg, S., and Berson, Y. (2019). Leaders' impact on organizational change: Bridging theoretical and methodological chasms. *Academy of Management Annals, 13*(1), 272–307.

Oreg, S., Vakola, M., and Armenakis, A. (2011). Change recipients' reactions to organizational change: A 60-year review of quantitative studies. *Journal of Applied Behavioral Science, 47,* 461–524.

Quinn, R., and Rohrbaugh, J. (1983). A spatial model of effectiveness criteria: Towards a competing values approach to organizational analysis. *Management Science, 29,* 363–377.

Rafferty, A., Jimmieson, N., and Restubog, S. (2013). When leadership meets organizational change: The influence of the top management team and supervisory leaders on change appraisal, change attitudes, and adjustment to change. In S. Oreg, A. Michel, and R. T. By (Eds), *The Psychology of Organizational Change: Viewing Change from the Employee's Perspective* (pp. 145–172). Cambridge University Press.

Russell, J. A. (2003). Core affect and the psychological construction of emotion. *Psychological Review, 110,* 145–172.

Saks, A. (2017). Translating employee engagement research into practice. *Organizational Dynamics, 46,* 76–86.

Saks, A. (2019). Antecedents and consequences of employee engagement revisited. *Journal of Organizational Effectiveness: People and Performance, 6*(1), 19–38.

Schaufeli, W. (2015). Engaging leadership in the jobs demands-resources model. *Career Development International, 20*(5), 446–463.

Schein, E. H. (2010). *Organizational Culture and Leadership* (4th ed.). Jossey-Bass.

Schneider, B. (1975). Organizational climates: An essay. *Personnel Psychology, 28,* 447–479.

Schneider, B., and Barbera, K. (2014a). Introduction. In B. Schneider and K. M. Barbera (Eds), *The Oxford Handbook of Organizational Culture and Climate* (pp. 3–20). Oxford University Press.

Schneider, B., and Barbera, K. (2014b). Summary and conclusion. In B. Schneider and K. M. Barbera (Eds), *The Oxford Handbook of Organizational Culture and Climate* (pp. 679–687). Oxford University Press.

Schneider, B., Brief, A., and Guzzo, R. (1996). Creating a climate and culture for sustainable organizational change. *Organizational Dynamics, 24*(4), 7–19.

Schneider, B., Ehrhart, M. G., and Macey, W. H. (2011). Perspectives on organizational climate and culture. In S. Zedeck (Ed.), *APA Handbook of Industrial and Organizational Psychology, Vol. 1: Building and Developing the Organization* (pp. 373–414). American Psychological Association.

Schneider, B., Ehrhart, M., and Macey, W. (2013). Organizational climate and culture. *Annual Review of Psychology, 64,* 361–88.

Schneider, B., Yost, A., Kropp, A., Kind, C., and Lam, H. (2017). Workforce engagement: What it is, what drives it, and why it matters for organizational performance. *Journal of Organizational Behavior, 39,* 462–480.

Schulte, M., Ostroff, C., Shmulyian, S., and Kinicki, A. (2009). Organizational climate configurations: Relationships to collective attitudes, customer satisfaction, and financial performance. *Journal of Applied Psychology*, *94*(3), 618–634.

Shea C., Jacobs, S., Esserman, D., Bruce, K., and Weiner, B. (2014). Organizational readiness for implementing change: A psychometric assessment of a new measure. *Implementation Science*, *9*(7). doi:10.1186/1748-5908-9-7.

Straatmann, T., Kohnke, O., Hattrup, K., and Muelle, K. (2016). Assessing employees' reactions to organizational change: An integrative framework of change-specific psychological factors. *Journal of Applied Behavioral Science*, *52*(3), 265–295.

Thundiyil, T., Chiaburu, D., Oh, I., Banks, G., and Peng, A. (2015). Cynical about change? A preliminary meta-analysis and future research agenda. *Journal of Applied Behavioral Science*, *51*(4), 429–450.

Tsaousis, I., and Vakola, M. (2018). Measuring change recipients' reactions: The development and psychometric evaluation of the CRRE scale. In M. Vakola and P. Petrou (Eds), *Organizational Change: Psychological Effects and Strategies for Coping* (pp. 114–127). Routledge.

Wanberg, C., and Banas, J. (2000). Predictors and outcomes of openness to change in a reorganizing workplace. *Journal of Applied Psychology*, *85*(1), 132–142.

Yukl, G., Mahsud, R., Prussia, G., and Hassan, S. (2019). Effectiveness of broad and specific leadership behaviors. *Personnel Review*, *48*(3), 774–783.

Zohar, D. (1980). Safety climate in industrial organizations: Theoretical and applied implication. *Journal of Applied Psychology*, *65*, 96–102.

PART III

Research strategies for the new agenda

11. Qualitative methods in engagement research

William H. Macey

Engagement research since the foundational work of Kahn (1990) has largely been quantitative, focusing on the antecedents and consequences of state engagement. This is even though work engagement reflects how people *experience* work (Bakker et al., 2011) and qualitative methods are most useful in understanding experiences, how people make sense of them, and their emotional reactions to them. As the relationship between employer and employee changes (Cappelli & Eldor, this volume) so will the nature of work experiences. Therefore, the use of qualitative methods to expand and perhaps even reframe the engagement construct will become increasingly important.

This chapter focuses on qualitative methods. However, it is not a primer. Readers with interest in how to actually do such work are referred to one of many detailed introductions to qualitative research, specific treatments of relevant methodologies (e.g., Charmaz, 2014, on grounded theory methodology; Smith et al., 1999, on interpretive phenomenological analysis), or specific data-collection methods. Instead, Kahn's (1990) effort is reviewed here with the purpose of highlighting the features of his inductive approach as a model for qualitative engagement research. A more general discussion of qualitative methods is presented after the Kahn review. Then, with that as background, several themes in qualitative engagement-related research are discussed. The chapter closes with an agenda for further qualitative engagement research emphasizing the changing nature of work experiences.

Kahn's foundational contribution

Much of qualitative management research is methodologically representative of an inductive approach labeled "grounded theory" (Glaser & Strauss, 1967). Starting with a general idea of the phenomenon of interest, the researcher iteratively collects data, evaluates those data, and considers next steps, including purposively sampling additional informants and modifying the data-collection protocol. Importantly, the researcher proceeds open to what might be discovered as the process evolves, constantly asking whether the data are supporting the emerging theoretical concept.

Using this approach, and building on existing theoretical frameworks from role theory and job design, Kahn (1990) defined engagement as "harnessing of organization members selves' to their work roles; in engagement, people employ and express themselves, physically, cognitively, and emotionally" (p. 694). Central to his thinking was that people vary in their engagement over time, and thus he differentiated his research from context-free attitudinal measurement studies. Kahn accordingly recognized the importance of contextual influences and thus the episodic nature of engagement.

Kahn (1990) conducted his first study in a summer camp where he also served as a counselor. Based on informal conversation, document review, observation, and self-reflection, he developed open-ended interview questions intending to reveal what people liked and disliked about their jobs and how people were involved in their work. He analyzed the resulting interview transcripts to frame a set of descriptive concept categories representing the episodes in which his informants seemed to engage or disengage at work. This analysis subsequently informed his second phase of research.

In that second study, Kahn (1990) conducted in-depth semi-structured interviews in an architectural firm. His interview questions included very specific references to a number of situations, focusing on times when employees felt attentive and interested, uninvolved or bored; and circumstances when people felt different or similar between work and non-work experiences. Other questions served to reveal job demands, interpersonal relationships, and support systems at work.

Kahn's (1990) final data set representing both studies comprised 86 engagement and 100 disengagement examples. From these, Kahn induced three sets of psychological factors influencing engagement and disengagement in role performances:

1. Meaningfulness (stemming from or influenced by task characteristics, role characteristics, and work interactions);
2. Safety (fostered or amplified through interpersonal relationships, group and intergroup dynamics, management-related factors, and organizational norms); and

3. Availability (influenced by the presence or depletion of physical or emotional energy, self-confidence or the lack thereof, or the distractions of insecurity and outside life).

More recently developed engagement frameworks are largely consistent with Kahn's (1990) explication of psychological meaningfulness, safety, and availability. For example, there is a clear degree of overlap in these three sets of work conditions with the antecedents of work engagement in the job demands-resources (JD-R) model (Bakker & Demerouti, 2017). This is not surprising in that the roots of Kahn's work were in role theory and the job design literature which stressed challenge, autonomy, and variety, and the initial JD-R model was presented as a framework similar to the job characteristics model of Hackman and Oldham (1980). Further, similarities to other frameworks such as the Gallup Q^{12} (Harter et al., 2003) can be traced to the qualitative origins in research focused on productive teams and individuals. Finally, although the Utrecht Work Engagement Scale (UWES; Schaufeli et al., 2002) is considered a measure of state engagement, some indicators comprising it reflect evaluations of the antecedent conditions identified by Kahn (e.g., the UWES item "I find the work that I do full of meaning and purpose" is conceptually consistent with Kahn's specification of psychological meaningfulness).

Several elements of Kahn's (1990) research are worth emphasizing:

- Multiple methods were used, including interviews, document review, observation, and direct in-role participation.
- He studied two significantly different organizations, seeking to generalize his findings.
- His interview plan evolved from a general effort in the first study to a more focused and situationally-based approach in the second to reflect what he learned from the first.
- He focused on informants' experiences in context. He worked inductively from quotations to identify the characteristics of "moments of personal engagement or disengagement" (p. 698).

Kahn's (1990) influence on subsequent study of engagement has been very important, but his methods have received much less attention. Given the general lack of attention to qualitative methods in engagement research, the following section provides a review of the techniques that might be used to further our understanding of engagement-related constructs.

Qualitative engagement-research methods

The number of different qualitative methods used in engagement-related research (and more generally occupational health and well-being) is somewhat limited; data are typically gathered directly from workers and obtained primarily through interviews, focus groups, surveys, and diaries. Informants commonly self-report as the data of interest are experiential, although reports of behavior are sometimes sought from observers. For example, Bakker and Demerouti (2008) cited Engelbrecht's (2006) unpublished study of Danish midwives who were asked to describe a highly engaged colleague.

Specific methods

Interviews

The semi-structured interview is arguably the most commonly used qualitative method to study engagement-related topics. Semi-structured interviews sacrifice a degree of consistency while still capturing a relatively complete narrative from the informant's perspective. The degree of structure varies widely, as does the extent to which questions are modified to reflect what is learned as the research proceeds. The key advantage of the interview over surveys is the option to follow up informants' responses to questions with probes to gain further detail.

Asking questions that reference the term "engagement" can be problematic as it is indefinite. Pilot testing questions with a sample of informants is essential to ensure that the questions are interpreted as intended. Flanagan (1954) suggested that even slight changes in an interview question can make for substantial differences in what is reported. Therefore, it can help to put the engagement topic in context. One approach is to provide a definition at the onset of the interview. For example, Bruning and Campion (2018) asked interviewees to provide examples of job crafting, both to improve effectiveness and to reduce stress. But pilot testing suggested that informants needed very specific guidance about what job crafting entails. Therefore, they began their interviews by providing a definition of job crafting, and discussed the definition until certain that informants understood its meaning.

The vignette interview is yet another way to provide appropriate context. Schaufeli et al. (2001) used four vignettes to guide their interviews, each vignette reflecting one quadrant of a circumplex model of affect representing the orthogonal dimensions of energy and pleasantness. Informants were then asked the extent to which they saw themselves in the vignettes.

Focus groups

This method is commonly used by survey research practitioners for the purpose of crafting survey items or seeking interpretive guidance with respect to survey results. Cucina and Gast (2020) offer an extensive review in that context. The method is particularly efficient when informants are asked to prepare written responses to questions. This requires an investment of group time in orienting informants to the task, but the return is considerable in terms of the amount of data collected relative to the individual interview. It is worth noting that focus groups can be conducted asynchronously using social medial platforms but at the expense of some loss of control, and may provide fewer opportunities for the deep level of probing that can be conducted in live sessions. Asynchronous focus groups differ from individual interviews in that focus group participants have access to other participants' comments.

Surveys

Open-ended survey questions can be a highly efficient means of data collection under the assumption that the responses provided are sufficiently detailed. The opportunity to follow up responses with clarifying questions is generally lost, although online solutions are now available for creating question hierarchies that probe based on initial responses. Open-ended surveys can be particularly useful when the intent is to explore the nomological net of a construct as a preliminary step in developing psychometric measures. Owens et al. (2016) provide an example in a study of relational energy transfer. They asked survey respondents "Have you ever had a coworker, boss/supervisor, or team member that you felt energized to be around?" (p. 37). Owens et al. identified several themes in the responses associated with psychological resources which then informed subsequent phases of their research. One limiting feature of this approach is that survey-generated narratives tend to be short and significantly less detailed than narratives obtained through interviews. For example, Owens et al. instructed respondents to type 100–200 words in their written response. Responses to questions in employee engagement open-ended surveys tend to be even shorter.

Diaries

Diaries allow for a relatively contemporaneous recording of events and experiences, and thus are less subject to retrospective biases. They are particularly useful for understanding how phenomena unfold over time. Poppleton et al. (2008) used the diary method to ask informants to describe events from the preceding 24 hours where work had affected their non-work life and vice versa. Among their findings, they discovered that negative interference at work can follow from thinking about personal problems during the day. Their observation clearly aligns with Kahn's (1990) "availability" dimension as a work condition essential to engagement.

Diaries can also be used to focus on both individual- and team-level phenomena. Amabile and Kramer (2011) included one open-ended question in a daily work-life survey asking participants to describe one event that day that stood out for them. Thematic coding of over 11,000 narratives revealed one particularly important theme in determining what the authors described as "inner work life," namely making progress toward goals as part of meaningful work. Their analyses indicated that progress (small wins, breakthroughs, goal attainment) and setbacks were the key determinants of informants' ratings of mood. Their approach was focused on teams within organizations, allowing them to interpret specific events related to interpersonal dynamics and leadership from multiple perspectives, both corroborating and reinforcing their observations.

Observation and participation

Direct observation can be particularly useful to fully understand the context in which engagement behavior is evident and thus to better understand what informants say. Tope et al. (2005) suggested that observation-based studies are more effective than interviews "in obtaining information about often-subtle workplace behaviors and attitudes" (p. 481). Grodal et al. (2015) thus shadowed engineers in a technology company to understand what they did, what they chose not to do, and how they interacted with others to understand help-giving and help-seeking behaviors.

Extant records and data

Rather than collect data directly from informants, researchers may wish to analyze narratives available through existing sources. These sources and corresponding methods might be useful in some future effort and are summarized in Table 11.1 for interested readers wishing to explore further.

Table 11.1   Citations to research using extant data

Source	Representative citation
Organizational ethnographies	Tope et al. (2005)
Employee reviews (e.g., Glassdoor)	Das Swain et al. (2020)
Emails	Srivastava et al. (2018)
Blogs	Peticca-Harris et al. (2015)

Coding and theme identification

Once the data are in hand, there is the issue of how to analyze them. It is customary to analyze narratives, field notes, and recorded observations by coding the text to represent the underlying patterns and themes. Coding is a complex process, typically conducted at multiple stages and degrees of specificity, and the sheer amount of data can be overwhelming. While software tools can relieve some of the burden, the complexity is not resolved through automation (Saldaña, 2016). Step-by-step guides to thematic analysis are available, including generating codes, identifying themes, and subsequent reporting (Braun & Clarke, 2012). Importantly, thematic analysis is often not a discrete activity; data collection and analysis are often treated as codependent processes. As an example, Merlo et al. (2020) revised their interview protocol multiple times as new insights emerged from the data.

Inductive research like Merlo et al. (2020) presupposes an organic evolution of the coding framework. That is, themes should capture the essence of the data as opposed to simply organizing examples to fit a pre-existing structure, although the latter is certainly appropriate in efforts to elaborate rather than create substantive theory. Braun and Clarke (2006) distinguished deductive approaches to thematic analysis as "top down" (fitting themes to an existing theory), whereas they considered inductive approaches as "bottom up" (p. 83). In the latter, themes emerge through a constant comparison of new data (i.e., narrative content) to existing categories, revision of the category structure, and so on in an iterative manner until the categorical structure represents the data as a whole. This may be done by a single researcher or by collaborating members of a research team. The number of themes that might be necessary to adequately fit the data clearly depends on the complexity of the topic, the characteristics of the informants, and the methods used.

Topic modeling

Given the complexity of thematic analysis, as well as the bias inherent in human coding, the potential for computationally-assisted solutions seems obvious. Topic modeling generally refers to the use of unsupervised machine learning algorithms (Banks et al., 2018) to identify the latent themes represented in a body of text, an application conceptually similar to the use of exploratory factor analysis to understand the latent structure of quantitative data. The interpretation of algorithmic output is complex, as subjective as any other form of content analysis, and sometimes leads to dissatisfying outcomes in practical application. Its benefits are realized when investigating very large data sets, and/or when applying previously developed models to new data. Potential applications for engagement research include the analysis of blog content that is often voluminous. Readers may wish to consult Hannigan et al. (2019) for considerations in using topic modeling for purposes of theory development. Fink and Macey (this volume) discuss topic modeling in more detail in the context of "big data."

Evaluative criteria in qualitative research

The adequacy of a qualitative research study is largely judged by the trustworthiness of the findings and methods used. For guidance, readers will find it worthwhile to visit the website of the Qualitative Research Guidelines Project (Cohen & Crabtree, 2006) which point to a variety of perspectives on evaluative criteria. Using evaluative criteria suggested by Lincoln and Guba (1985), Klotz and Bolino (2016) addressed issues of credibility, transferability, dependability, and confirmability in their development of a taxonomy of voluntary job resignation styles.

Themes in qualitative engagement research

What follows is a description of select research efforts relevant to (1) the episodic and contextually-driven nature of engagement as suggested by Kahn (1990); (2) components of the JD-R model, including job crafting; and/or (3) the investigation of what can be reasonably if not explicitly regarded as engagement behavior.

Episodic engagement

As noted earlier, Kahn (1990) emphasized the in-the-moment nature of engagement experiences. The dynamic aspect of engagement has been an evolving theme both in the quantitative (Sonnentag et al., and McLarnon et al., this volume) and in the qualitative engagement literature.

Task-specific engagement

Qualitative methods are particularly appropriate for investigating engagement as it relates to specific tasks or in specific contexts. For example, Margolis and Molinsky (2008) interviewed managers, doctors, police officers, and counselors about how they responded to their subjective experience of performing emotionally burdensome tasks such as firing employees or evicting people from their homes, precisely the kinds of tasks from which people might be expected to psychologically disengage. They identified engagement indicators that were task-specific, such as the experience of sympathy or guilt and attending to the negative consequences of their necessary actions. The authors also identified indicators of disengagement, such as denying prosocial emotion, and minimizing the impact of one's actions. Perhaps contrary to expectations, they found that many informants invested significant emotional energy in performing necessary evils rather than disengaging, and suggested that by psychologically engaging in such tasks people can be authentic and actually forestall burnout. A reasonable question is whether those who do invest themselves in performing such tasks experience a deficit in other aspects of their work; that is, whether there is spillover on a task-level basis and whether that spillover impacts all or uniquely some components of engagement.

Newton et al. (2020) collected critical incident data (Flanagan, 1954) using open-ended surveys administered to NASA flight crew members, asking them to report on transitions between two recent tasks. Based on these data they subsequently hypothesized two primary mechanisms by which engagement on one task might impact engagement on subsequent tasks, namely spillover from positive affect and attention residue. The first would be expected to enhance subsequent task engagement and the latter to negate those benefits. An extension of their research to less tightly constrained work would be valuable as cognitive disengagement might often be expected at transition points between tasks (Merlo et al., 2020; see below).

The research described above highlights the value of qualitative methods for identifying events that influence the rhythm of engagement throughout the day and longer as well as task transfer issues and engagement. Yet, further research is clearly needed exploring how the physical, cognitive, and emotional components of engagement interrelate across task and event boundaries (Saks, this volume).

Reactions to misfit unfold over time

As Kahn (1990) suggested, the alignment of roles with preferred self-image should contribute to the sense of meaningfulness in one's role and therefore engagement. Conversely, misfit can be visible to others and that in turn can lead to a loss of psychological safety contributing to disengagement. Follmer et al. (2018) conducted an inductive, multi-phase, qualitative investigation of how people respond to perceived misfit. In their first study, they conducted interviews with workers who described experiences of both fit and misfit. As their efforts to code transcriptions proceeded, they noticed how misfit experiences were more unusual and described in more elaborate terms than fit experiences. Therefore, they focused their second research phase to identify different strategies that workers take in response to misfit. Accordingly, they used a theoretical sampling procedure to identify individuals who were most likely to experience misfit; that is, those who had recently experienced organizational change. This sampling strategy represents a critical feature of inductive research, namely identifying informants who can best speak to the issue of interest.

Follmer et al. (2018) coded interview narratives to reveal resolution, adjustment, relief-seeking, and resignation approaches and specific strategies within those approaches. Some of the adjustment strategies they identified are arguably more aligned with a positive, proactive form of engagement behavior (e.g., job crafting) than withdrawal or disengagement. The value of qualitative research in this specific effort was that it was used to understand how informants adjusted to misfit over time and in relation to specific events. Extrapolated to the other (dis)engagement-relevant contexts, interview questions such as "When did you realize you no longer felt energized by your work?" might be used to surface precipitating events, the reactions to those experiences, and so on as individually-specific dynamic sequences of engagement episodes.

Negative events have greater impact than positive events

One significant issue that emerges when investigating engagement-related themes is negativity bias. That is, holistic judgments are more significantly impacted by negative than positive events. As experienced survey practitioners know, open-ended survey responses tend to be disproportionately negative and dissatisfied employees are more likely to comment than those who are satisfied (Poncheri et al., 2008). Along similar lines, Follmer et al. (2018) found that episodes characterized by misfit were more novel and described more elaborately. Amabile and Kramer (2011) also stressed the asymmetry in positive vs negative events in determining the quality of work life. Colquitt et al. (2015) found that the frequency distribution of themes varied meaningfully depending on whether interview questions asked for reactions to just or unjust supervisory behavior; reactions to unjust supervisory actions disproportionately represented themes of contingent reactions, hostility, and distraction whereas recounted reactions to supervisory justice disproportionately represented self-esteem and reciprocation. This cumulative pattern of research and practical experience illustrates the need to craft interview questions that invite informants to reflect on experiences revealing the full meaning of the engagement construct and not just a positive or negative interpretation.

Disengagement may be helpful even if temporary

Merlo et al. (2020) investigated the experience of mind-wandering or day dreaming using a semi-structured interview protocol. They found these episodes to begin following one of three internal conditions: (1) positive or negative emotional experiences; (2) work overload; and (3) boredom. They also noted that daydreaming could be prompted by external events such as email notifications, and by certain work contexts such as meetings and breaks that follow a change in task focus. Some informants reported daydreaming to be refreshing even if others reported feelings of guilt. Thus, cognitive disengagement may not necessarily result in a performance deficit but rather may serve as a useful if temporary means to cope with job demands.

Research elaborating JD-R theory

The JD-R theory is arguably the most researched engagement framework, predominately reflecting the use of quantitative methods, especially with regard to the facets of the UWES: absorption, dedication, and vigor. Nonetheless, there is a large body of qualitative research on the subject of job crafting (cf., Lazazzara et al.. 2020), a key component of the JD-R framework. I explore qualitative work on both the facets in the UWES and job crafting in what follows.

Absorption is an outcome and not a facet of engagement

Absorption is one of the three facets of the UWES, although some question exists as to whether it is better considered an engagement outcome (Bakker et al., 2011). Two qualitative studies speak to this. In the first, Albrecht and Wilson-Evered (2012) trained nine internal-company employees to act as interviewers. They asked 51 senior employees in a multi-national organization questions such as "What does employee engagement mean to you?" "Tell me about times you have felt particularly engaged," and "What are the conditions or factors which enabled you or your colleagues to be engaged?" (p. 64). Coded themes included reciprocal relationships, respectful and supportive leadership, discretionary effort, organizational commitment and identification, the full expression of self in the work role, alignment with work objectives – what the authors call "focused striving" – and open and respectful relationships. However, when informants were probed as to when they feel "really engaged" (p. 65), absorption did not emerge as a theme, although energy and enthusiasm were clearly evident in their responses. Thus, their modification to the JD-R model did not include absorption as a component.

In a second study, Medhurst and Albrecht (2016) interviewed 15 sales professionals, asking what engagement meant to them and following up by asking how the experience of engagement was similar or dissimilar to vigor, energy, dedication, and absorption. Their interpretation of results suggested that, while job and personal resources are antecedents of engagement consistent with JD-R theory, engagement is a precursor to a state of flow within which absorption might be better represented as an "amplified expression of focus, concentration and attention" (p. 31). However, they also did note that what emerged for them as a "focused" theme was more similar to the absorption facet of engagement as defined by Schaufeli et al. (2002). This distinction is clearly subtle and would benefit from further exploration.

Job crafting is proactive and self-serving

Within JD-R theory, job crafting is a mechanism by which individuals proactively address both demands and resource availability, thereby reducing hindrances or enhancing the motivational qualities of work. Bruning and Campion (2018) used a qualitative research strategy to develop a taxonomy of job crafting. They asked 246 informants to provide examples of job-crafting actions taken to improve their effectiveness and also actions taken to reduce personal stress. Based on thematic coding, Bruning and Campion identified a taxonomy of role and resource job crafting, further distinguishing between approach-crafting activities that are problem focused and oriented toward improving work experiences and avoidance-crafting activities that evade or eliminate part of one's work.

Research focusing on behavioral engagement

Macey and Schneider (2008) suggested that engagement in its behavioral form can be taken to mean going beyond what is commonly expected and is thus discretionary. As they noted, this implies a frame of reference as to what is normal or typical. To that point, Carsten et al. (2010) studied the notion of followership as a social construction yielding data that can be interpreted within an engagement framework. Their coded themes derived from the data included categories such as "taking ownership," "initiative/proactive behavior," and "deference," which was defined as "not participating readily or actively" (p. 549). Informant responses suggested passive, active, and proactive social constructions of followership, the latter of which is characterized by giving feedback to leaders and challenging leader assumptions. The point here is that what might be considered "engagement behavior" is influenced by what employees think it means to follow those in a leadership role, and that this social construction may be a reflection of group climate. Thus, what is discretionary to some is not to others, from both worker and observer perspectives.

Dekas et al. (2013) further illustrate the importance of frame of reference in a study of organizational citizenship behavior (OCB) among Google employees. In an effort to elaborate on existing themes to better fit knowledge work, they conducted focus groups to collect examples of OCBs. They inductively content-analyzed the resulting examples by classifying them into existing categories, creating new categories as needed to reflect the data. Dekas et al. arrived at a solution comprising eight dimensions of OCB specific to Google. Several of these dimensions did not correspond to existing frameworks in the literature, such as "social participation," which refers to taking part in social activities. Their research demonstrates how qualitative techniques can be useful to verify and, if needed, elaborate existing conceptualizations of behavioral engagement in a new world of work.

A qualitative engagement-research agenda

This chapter has emphasized that qualitative methods are particularly relevant to engagement research when the goal is to understand how workers make sense of their experiences, understand the temporal dynamics of engagement episodes, and/or examine what it means to be engaged from an observer's point of view. Given the changes in the employment context and in particular the new work routines that have emerged for those working from home, much of what is accepted wisdom regarding the engagement experience, as well as its antecedents and consequences, may be questioned. Thus, some areas of inquiry particularly amenable to qualitative research questions include:

- What are the organizational referents of engagement for freelance workers whose primary source of income is arranged through an online platform (Cappelli & Eldor, this volume)?
- How do managers gauge employee engagement as their teams have shifted to working from home as the result of the Covid-19 pandemic (see Gagné et al., this volume)?
- What are the spillover effects on work engagement that originate from family–work conflict as a result of the shift to working from home (Speights et al., 2020)?
- What is the meaning of discretionary effort for those in contractor or temporary roles working alongside regular employees (Boudreau and Cappelli & Eldor, this volume)?
- How do freelancers experience engagement? How does that differ from the experiences of those in more traditional entrepreneurial roles (Schonfeld & Mazzola, 2015)?
- How do workers predisposed to be engaged (Hough & Oswald, this volume) make sense of change and uncertainty (Gagné et al., this volume)? How does that differ from those not so predisposed?
- What are the thematic differences in narratives of disengaged vs engaged workers? Are disengagement and engagement endpoints of the same continuum (Kahn, 1990)?
- How do workers make sense of and interpret leaders' motives in a highly monitored work environment (Gagné et al., this volume)?
- What team experiences define the emergence of group norms for discretionary effort (Albrecht, this volume)?
- How do freelance workers cope with and make sense of the unethical behaviors of their customers (Cappelli & Eldor, this volume)?

References

Albrecht, S.L., and Wilson-Evered, E. (2012). Bridging the practice and science of employee engagement: A qualitative investigation. *Ciencia y Trabajo, 2012*(14), 61–71.

Amabile, T., and Kramer, S. (2011). *The Progress Principle: Using Small Wins to Ignite Joy, Engagement, and Creativity at Work*. Harvard Business Publishing.

Bakker, A.B., Albrecht, S.L., and Leiter, M.P. (2011). Key questions regarding work engagement. *European Journal of Work and Organizational Psychology, 20*(1), 4–28.

Bakker, A.B., and Demerouti, E. (2008). Towards a model of work engagement. *Career Development International*, *13*, 209–223.

Bakker, A.B., and Demerouti, E. (2017). Job demands–resources theory: Taking stock and looking forward. *Journal of Occupational Health Psychology*, *22*(3), 273–285.

Banks, G.C., Woznyj, H.M., Wesslen, R.S., and Ross, R.L. (2018). A review of best practice recommendations for text analysis in R (and a user-friendly app). *Journal of Business and Psychology*, *33*(4), 445–459.

Braun, V., and Clarke, V. (2006). Using thematic analysis in psychology. *Qualitative Research in Psychology*, *3*(2), 77–101.

Braun, V., and Clarke, V. (2012). Thematic analysis. In H. Cooper, P. M. Camic, D. L. Long, A. T. Panter, D. Rindskopf, & K. J. Sher (Eds), *APA Handbook of Research Methods in Psychology, Vol. 2. Research Designs: Quantitative, Qualitative, Neuropsychological, and Biological* (pp. 57–71). American Psychological Association.

Bruning, P.F., and Campion, M.A. (2018). A role–resource approach–avoidance model of job crafting: A multimethod integration and extension of job crafting theory. *Academy of Management Journal*, *61*(2), 499–522.

Carsten, M.K., Uhl-Bien, M., West, B.J., Patera, J.L., and McGregor, R. (2010). Exploring social constructions of followership: A qualitative study. *Leadership Quarterly*, *21*(3), 543–562.

Charmaz, K. (2014). *Constructing Grounded Theory: A Practical Guide through Qualitative Analysis*. Sage.

Cohen, D., and Crabtree, B. (2006, July). *Qualitative Research Guidelines Project*. Robert Wood Johnson Foundation. www.qualres.org/index.html.

Colquitt, J.A., Long, D.M., Rodell, J.B., and Halvorsen-Ganepola, M.D.K. (2015). Adding the "in" to justice: A qualitative and quantitative investigation of the differential effects of justice rule adherence and violation. *Journal of Applied Psychology*, *100*(2), 278–297.

Cucina, J., and Gast, I. (2020). Focus groups: Blending qualitative and quantitative methodology to improve the survey process. In W.H. Macey and A.A. Fink (Eds), *Employee Surveys and Sensing: Challenges and Opportunities*. Oxford University Press.

Das Swain, V., Saha, K., Reddy, M.D., Rajvanshy, H., Abowd, G.D., and De Choudhury, M. (2020, April). Modeling organizational culture with workplace experiences shared on Glassdoor. In *Proceedings of the 2020 CHI Conference on Human Factors in Computing Systems* (pp. 1–15). https://dl.acm.org/doi/abs/10.1145/3313831 .3376793.

Dekas, K.H., Bauer, T.N., Welle, B., Kurkoski, J., and Sullivan, S. (2013). Organizational citizenship behavior, version 2.0: A review and qualitative investigation of OCBs for knowledge workers at Google and beyond. *Academy of Management Perspectives*, *27*(3), 219–237.

Engelbrecht, S. (2006). Motivation and burnout in human service work: The case of midwifery in Denmark [Unpublished doctoral dissertation, Roskilde University].

Flanagan, J.C. (1954). The critical incident technique. *Psychological Bulletin*, *51*(4), 327–358

Follmer, E.H., Talbot, D.L., Kristof-Brown, A.L., Astrove, S.L., and Billsberry, J. (2018). Resolution, relief, and resignation: A qualitative study of responses to misfit at work. *Academy of Management Journal*, *61*(2), 440–465.

Glaser, B.G., and Strauss, A.L. (1967). *The Discovery of Grounded Theory*. Aldine.

Grodal, S., Nelson, A.J., and Siino, R.M. (2015). Help-seeking and help-giving as an organizational routine: Continual engagement in innovative work. *Academy of Management Journal*, *58*(1), 136–168.

Hackman, J.R., and Oldham, G.R. (1980). *Work Redesign*. Addison-Wesley.

Hannigan, T.R., Haans, R.F., Vakili, K., Tchalian, H., Glaser, V.L., Wang, M.S., Kaplan, S., and Jennings, P.D. (2019). Topic modeling in management research: Rendering new theory from textual data. *Academy of Management Annals*, *13*(2), 586–632.

Harter, J.K., Schmidt, F.L., and Keyes, C.L.M. (2003). Well-being in the workplace and its relationship to business outcomes: A review of the Gallup studies. In C.L.M. Keyes and J. Haidt (Eds), *Flourishing: Positive Psychology and the Life Well-lived* (pp. 205–224). American Psychological Association.

Kahn, W.A. (1990). Psychological conditions of personal engagement and disengagement at work. *Academy of Management Journal*, *33*(4), 692–724.

Klotz, A.C., and Bolino, M.C. (2016). Saying goodbye: The nature, causes, and consequences of employee resignation styles. *Journal of Applied Psychology*, *101*(10), 1386–1404.

Lazazzara, A., Tims, M., and de Gennaro, D. (2020). The process of reinventing a job: A meta-synthesis of qualitative job crafting research. *Journal of Vocational Behavior*, *116*(Part B), Article 103267.

Lincoln, Y.S., and Guba, E.G. (1985). *Naturalistic Inquiry*. Sage.

Macey, W.H., and Schneider, B. (2008). The meaning of employee engagement. *Industrial and Organizational Psychology: Perspectives on Science and Practice*, *1*, 3–30.

Margolis, J.D., and Molinsky, A. (2008). Navigating the bind of necessary evils: Psychological engagement and the production of interpersonally sensitive behavior. *Academy of Management Journal*, *51*(5), 847–872.

Medhurst, A.R., and Albrecht, S.L. (2016). Salesperson work engagement and flow. *Qualitative Research in Organizations and Management: An International Journal*, *11*(1), 22–45.

Merlo, K.L., Wiegand, K.E., Shaughnessy, S.P., Kuykendall, L.E., and Weiss, H.M. (2020). A qualitative study of daydreaming episodes at work. *Journal of Business and Psychology*, *35*(2), 203–222.

Newton, D.W., LePine, J.A., Kim, J.K., Wellman, N., and Bush, J.T. (2020). Taking engagement to task: The nature and functioning of task engagement across transitions. *Journal of Applied Psychology*, *105*(1), 1–18.

Owens, B.P., Baker, W.E., Sumpter, D.M., and Cameron, K.S. (2016). Relational energy at work: Implications for job engagement and job performance. *Journal of Applied Psychology*, *101*(1), 35–49.

Peticca-Harris, A., Weststar, J., and McKenna, S. (2015). The perils of project-based work: Attempting resistance to extreme work practices in video game development. *Organization*, *22*(4), 570–587.

Poncheri, R.M., Lindberg, J.T., Thompson, L.F., and Surface, E.A. (2008). A comment on employee surveys: Negativity bias in open-ended responses. *Organizational Research Methods*, *11*(3), 614–630.

Poppleton, S., Briner, R.B., and Kiefer, T. (2008). The roles of context and everyday experience in understanding work-non-work relationships: A qualitative diary study of white-and blue-collar workers. *Journal of Occupational and Organizational Psychology*, *81*(3), 481–502.

Saldaña, J. (2016). *The Coding Manual for Qualitative Researchers*. Sage.

Schaufeli, W.B., Salanova, M., González-Romá, V., and Bakker, A.B. (2002). The measurement of engagement and burnout: A two sample confirmatory factor analytic approach. *Journal of Happiness Studies*, *3*(1), 71–92.

Schaufeli, W.B., Taris, T., Le Blanc, P., Peeters, M., Bakker, A., and De Jonge, J. (2001). Maakt arbeid gezond? Op zoek naar de bevlogen werknemer [Does work make one healthy? In search of the engaged worker]. *De Psycholoog*, *36*, 422–428.

Schonfeld, I.S., and Mazzola, J.J. (2015). A qualitative study of stress in individuals self-employed in solo businesses. *Journal of Occupational Health Psychology*, *20*(4), 501–513.

Smith, J.A., Jarman, M., and Osborn, M. (1999). Doing interpretative phenomenological analysis. In M. Murray and K. Chamberlain (Eds), *Qualitative Health Psychology: Theories and Method* (pp. 218–240). Sage.

Speights, S.L., Bochantin, J.E. and Cowan, R.L. (2020). Feeling, expressing, and managing emotions in work-family conflict. *Journal of Business and Psychology*, *35*, 363–380.

Srivastava, S.B., Goldberg, A., Manian, V.G., and Potts, C. (2018). Enculturation trajectories: Language, cultural adaptation, and individual outcomes in organizations. *Management Science*, *64*(3), 1348–1364.

Tope, D., Chamberlain, L.J., Crowley, M., and Hodson, R. (2005). The benefits of being there: Evidence from the literature on work. *Journal of Contemporary Ethnography*, *34*(4), 470–493.

12. Investigating employee engagement at multiple levels

Vicente González-Romá

Employee engagement is a positive, fulfilling, work-related, affective-cognitive state, characterized by vigor (i.e., high levels of energy, effort, resilience, and persistence while working), dedication (i.e., a sense of significance, enthusiasm, inspiration, pride, and challenge), and absorption (i.e., concentrating fully on one's work and having difficulty detaching from it) (González-Romá et al., 2006). As the term *"employee* engagement" suggests, engagement has generally been investigated and operationalized at the individual level (see Bakker et al., 2014, for a review). However, some researchers have also examined engagement at higher levels of analysis, generally at the work-team level (e.g., Costa et al., 2014). These studies show that: (a) engagement is a multilevel construct, (b) it has antecedents and consequences at multiple levels of analysis, and (c) to obtain a richer understanding of engagement's nomological network (i.e., the set of its relationships with hypothetical antecedents and consequences), it has to be investigated with a multilevel approach (see Xanthopoulou & Bakker, this volume).

Therefore, the goals of this chapter are:

1. To show that engagement can be conceptualized and operationalized at different levels of analysis following distinct emergence models; and
2. To show how the influence of engagement at higher levels of analysis (e.g., the work-team) on individual variables can be investigated by using multilevel methods.

Engagement at higher levels

When investigated at higher levels of analysis, engagement has been conceptualized as an emergent construct (e.g., García-Buades et al., 2016). Emergent constructs originate in lower-level properties (such as cognitions, affect, behaviors, or other characteristics of individuals), they are amplified by their interactions, and they manifest as higher-level, collective phenomena (Kozlowski & Klein, 2000, p. 55). Two general types of emergence can be distinguished: composition and compilation (Kozlowski & Klein, 2000).

Composition emergence describes how individual-level properties (e.g., employee engagement) combine "to yield a higher-level property [e.g., team engagement] that is essentially the same as its constituent elements" (Kozlowski & Klein, 2000, p. 16). In composition emergence, the *type and amount* of the lower-level property involved is assumed to be similar for all the individuals in the work unit. In the case of team engagement, the higher-level construct is formed from the same type of individual property (employee engagement), and all the employees in the team experience a similar (shared) amount of engagement. To fully understand the nature of higher-level constructs, it is *crucial* to explain the psychosocial factors and processes through "which lower-level properties emerge to form collective phenomena" (Kozlowski & Klein, 2000, p. 15). In composition emergence, these factors and processes explain how convergence, sharing, and within-unit agreement develop to yield a *shared* unit property (Kozlowski & Klein, 2000). In the case of engagement, working in the same environment (e.g., a given work unit), having the same leader, social interaction among unit members, and emotional contagion are some of the factors and processes that explain why work-unit members may develop similar (shared) levels of engagement (Costa et al., 2014). These factors and processes yield a *shared* higher-level property that manifests at a higher level (e.g., *team engagement*). Once within-unit agreement among unit members' scores is shown, the aforementioned shared property is operationalized by computing the average of individual engagement scores. This average is obtained following a direct consensus model of composition (Chan, 1998), and using engagement items in which the referent is the respondent (e.g., "At work, *I* feel full of energy"; Salanova et al., 2005). In this case, the average that is used to operationalize team engagement represents a *shared individual state of engagement*.

In other cases, researchers assuming composition emergence operationalize team engagement following a different procedure (e.g., Barrick et al., 2015; Costa et al., 2014). They first use engagement items in which the referent is a collective that the researchers are interested in ("my team", "my organization", "we", "my coworkers and I" – for example, "My team is bursting with energy at work"; Tims et al., 2013). They then obtain a unit average following a referent-shift consensus model of composition once within-unit agreement among unit members' scores is shown (Chan, 1998). Here, the average that is used to operationalize team engagement represents *a shared individual belief about the unit state of engagement.* Note how the change in the referent of engagement items results in different unit-level constructs (Chan, 1998). To distinguish between them, Barrick and colleagues (2015) refer to the unit scores obtained by following a direct consensus model as indicators of aggregated individual-level engagement, and the unit scores obtained by following a referent-shift consensus model as indicators of collective unit engagement. Interestingly, although different, the two indicators tend to be highly correlated (0.88 in Costa et al. (2014) and 0.57 in Barrick et al. (2015)).

Previous research on engagement at higher levels of analysis has generally adopted the composition type of emergence, showing that team engagement has important influences on team performance and is affected by team resources and demands and team states and processes (e.g., Rodríguez-Sánchez et al., 2017; Salanova et al., 2005; Tims et al., 2013).

Compilation emergence describes how different *types or/and amounts* of individual properties combine to form higher-order *configural* properties (Kozlowski & Klein, 2000). In compilation emergence, a number of factors and processes promote variability and different patterns of individual-level properties within the team (Kozlowski & Klein, 2000). For instance, regarding within-team variability, different levels of emotional contagion within teams in a sample of work teams may yield different levels of within-team agreement on engagement. These latter differences can be represented by a *configural* team-level property: *team engagement homogeneity* (or its opposite: team engagement heterogeneity). Assuming a single mode distribution (Chan, 1998), team engagement homogeneity can be represented by computing the within-team standard deviation in engagement.

Regarding the emergence of different patterns of individual-level properties within the team, and based on the relationship between leader–member exchange quality and employee engagement (Christian et al., 2011), we can suppose that if a leader develops different quality relationships with his/her collaborators, he or she can contribute to forming distinct engagement patterns within his or her team. If the leader has high-/low-quality relationships with all the team members, the pattern or distribution of individual engagement scores within the team will be *uniform*, showing a single grouping of high/low engagement scores comprising all the unit members. If he or she has high-quality relationships with only one or a few of his or her collaborators, and low-quality relationships with the others, the pattern will be *non-uniform*, with one or a few collaborators with high engagement scores and the rest with low scores. Other factors, such as demographic faultlines and different socialization processes, might also yield distinct engagement patterns.

The existence of distinct patterns of within-team engagement can be represented by another configural team-level property: *team engagement uniformity*. The operationalization of this property is based on the identification of different types of within-team configurations of the specific individual property involved (e.g., uniform and non-uniform types or patterns). This can be done by implementing different methods (see González-Romá & Hernández, 2014; Loignon et al., 2019; Seo et al., 2018). For instance, based on González-Romá and Hernández's (2014) method, researchers can use raters that are asked to classify within-team distributions of individual engagement scores into uniform and non-uniform patterns with the help of a set of guidelines. Another approach is to use latent profiles analysis (LPA) to identify different types of within-team engagement patterns in survey responses (see Seo et al. (2018) and McLarnon et al., this volume, for an application of this method). In this case, LPA identifies different patterns based on the four statistical moments (mean, variance, skewness, and kurtosis) of each team, which provide information about the shape of the within-team distribution.

Unfortunately, employee engagement has not been conceptualized and operationalized at higher levels of analysis following compilation models of emergence. This is unfortunate for several reasons. First, although there are several factors and processes that foster convergence among unit members' cognitions and responses, research on perceptions (e.g., work-unit climate; González-Romá & Hernández, 2014), affect (e.g., positive affect; Barsade et al., 2000), and attitudes (e.g., job/team satisfaction; Dineen et al., 2007; Loignon et al., 2019) has shown that there can be substantial variability and non-uniform patterns within units. Thus, the same thing can occur in the case of employee engagement.

To investigate this possibility, I examined the within-team distributions of individual-level engagement, as measured by the Utrecht Work Engagement Scale (UWES; Schaufeli et al., 2002), in a sample composed of 65 bank branches of a savings bank. The average team size (excluding the team manager) was 4.8 (standard deviation, or SD = 1.63; range = 3 to 9 members). The average response rate across teams was 92 percent (SD = 14.9). After obtaining the average total engagement score for each branch member, I computed the SD in engagement for each branch. The average SD in the sample of branches was 0.68 (SD = 0.40; observed range = 0 to 1.74[1]). These results indicated that team engagement homogeneity showed substantial variability across branches. Then, in order to ascertain which branches had uniform and non-uniform patterns, I examined the form of the within-unit distribution shown by employee engagement scores using González-Romá and Hernández's (2014) guidelines. As expected, most branches showed a uniform pattern (51; 78.5

percent). However, 14 (21.5 percent) of the 65 branches showed non-uniform patterns. Among them, 14 branches had a *weak dissimilarity* pattern (i.e., one homogenous subgroup with the excluded members not forming a coherent cluster), and 5 branches (7.7 percent) had a *strong dissimilarity* pattern (i.e., two homogenous subgroups within the unit). These observed patterns are represented in Figure 12.1. All these results showed that employee engagement can also emerge at higher levels following compilation emergence.

Figure 12.1   Observed patterns of employee engagement scores in three bank branches

Second, previous research has found that homogeneity and uniformity are higher-level properties that have consequences for team functioning. For instance, González-Romá and Hernández (2014) showed that uniformity in organizational support climate affected team communication quality. Loignon et al. (2019) found that within-team patterns in team satisfaction were related to willingness to work together in the future. Dineen et al. (2007) showed that the team mean and homogeneity in job satisfaction interacted to predict absenteeism. These results suggest that, in addition to team (average) engagement, team engagement homogeneity and uniformity may also have important consequences for team functioning and outcomes. This idea represents a pressing research question that future studies should address.

I finish this section by recommending that when investigating employee engagement at multiple levels, researchers should, in a first stage, do the following:

1.   Specify the level(s) at which engagement will be investigated;
2.   Define engagement at these levels;
3.   *Theoretically* explain how engagement emerges at higher levels, yielding higher-level constructs;
4.   Specify the type of emergence involved; and
5.   Show how engagement will be operationalized at the respective levels.

Following this process will contribute to gaining clarity in multilevel engagement research.

After constructs and variables are defined and operationalized, the research effort can focus on estimating the relationships between engagement and hypothesized antecedents and consequences at multiple levels. To do so, an understanding of multilevel methods is required. The logic of these methods is presented in the next section.

The logic of multilevel methods

An assumption of multilevel methods is that the relationship between two *individual*-level variables (X and Y) can vary across units, and that the parameters that define this relationship depend on certain *unit* properties. The aforementioned relationship can be formalized in a simple regression equation: $Y = a + bX + e$, where Y is the outcome variable, X is the predictor variable, a is the regression intercept, b is the regression coefficient or slope, and e is the residual term. Suppose that X refers to individual workload and Y refers to employee job satisfaction. If this simple regression equation is estimated in each unit in a sample of units, it is likely that the values obtained for the intercept and the slope will vary across units. This means that: for a certain value of X (workload), different units may have different expected values (i.e., intercepts) of Y (satisfaction), and the magnitude and sign of the relationship (i.e., the slope) may be different for distinct units. The former simple regression equation can be rewritten using multilevel notation and considering the nested structure of the data (i.e., employees nested within units):

$$Y_{ij} = \beta_{0j} + \beta_{1j} X_{ij} + r_{ij} \tag{1}$$

where Y_{ij} is the score on the outcome variable (job satisfaction) of subject i from unit j, X_{ij} is the score on the predictor variable (workload) of subject i from unit j, β_{0j} is the regression intercept estimated in each unit (j), β_{1j} is the regression coefficient (slope) estimated in each unit (j), and r_{ij} is the residual term of the regression equation in each unit (j). Because in this equation the outcome and the predictor are individual-level variables, equation 1 is an individual-level (or Level-1, L1) equation. The j subscript of the intercept (β_{0j}) and the slope (β_{1j}) denotes that they may vary across the j units. An interesting question then is to identify factors that explain variability in β_{0j} and β_{1j}. Imagine that we think that unit shared engagement (E, a unit-level property) is one of these factors. Thus, we can write a couple of simple regression equations with the form $Y = a + b X + e$ that show this idea:

$$\beta_{0j} = \gamma_{00} + \gamma_{01} E_j + U_{0j} \tag{2}$$

$$\beta_{1j} = \gamma_{10} + \gamma_{11} E_j + U_{1j} \tag{3}$$

where E_j represents the score on the predictor (unit engagement) of unit j, γ_{00} and γ_{10} are two regression intercepts, γ_{01} and γ_{11} are two regression slopes that estimate the relationship between E_j and β_{0j}, and E_j and β_{1j}, respectively, and U_{0j} and U_{1j} are the corresponding residual terms. These equations have two special characteristics:

1. The outcome variables (β_{0j} and β_{1j}) are the regression intercepts and slopes, not the typical substantive variables (as in equation 1); and
2. The outcome and predictor variables are unit-level variables.

Therefore, equations 2 and 3 are unit-level (or Level-2, L2) equations.

Equations 1, 2, and 3 constitute a multilevel model in which different relationships are specified at different levels of analysis. Multilevel methods are used to estimate the parameters involved in Level-1 and Level-2 equations. These parameters and other components of multilevel models are denoted by specific terms. *Random coefficients* are parameters that vary across Level-2 units (β_{0j} and β_{1j}; they carry the j subscript). *Fixed effects* are parameters that do not vary across Level-2 units ($\gamma_{00}, \gamma_{01}, \gamma_{10},$ and γ_{11}; they do not carry a j subscript). *Random effects* represent the variation in random coefficients across Level-2 units (U_{0j} and U_{1j}). It is assumed that these residuals follow a normal distribution, with a zero mean and variances $\sigma^2_{\tau_{00}}$ and $\sigma^2_{\tau_{11}}$ respectively. The *variance-covariance components* of the specified multilevel model are: the variances of the Level-2 residuals ($\sigma^2_{\tau_{00}}$ and $\sigma^2_{\tau_{11}}$), the covariance of the Level-2 residuals ($\sigma^2_{\tau_{10}}$), and the variance of the Level-1 residual r_{ij} (see equation 1), which is denoted by σ^2. It is also assumed that r_{ij} follows a normal distribution with a zero mean. σ^2 represents the variance in the outcome variable within units; $\sigma^2_{\tau_{00}}$ represents the variance in the intercept (β_{0j}) between units; and $\sigma^2_{\tau_{11}}$ represents the variance in the slope (β_{1j}) between units.

Multilevel models to examine the influence of engagement at multiple levels

Generally, multilevel researchers build models to be tested in a progressive way, starting with a simple model in which the variance of the outcome variable is decomposed into its within (σ^2) and between ($\sigma_{\tau_{00}}^2$) components, and finishing with a model that tests the specific study hypotheses. Due to space limitations, in this chapter I only focus on two models that can be used to estimate the influence of engagement across levels. Interested readers can consult González-Romá and Hernández's (2019) article to see how to specify and test other multilevel models, as well as Xanthopoulou and Bakker (this volume) for sample multilevel findings.

Examining the cross-level direct effect of team engagement

Researchers are often interested in ascertaining whether a higher-level construct is related to a given outcome after controlling for the predictor's individual-level counterpart. Imagine that a researcher wants to see whether, after controlling for the influence of employee engagement (X) on job satisfaction (Y), team shared engagement (E) adds predictive power. The corresponding research model is typically represented as shown in Figure 12.2, panel A.

The corresponding multilevel model is:

$$\text{L1: } Y_{ij} = \beta_{0j} + \beta_{1j} x_{ij} + r_{ij} \tag{4}$$

$$\text{L2: } \beta_{0j} = \gamma_{00} + \gamma_{01} E_j + U_{0j} \tag{5}$$

$$\beta_{1j} = \gamma_{10} \tag{6}$$

This model is known as an intercepts-as-outcomes model with fixed slopes. In equation 4 (the L1 equation), the values for employee engagement (X_{ij}) have been Centered Within Cluster (CWC), following this expression: $x_{ij} = \bar{X}_{ij} - \bar{X}_{j}$. By so doing, x_{ij} and E_j become two orthogonal predictors.[2] β_{1j} estimates the engagement-satisfaction individual-level relationship. Note that in equation 6, β_{1j} is assumed to not vary across units (there is no residual term, U_{1j}); thus, the slope (β_{1j}) is said to be fixed. This typically occurs when researchers are not interested in modeling the slope variability, as in the present case. It also shows that the final form of multilevel models depends on the researcher's specific goals, hypotheses, and assumptions.[3]

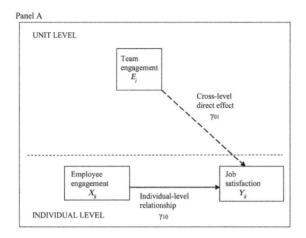

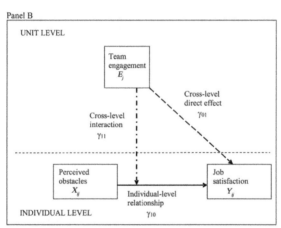

Figure 12.2   Typical representation of multilevel models including a cross-level direct effect (Panel A) and a cross-level interaction (Panel B)

In equation 5, the values for team shared engagement (E_j) are each unit's average score on engagement. γ_{01} estimates the relationship between E_j and β_{0j}. Note that the intercept is an estimation of the unit's mean on the outcome variable[4] (see Enders & Tofighi, 2007; González-Romá, 2019; LoPilato & Vandenberg, 2015). The fact that x_{ij} and E_j appear in two different equations points out that they explain different components of the outcome variance: x_{ij} explains the variance that Y shows *within* units (i.e., the within variance), whereas E_j explains the variance shown by the intercept *between* units. Because the intercept is an estimation of the units' mean on the outcome variable, we can say that E_j explains variance in units' average satisfaction. These differences between the variances explained by L1 and L2 predictors are often neglected and frequently lead researchers to inaccurate conclusions; for example, that an L2 predictor explains the variance in an L1 outcome (González-Romá, 2019; LoPilato & Vandenberg, 2015). By definition, an L2 predictor cannot explain within-unit variance in a given outcome because the L2 predictor is constant within a specific unit. More accurately, as equation 5 shows, an L2 predictor explains variance in the intercept across units. Knowing the substantive meaning of the intercept allows researchers to draw more precise conclusions based on their findings.

I estimated the multilevel model shown above in the subsample of 51 branches with a uniform distribution of engagement scores. Before that, I determined whether it was empirically justified to aggregate branch members' engagement scores to operationalize team shared engagement. The average within-unit agreement index ($r_{WG(J)}$) obtained assuming a slightly skewed null distribution was 0.94 (SD = 0.06). Therefore, aggregation was justified.

The multilevel model was estimated using the software package SPSS.[5] The results obtained showed that:

- the parameter estimating the individual-level relationship between engagement and satisfaction was positive and statistically significant ($\gamma_{10} = 0.56$, $p < 0.01$); and
- the parameter estimating the unit-level relationship between team engagement and the units' intercept was positive and statistically significant ($\gamma_{01} = 0.26$, $p < 0.05$).

These results showed that engagement was positively related to satisfaction at both the individual and unit levels of analysis.

Examining the cross-level moderator influence of team engagement

Higher-level constructs can moderate individual-level relationships. Imagine that a researcher thinks the negative relationship between employees' perceived obstacles to good performance (x_{ij}) and job satisfaction (Y_{ij}) is buffered by team engagement (E_j). Because the individual-level relationship is moderated by a variable that resides at a higher level, we refer to this moderation as a *cross-level interaction*. The corresponding research model is typically represented as shown in Figure 12.2, panel B. The corresponding multilevel model is:

L1: $Y_{ij} = \beta_{0j} + \beta_{1j} x_{ij} + r_{ij}$ (7)

L2: $\beta_{0j} = \gamma_{00} + \gamma_{01} E_j + U_{0j}$ (8)

$\beta_{1j} = \gamma_{10} + \gamma_{11} E_j + U_{1j}$ (9)

This model is known as an intercepts-and-slopes-as-outcomes model. Compared with the previous model, this kind of model shows the following new key features. First, it shows that the slope (β_{1j}) that estimates the individual-level relationship between x_{ij} and Y_{ij} can vary across units. Thus, equation 9 includes a residual term (U_{1j}). Second, it assumes that the variability of β_{1j} across units is explained by an L2 predictor (E_j). γ_{11} is the parameter that estimates whether β_1 is affected by E_j (it tests the expected cross-level interaction).

Using the aforementioned subsample of branches, I estimated this multilevel model. The results obtained showed:

- the parameter estimating the individual-level relationship between obstacles and satisfaction was negative and statistically significant (γ_{10} = -0.23, $p < 0.05$);
- the parameter estimating the unit-level relationship between team engagement and units' intercept was positive and statistically significant (γ_{01} = 0.26, $p < 0.05$); and
- the parameter estimating the unit-level relationship between team engagement and units' slope was negative and statistically significant (γ_{11} = -0.73, $p < 0.01$).

Based on this latter result, we can say that there is empirical support for a cross-level interaction: team engagement moderates the individual-level relationship between perceived obstacles and satisfaction. The negative signs of γ_{10} and γ_{11} suggest that the negative relationship between obstacles and satisfaction becomes weaker as team engagement increases. To more precisely interpret cross-level interactions, readers can use the tools available on Preacher's website (www.quantpsy.org/interact/index.htm).

Extending multilevel models to include configural properties

The models presented above can be extended to include configural team-level properties (team engagement homogeneity and team engagement uniformity). To do so, researchers have to obtain operationalizations of these properties and include them in the corresponding multilevel equation. For instance, imagine that a researcher thinks the following: (a) team engagement homogeneity (H_j, a L2 property operationalized as the within-team SD in individual engagement scores) is related to job satisfaction after controlling for the impact of team shared engagement, and (b) the negative relationship between employees' perceived obstacles to good performance (x_{ij}) and job satisfaction (Y_{ij}) depends on team engagement homogeneity (H_j), once the influence of team shared engagement (E_j) on the mentioned individual-level relationship is controlled for. The corresponding multilevel model is:

$$\text{L1: } Y_{ij} = \beta_{0j} + \beta_{1j} x_{ij} + r_{ij} \tag{10}$$

$$\text{L2: } \beta_{0j} = \gamma_{00} + \gamma_{01} E_j + \gamma_{02} H_j + U_{0j} \tag{11}$$

$$\beta_{1j} = \gamma_{10} + \gamma_{11} E_j + \gamma_{12} H_j + U_{1j} \tag{12}$$

The new fixed parameters γ_{02} and γ_{12} estimate the relationships presented above in points (a) and (b).

Applying multilevel models to intensive longitudinal designs

Multilevel models can be applied to model data collected in Intensive Longitudinal Designs (ILD) (see Sonnentag et al., this volume). In these designs, many repeated measures across time of each subject are collected. An example of ILDs is diary studies, in which data on engagement and its antecedents and consequences are collected across one or two work weeks (e.g., Xanthopoulou et al., 2009). In these cases, there is also a nested structure in the data: measurement occasions (i, L1) are nested within subjects (j, L2). In studies with these designs, multilevel modeling can be applied to investigate, for instance, whether:

1. Occasion-level engagement (Y_{ij}) (e.g., daily engagement) is predicted by occasion-level antecedents (x_{ij}) (e.g., a job resource–daily social support);

2. Subjects' average engagement across occasions is influenced by certain person-level variables (P_j) (e.g., neuroticism); and
3. The relationship between occasion-level engagement and one of its antecedents depends on a person-level variable (P_j) (see Beattie & Griffin, 2014; McLarnon et al., and Xanthopoulou & Bakker, this volume).

Finally, multilevel analysis of engagement data collected in ILDs allows researchers to estimate the proportion of within-subject variability over time. When this proportion of variance is substantive (as in Xanthopoulou et al., 2009), researchers can estimate subjects' variability in engagement scores over time (e.g., by computing the corresponding SD) and examine what factors predict this variability (see Kampf et al., in press). This approach opens new lines of inquiry that researchers should consider.

Conclusion

The fact that engagement can emerge at higher levels following different models of emergence suggests that different higher-level engagement properties (shared engagement, engagement homogeneity, and engagement uniformity) can be investigated. To date, we have some empirical evidence about the antecedents and consequences of shared engagement. But there is a notable scarcity of studies about the nomological network of engagement homogeneity and uniformity. I hope this chapter will help researchers to find ways to extend and enrich the study of engagement at multiple levels.

Notes

1. Note that the response scale ranged from 1 ("never") to 7 ("always"). Therefore, the maximum value for the standard deviation was 3.
2. I recommend Enders & Tofighi's (2007) article on centering predictor variables in multilevel models.
3. Nevertheless, understanding a sequence of basic models is useful in building more specific models (see González-Romá & Hernández, 2019).
4. The exact meaning of the intercept depends on the centering option implemented (see Enders and Tofighi, 2007; González-Romá & Hernández, 2019).
5. See González-Romá and Hernández (2019) for SPSS syntax useful for estimating all the models examined here.

References

Bakker, A. B., Demerouti, E., and Sanz-Vergel, A. I. (2014). Burnout and work engagement: The JD–R approach. *Annual Review of Organizational Psychology and Organizational Behavior, 1,* 389–411.

Barrick, M. R., Thurgood, G. R., Smith, T. A., and Courtright, S. H. (2015). Collective organizational engagement: Linking motivational antecedents, strategic implementation, and firm performance. *Academy of Management Journal, 58,* 111–135.

Barsade, S. G., Ward, A. J., Turner, J. D., and Sonnenfeld, J. A. (2000). To your heart's content: A model of affective diversity in top management teams. *Administrative Science Quarterly, 45,* 802–836.

Beattie, L., and Griffin, B. (2014). Day-level fluctuations in stress and engagement in response to workplace incivility: A diary study. *Work & Stress, 28,* 124–142.

Chan, D. (1998). Functional relationships among constructs in the same content domain at different levels of analysis: A typology of composition models. *Journal of Applied Psychology, 83,* 234–246.

Christian, M. S., Garza, A. S., and Slaughter, J. E. (2011). Work engagement: A quantitative review and test of its relations with task and contextual performance. *Personnel Psychology, 64,* 89–136.

Costa, P. L., Passos, A. M., and Bakker, A. B. (2014). Team work engagement: A model of emergence. *Journal of Occupational and Organizational Psychology, 87,* 414–436.

Dineen, B. R., Noe, R. A., Shaw, J. D., Duffy, M. K., and Wiethoff, C. (2007). Level and dispersion of satisfaction in teams: Using foci and social context to explain the satisfaction-absenteeism relationship. *Academy of Management Journal, 50,* 623–643.

Enders, C. K., and Tofighi D. (2007). Centering predictor variables in cross-sectional multilevel models: A new look at an old issue. *Psychological Methods, 12,* 121–138.

García-Buades, E., Martínez-Tur, V., Ortiz-Bonnín, S., and Peiró, J. M. (2016). Engaged teams deliver better service performance in innovation climates. *European Journal of Work and Organizational Psychology, 25,* 597–612.

González-Romá, V. (2019). Three issues in multilevel research. *Spanish Journal of Psychology, 22,* e4, 1–7.

González-Romá, V., and Hernández, A. (2014). Climate uniformity: Its influence on team communication quality, task conflict, and team performance. *Journal of Applied Psychology, 99,* 1042–1058.

González-Romá, V., and Hernández, A. (2019). Multilevel modeling methods. In O. Braddick (Ed.), *Oxford Research Encyclopedia of Psychology* (pp. 1–37). New York: Oxford University Press.

González-Romá, V., Schaufeli, W. B., Bakker, A. B., and Lloret, S. (2006). Burnout and work engagement: Independent factors or opposite poles? *Journal of Vocational Behavior, 68,* 165–174.

Kampf, P., Hernández, A., and González-Romá, V. (in press). Antecedents and consequences of workplace mood variability over time: A weekly study over a three-month period. *Journal of Occupational and Organizational Psychology.*

Kozlowski, S. W. J., and Klein, K. J. (2000). A multilevel approach to theory and research in organizations: Contextual, temporal, and emergent processes. In K. J. Klein and S. W. J. Kozlowski (Eds), *Multilevel Theory, Research, and Methods in Organizations* (pp. 3–90). San Francisco: Jossey-Bass.

Loignon, A. C., Woehr, D. J., Loughry, M. L., and Ohland, M. W. (2019). Elaborating on team-member disagreement: Examining patterned dispersion in team-level constructs. *Group & Organization Management, 44,* 165–210.

LoPilato, A. C., and Vandenberg, R. J. (2015). The not so-direct cross-level direct effect. In C. E. Lance and R. J. Vandenberg (Eds), *More Statistical and Methodological Myths and Urban Legends* (pp. 292–310). New York, NY: Routledge.

Rodríguez-Sánchez, A. M., Devloo, T., Rico, R., Salanova, M., and Anseel, F. (2017). What makes creative teams tick? Cohesion, engagement, and performance across creativity tasks: A three-wave study. *Group & Organization Management, 42,* 521–547.

Salanova, M., Agut, S., and Peiró, J. M. (2005). Linking organizational resources and work engagement to employee performance and customer loyalty: The mediation of service climate. *Journal of Applied Psychology, 90,* 1217–1227.

Schaufeli, W. B., Salanova, M., González-Romá, V., and Bakker, A. B. (2002). The measurement of engagement and burnout: A two sample confirmatory factor analytic approach. *Journal of Happiness Studies, 3,* 71–92.

Seo, J. J., Nahrgang, J. D., Carter, M. Z., and Hom, P. W. (2018). Not all differentiation is the same: Examining the moderating effects of leader-member exchange (LMX) configurations. *Journal of Applied Psychology, 103,* 478.

Tims, M., Bakker, A. B., Derks, D., and Van Rhenen, W. (2013). Job crafting at the team and individual level: Implications for work engagement and performance. *Group & Organization Management, 38,* 427–454.

Xanthopoulou, D., Bakker, A. B., Demerouti, E., and Schaufeli, W. B. (2009). Work engagement and financial returns: A diary study on the role of job and personal resources. *Journal of Occupational and Organizational Psychology, 82,* 183–200.

13. Empirical approaches to address the dynamic aspects of work engagement: study design and data analyses

Sabine Sonnentag, Monika Wiegelmann, and Maike Czink

Work engagement is a popular concept within organizational research and organizational practice. When introducing the engagement concept, Kahn (1990, p. 692) described how "people personally engage, or express and employ their personal selves" in task behaviors. He studied how people invest themselves physically, cognitively, and emotionally into their work roles and how they express themselves at work. More recent research conceptualizes work engagement as an aspect of work-related well-being (Schaufeli & Bakker, 2004) and describes it "as a positive, fulfilling, work-related state of mind that is characterized by vigor, dedication, and absorption" (Schaufeli & Bakker, 2004, p. 295). In essence, work engagement captures the experience of actively immersing one's self into work (Rich et al., 2010) and feeling vigorous, absorbed, and dedicated at work.

Concepts of dynamism: variability and change over time

Like most experiential psychological constructs, work engagement shows variability and change over time. *Variability* refers to relatively short-term fluctuations in work engagement that are "more or less reversible" (Nesselroade, 1991, p. 215), occurring from moment to moment, from day to day, or from week to week (Nesselroade & Ram, 2004). *Change* refers to more enduring increases or decreases in work engagement, usually happening over longer periods of time. Of course, changes can be reversible as well, but generally they span larger time periods than day-to-day or week-to-week fluctuations.

Variability and change are not necessarily independent. Within longer-term upward or downward trajectories of work engagement, there may be day-to-day or week-to-week fluctuations in work engagement as well. In addition, short-term fluctuations in work engagement may even stimulate longer-term changes in work engagement. For instance, a person may observe that his or her work engagement fluctuates from day to day and may interpret this fluctuation as a sign of boring tasks occurring on some days but not on others. In an attempt to end this dissatisfying situation, the person might engage in job crafting to decrease boredom and increase work engagement over time (see Xanthopoulou & Bakker, this volume).

Although fluctuations in work engagement usually happen within rather short time frames, and changes over longer time periods, some fluctuations may occur over longer periods as well and changes may happen rather quickly. For instance, work engagement may fluctuate in parallel to economic cycles and may fluctuate in parallel to economic cycles and may change quite instantaneously after a negative major work event.

The dynamic perspective on work engagement does not imply that there are no between-person differences in work engagement. These differences are due to differences in personality (Young et al., 2018; see Hough & Oswald, this volume) and job characteristics (Christian et al., 2011; Salanova, this volume). Moreover, between-person differences in work engagement are relatively stable over time.

Research on dynamic work engagement has made substantial progress during recent years, but is still in its infancy. Accordingly, some of the research designs and analytical approaches that we cover in this chapter have not yet been used in empirical research on work engagement. We will start our descriptions with actual empirical examples of variability and change in work engagement. We then discuss more generally some of the issues that arise in the planning and data-collection phases of research on variability and change. This is followed by a discussion of the statistical analyses available to researchers once the data have been collected. We conclude by identifying yet other strategies and data analytic techniques that can be used when investigating engagement as a dynamic process.

Empirical examples

Examples for studying variability

Research on variability in work engagement often examines day-, week-, or event-level data. For example, Venz et al. (2018) investigated mechanisms counteracting the negative consequences of a lack of resources on work engagement on a day-to-day level. In a daily diary, employees answered two online questionnaires a day over the course of one workweek. They reported experienced resources (state of being recovered, role clarity) as predictors, use of self-management strategies as a moderator, and work engagement as an outcome on a daily basis. Multilevel regression modeling showed that resources and self-management strategies were positively related to work engagement. Additionally, on days characterized by a relative lack of resources, self-management strategies served as a moderator in the relationship between resources and daily work engagement.

In another day-level study, Ilies et al. (2017) conceptualized daily work engagement as a predictor variable and examined if employees shared more positive work events with their spouses at home (i.e., work–family interpersonal capitalization) after they had experienced high engagement at work. Data collected over 10 workdays showed that this was indeed the case. Moreover, the authors reported that sharing positive events predicted family satisfaction and work–family balance, and that the relationship between work engagement and sharing positive events was particularly strong for employees with high intrinsic work motivation.

Examples for studying change

De Wind et al. (2017) examined work engagement of employees approaching retirement. More specifically, they examined how work engagement changes over time among older workers and if there exist subsamples that differ in the trajectories of work engagement. Participants answered four online surveys at intervals of one year. The authors performed latent class growth mixture modeling which allowed them to identify subgroups that showed different patterns of change in work engagement over time. They found four subgroups that experienced either a constant high level, a constant low level, a decrease, or an increase in work engagement over time. In addition, de Wind et al. examined early retirement as a potential outcome of the distinct change trajectories, finding that early retirement was more likely for persons with a steady low work engagement, compared to persons with a steady high work engagement (after adjusting for age, gender, and educational level).

Another study on change in work engagement used a much shorter time frame. Luta et al. (2019) tested if work engagement systematically changes over the course of the week (Monday through Friday) and if the specific change pattern can be explained by personality variables (see Hough & Oswald, this volume). These authors assessed personality and then collected engagement data over the course of two workweeks. Luta et al. found across the sample an inverted U-shaped pattern of work engagement over time overall, with the peak around midweek. Interestingly, however, it was persons high on neuroticism who most strongly showed this curvilinear pattern; persons low on neuroticism had generally higher and rather stable work engagement over the workweek. This study illustrates that it is not necessarily the time frame that differentiates the change perspective from the variability perspective, but the change perspective's focus on patterns spanning several measurement occasions – as opposed to the variability perspective's focus on the ups and downs at specific occasions.

Study planning and data collection

Study planning and data collection when studying variability of work engagement

When addressing the variability of work engagement, researchers focus on the association between fluctuating states, experiences, and behaviors (Ohly et al., 2010). Depending on the specific research question, work engagement might be a predictor, outcome, covariate, or mediator. To answer research questions related to variability, different types of diary studies can be used. In the *experience-sampling methodology*, individuals report their current behavior, feelings, or thoughts as well as the situational context at specific or random time points (Fisher & To, 2012). *Event-sampling methodology* captures the experiences immediately after a specific event has occurred (Ohly et al., 2010). *Daily diaries* – as used in the study by Venz et al. (2018) – involve behavior, feelings or thoughts happening during the whole (work) day (Ohly et al., 2010).

Diary studies have important advantages over cross-sectional studies. First, they assess experiences in their natural context and measure them within temporal proximity to the corresponding time point, time interval, or event (Reis & Gable, 2000). Thereby, retrospective biases that can impact the validity of cross-sectional survey measures are reduced. Second, diary studies allow researchers to capture the situational context (Reis & Gable, 2000) that can be a potential cause for variability in work engagement.

When designing and conducting diary studies, there are different methodological aspects to consider. First, it is important to decide about the units of analysis (i.e., organization, individual, day, event) the research questions focus on. These units define the data structure. Researchers mainly use diary studies to capture within-person fluctuations between days, resulting in a data structure with two levels (person, day). However, diary designs can also be applied to examine fluctuations from event to event or from task to task, with events or tasks nested within days, resulting in a three-level data structure. Second, the specific measurement occasions have to be defined based on the research question and the units of analysis. Of course, it is important to assess the constructs close in time to their occurrence.

Because examining dynamics in work engagement requires multiple measurement occasions, various problems during data collection may arise. It can happen that participants fill out the surveys but respond carelessly; that is, do not pay (full) attention to the item content. Moreover, participants might not complete the surveys on all occasions, or might miss some items, which can cause missing data at various levels of analysis (for countermeasures, see Meade & Craig, 2012; Newman, 2014).

Research on engagement variability may be extended to dyadic and team processes. Whereas most studies addressing variability of work engagement have focused on variability within the individual, variability may occur in dyads (Bakker & Xanthopoulou, 2009) or even teams (Barnes et al., 2015), thereby requiring data collection and analysis at higher levels (see González-Romá, this volume).

Study planning and data collection when studying change of work engagement

Researchers pursue two main goals when studying change. First, they investigate intra-individual change over time and describe individual growth trajectories. Second, they predict interindividual differences in the individual growth trajectories. Change is mostly researched as an outcome of some processes, but it can also be a predictor or a mediator.

Obviously, the study of change demands longitudinal data, with the constructs of interest measured on several occasions (Nesselroade & Ram, 2004). The number of measurement occasions determines the complexity of the models that can be fitted to the data. With few measurement occasions, only rather simple models (e.g., linear change) can be fitted, whereas more measurement occasions allow more complex models (e.g., quadratic or cubic change) to be fitted (Singer & Willett, 2003).

A further important topic is the spacing of measurement occasions. The decision about the spacing intervals should depend on the research question and on the expectations of when change will occur (Mitchell & James, 2001). Determining the optimal time lag is important as otherwise change might exist but would not be observed in the data (Dormann & Griffin, 2015). Furthermore, measurement occasions do not necessarily need to be equally spaced (for analyzing unequally spaced longitudinal data, see Voelkle et al., 2012; cf. section on Future Directions).

Statistical approaches

Assessing variability or change in work engagement requires measuring work engagement at multiple occasions, resulting in measurement occasions nested in persons. To account for this nestedness, specific analytical approaches are needed. In this chapter, we present two classes of models for analyzing variability and change: multilevel modeling (MLM) and structural equation modeling (SEM), either in a multilevel or a unilevel approach. MLM estimates parameters based on manifest variables, whereas SEM involves latent variables (Heck & Thomas, 2015). In MLM the variance of the outcome variable is decomposed and accounted for by having different equations for each level (e.g., day level [Level 1] and person level [Level 2]). In contrast to a more traditional multilevel approach where Level 1 refers to persons and Level 2 refers to teams (González-Romá, this volume), Level 1 refers to occasions and Level 2 refers to persons.

SEM typically consists of a measurement model and a structural model (Heck & Thomas, 2015). Due to the inclusion of multiple indicators in measurement models, realizing SEM is rather complex compared to MLM, and convergence problems may arise (Heck & Thomas, 2015). To analyze MLM and SEM, software such as R or MPlus can be used (for guidelines on R, see Bliese, 2016; Finch & French, 2015; for guidelines on MPlus, see Heck & Thomas, 2015).

Statistical approaches when analyzing variability in work engagement

Multilevel regression modeling

Typically, multilevel regression modeling (MRM) is used to analyze variability in a single outcome variable at multiple levels (Gross et al., 2013). Thereby, researchers usually analyze their data with a stepwise procedure. In a first step, they start with a null model (intercept-only model) containing only the outcome variable (Heck & Thomas, 2015). For instance, in the Venz et al. (2018) study described earlier, the variance of work engagement was decomposed into day-level (within-person) and person-level (between-person) variance, with 38 percent of the variance being at the day level and 62 percent being at the person level. In the following steps, predictors and moderators are added to the null model. To add predictors, a random-intercept model (i.e., a model that allows for variance in the intercepts; Heck & Thomas, 2015) has to be specified.

Moderator hypotheses can be directly tested with MRM. For instance, the Venz et al. (2018) study tested self-management strategies as a day-level moderator variable. The Ilies et al. (2017) study tested intrinsic motivation as a person-level moderator, depicting a so-called cross-level interaction. When testing cross-level interactions, it is important to define a random-slope model (i.e., to allow for variance in the Level 1 slopes; Heck & Thomas, 2015).

To test mediation hypotheses, it is recommended to extend MRM to multilevel path models (Zhang et al., 2009). Additionally, multilevel path models allow for the simultaneous test of more than one outcome variable (Heck & Thomas, 2015). For instance, researchers might want to test the three sub-dimensions of work engagement (vigor, dedication, absorption), instead of an overall work-engagement score, as outcome variables.

In MLM in general, it is important to be aware of the scaling of variables. While raw metric scaling is used for the outcome, the scaling of all predictors has to be adjusted by centering them at the grand or group mean, depending on the specific research question (Enders & Tofighi, 2007). "Group mean" in the terminology of Enders and Tofighi is the person mean in a day-level study (for a discussion on centering in within-person research, see Gabriel et al., 2019).

Multilevel structural equation modeling

Multilevel structural equation modeling (MSEM) combines the advantages of confirmatory factor analyses (i.e., measurement model) with multilevel path modeling (i.e., structural model; Preacher et al., 2010). In general, the analytical procedure is similar to MRM and multilevel path modeling. However, there are two main differences. First, the relationships in the structural model are specified between latent variables. Second, all latent variables and relationships involving lower-level predictors are not only defined on the corresponding level of the predictor but also on the upper levels. Therefore, the variance of these variables is decomposed into within-person and between-person components. This decomposition leads to within-person and between-person covariance matrices, with no need to explicitly center variables in MSEM (Heck & Thomas, 2015).

Due to the complexity of SEM procedures (Heck & Thomas, 2015), problems of convergence may arise. The measurement model (i.e., the first-order factors) may cause these problems. One possible solution is to estimate relationships between the manifest variables. Manifest variables still offer the advantages of MSEM, such as the decomposition of variances, the specification of indirect effects, and the investigation of relationships on various levels. Alternatively, one might use a two-step procedure by first computing factor scores in a confirmatory factor analysis and then using these factor scores in MSEM.

MSEM provides advantages over multilevel path modeling (as a specific instantiation of MRM). Testing multilevel mediation with MSEM is more straightforward than testing it with multilevel path models (Zhang et al., 2009) and overcomes potential biases when creating interaction terms for moderator analysis (for ways to test multilevel moderation with MSEM, see Preacher et al., 2016). Finally, modeling the relationship on both levels simultaneously provides the chance to directly test cross-level isomorphism and homology (Gabriel et al., 2019; Xanthopoulou & Bakker, this volume).

Statistical approaches when analyzing change in work engagement

When modeling change, it is important to first test whether the construct of interest is measurement-invariant across time (i.e., whether the scores that were measured at different time points represent the same construct). In general, three aspects of measurement invariance, namely configural, metric, and scalar invariance, are tested via model constraints (for the stepwise procedures involved, see Vandenberg & Lance, 2000).

Furthermore, the coding of time needs special attention. Because the intercept reflects the work-engagement score at the point when the value of the time variable equals zero, it might be useful to rescale the time variable to give it a meaningful zero (Biesanz et al., 2004). For instance, when interested in the development of work engagement following individuals' entry into the labour market, researchers might want to use a time variable that codes the amount of time since the entry with the score of zero reflecting the entry time point.

Change can be continuous (i.e., smooth) or discontinuous (i.e., occurring in "steps"). Growth models for both continuous and discontinuous change can be either fitted within MLM (Raudenbush & Bryk, 2002) or within SEM (Duncan et al., 2006). Figure 13.1 illustrates continuous and discontinuous change.

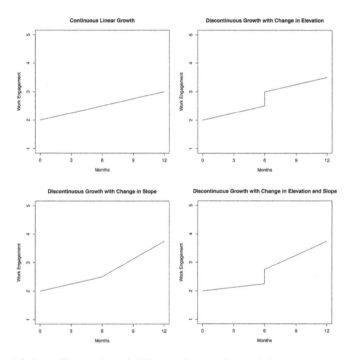

Figure 13.1   Illustration of different forms of growth in work engagement over the course of one year

Note: Scale for work engagement: 1 = completely disagree, 5 = completely agree.

Continuous change

Multilevel growth curve modeling

Multilevel growth curve modeling (MGCM) belongs to the model class of MLM. In MGCM, time is modeled by including the time variable as a predictor in the Level 1 equation. The resulting Level 1 model describes an individual growth model representing the trajectory of an individual over time (e.g., a linear increase or decrease in work engagement over time). The Level 2 model describes the individual differences in the change trajectories (Raudenbush & Bryk, 2002). MGCM allows one to test not only for linear growth, but also for nonlinear growth (e.g., quadratic or cubic time trends; Heck & Thomas, 2015).

A so-called unconditional growth model (i.e., a model including time variables only) can be extended by adding more predictors or more levels. For instance, in most studies employees experience different levels of work engagement at the first measurement occasion. Researchers might be interested in personality variables (which are assumed to be stable across all measurement occasions) that predict employees' intercepts of work engagement. Therefore, personality variables (see Hough & Oswald, this volume) would be added as predictors into the Level 2 equation. Furthermore, these variables might also explain interindividual differences in the slopes (e.g., increasing, stable, and decreasing work engagement). Accordingly, the interaction term of the time trend and the respective Level 2 variables are added into the model. Furthermore, additional Level 1 predictors (i.e., variables that vary across measurement occasions) can be included in the model. For instance, an employee's interest in the projects he or she is currently working on might explain variance over and above the variance that is already explained by the growth trajectories.

Latent growth curve modeling

Latent growth curve modeling (LGCM) belongs to the model class of SEM and explains change over time as a latent process (Duncan & Duncan, 2004). In contrast to MLM, the outcomes are multivariate data and therefore the differentiation in two levels is not necessary (Heck & Thomas, 2015). In the structural model, the change process is modeled by two (or more) latent parameters (i.e., intercept and slope(s)) which are specified by the first-order factors and the respective factor loadings (Gross et al., 2013). The first-order factors are usually specified by using the items as indicators. However, in order to avoid convergence problems, manifest variables can also be used as indicators of the latent intercept and slope parameters. As described earlier, one might also use factor scores based on the results of confirmatory factor analyses.

In the basic linear LGCM, two latent parameters are specified in the structural model: intercept and slope. The latent intercept parameter represents the baseline point of the underlying change process and is specified by fixing the factor loading of each indicator to 1 (Heck & Thomas, 2015). The latent slope parameter represents the latent trajectory of work engagement. In LGCM, the passage of time is included by the factor loadings of the indicators on the latent slope parameter. These loadings can either be freely estimated or fixed according to the expected shape of change (Heck & Thomas, 2015). A latent linear slope parameter might, for instance, be specified by fixing the factor loadings of the first-order factors on this latent parameter at 0, 1, 2, and 3.

LGCM can be extended by adding time-invariant and time-variant covariates to the model as predictors of the latent intercept and slope parameters (Gross et al., 2013). Similar to Level 2 predictors in MGCM, time-invariant covariates (e.g., personality variables) can explain interindividual differences in work engagement intercepts and slopes. For instance, the study by Luta et al. (2019) described earlier identified neuroticism as such a time-invariant covariate. Similar to Level 1 predictors in MGCM, time-variant covariates (e.g., an employee's momentary interest in the project he or she is currently working on) can predict variance in the latent true scores at the respective time point above and beyond the underlying trajectory (Gross et al., 2013).

This LGCM approach may be extended by simultaneously testing several growth curves and their empirical interdependence, an approach discussed as a parallel-growth process (McArdle, 2009). For example, one could examine if organizational newcomers' positive social interactions on the job increase over the first weeks upon organizational entry and if this increase in positive social interactions is associated with a parallel increase in work engagement over time.

Discontinuous change

Discontinuous change trajectories are characterized by at least one shift in slope and/or in elevation (Singer & Willett, 2003). To model discontinuous change, data from before and after the occurrence of a certain event are needed. For instance, experiencing a promotion might lead to such a discontinuous change in work engagement, as shown on the bottom right of Figure 13.1.

Discontinuous multilevel growth curve modeling
To specify a discontinuous MGCM, elevation and/or shift variables are added as predictors into the model. The elevation variable codes the time before and after the event occurrence and thus describes the change at event occurrence; the shift variable codes the additional slope after the event occurrence and denotes the additional change since the event occurrence (Singer & Willett, 2003).

Piecewise latent growth curve modeling
Within piecewise LGCM, longitudinal data are divided into meaningful segments. For each segment, separate intercept and slope factors are specified (Duncan & Duncan, 2004) and each segment may follow a different growth

shape. Different assumptions on the data can then be tested by using equality constraints (Heck & Thomas, 2015).

Within both discontinuous MGCM and piecewise LGCM, further predictors can be added to the models and more than two segments can be examined. For instance, comparing the development of work engagement before, during, and after an organizational health intervention would imply an investigation of three segments.

Performing (discontinuous) MGCM and (piecewise) LGCM often leads to the same results. However, there are some situations in which one approach might be preferred over the other. MGCM has the advantage that, when the sample size is relatively small, convergence problems are less likely than when conducting a LGCM. In contrast, LGCM allows one to more easily examine change in two or more constructs simultaneously (Duncan et al., 2006) and to test complex mediations (e.g., using the growth curve as mediator).

Future directions

Depending on the specific research question, researchers may want to go beyond the approaches described thus far. Here, we mention a few options.

Person-centered approach

Variability and change in work engagement can be investigated with a person-centered approach as well. This approach starts from the assumption that not all study participants come from the same population, but that different subpopulations may exist and that these subpopulations can be best described by different sets of parameters (for more information, see McLarnon et al., this volume).

Within-person variability in work engagement

Research on work engagement might gain from explicitly addressing variability as a between-person variable. Technically speaking, variability could be assessed by using the within-person standard deviation (Houben et al., 2015). With respect to substantive research questions, it could be fruitful to examine the predictors and consequences of a high versus a low variability in work engagement.

Continuous time modeling

Fluctuations and change in psychological experiences occur continuously over time. Traditional methods of data collection and analysis, however, capture these continuous fluctuations and changes by discrete "snapshots" (Voelkle et al., 2012, p. 176), often assuming equal spacing of measurement points. In many studies, however, this might not be the case. Not taking into account the actual time lag between various measurement points may result in biased parameter estimates (de Haan-Rietdijk et al., 2017).

To address situations of unequally spaced measurement points, continuous time modeling should be used. This approach helps to arrive at more precise parameter estimates and enables researchers to learn more about the dynamics of work engagement. For instance, research has shown that momentary states experienced in the morning predict work engagement later during the workday (Sonnentag, 2003). Continuous time modeling would allow researchers to test how long such effects endure and when they fade out (for use of continuous time modeling when analyzing panel data, see Voelkle et al., 2012; for incorporating continuous time modeling into the analysis of experience-sampling data, see de Haan-Rietdijk et al., 2017).

Conclusion

Work engagement is a fascinating concept for researchers interested in identifying job-related experiences that benefit the individual worker and the organization alike. Work engagement is a dynamic experience that fluctuates within person and can change over time. To capture the dynamic nature of work engagement, specific study designs and statistical methods are needed. Advancements in statistical methods – as described in this chapter – provide helpful approaches for analyzing the dynamic nature of work engagement. We hope that researchers are motivated by our chapter to use these methods in their own research.

Acknowledgement

Preparation of this chapter was partly supported by a grant from the German Research Foundation (Research Training Group, GRK 2277).

References

Bakker, A. B., and Xanthopoulou, D. (2009). The crossover of daily work engagement: Test of an actor-partner interdependence model. *Journal of Applied Psychology*, 94(6), 1562–1571. https://doi.org/10.1037/a0017525.

Barnes, C. M., Lucianetti, L., Bhave, D. P., and Christian, M. S. (2015). "You wouldn't like me when I'm sleepy": Leaders' sleep, daily abusive supervision, and work unit engagement. *Academy of Management Journal*, 58(5), 1419–1437. https://doi.org/10.5465/amj.2013.1063.

Biesanz, J. C., Deeb-Sossa, N., Papadakis, A. A., Bollen, K. A., and Curran, P. J. (2004). The role of coding time in estimating and interpreting growth curve models. *Psychological Methods*, 9(1), 30–52. https://doi.org/10.1037/1082-989X.9.1.30.

Bliese, P. D. (2016). *Multilevel Modeling in R (2.6): A Brief Introduction to R, the Multilevel Package and the nlme Package*. Walter Reed Army Institute of Research.

Christian, M. S., Garza, A. S., and Slaughter, J. E. (2011). Work engagement: A quantitative review and test of its relations with task and contextual performance. *Personnel Psychology*, 64(1), 89–136. https://doi.org/10.1111/j.1744-6570.2010.01203.x.

De Haan-Rietdijk, S., Voelkle, M. C., Keijsers, L., and Hamaker, E. L. (2017). Discrete- vs. continuous-time modeling of unequally spaced experience sampling method data. *Frontiers in Psychology*, 8, Article 1849. https://doi.org/10.3389/fpsyg.2017.01849.

De Wind, A., Leijten, F. R., Hoekstra, T., Geuskens, G. A., Burdorf, A., and van der Beek, A. J. (2017). "Mental retirement?" Trajectories of work engagement preceding retirement among older workers. *Scandinavian Journal of Work, Environment & Health*, 43(1), 34–41. https://doi.org/10.5271/sjweh.3604.

Dormann, C., and Griffin, M. A. (2015). Optimal time lags in panel studies. *Psychological Methods*, 20(4), 489–505. https://doi.org/10.1037/met0000041.

Duncan, T. E., and Duncan, S. C. (2004). An introduction to latent growth curve modeling. *Behavior Therapy*, 35(2), 333–363. https://doi.org/10.1016/S0005-7894(04)80042-X.

Duncan, T. E., Duncan, S. C., and Strycker, L. A. (2006). *An Introduction to Latent Variable Growth Curve Modeling: Concepts, Issues, and Application*. Lawrence Erlbaum.

Enders, C. K., and Tofighi, D. (2007). Centering predictor variables in cross-sectional multilevel models: A new look at an old issue. *Psychological Methods*, 12(2), 121–138. https://doi.org/10.1037/1082-989X.12.2.121.

Finch, W. H., and French, B. F. (2015). *Latent Variable Modeling with R*. Routledge.

Fisher, C. D., and To, M. L. (2012). Using experience sampling methodology in organizational behavior. *Journal of Organizational Behavior*, 33(7), 865–877. https://doi.org/10.1002/job.1803.

Gabriel, A. S., Podsakoff, N. P., Beal, D. J., Scott, B. A., Sonnentag, S., Trougakos, J. P., and Butts, M. M. (2019). Experience sampling method: A discussion of critical trends and considerations for scholarly advancement. *Organizational Research Methods*, 22(4), 969–1006. https://doi.org/10.1177/1094428118802626.

Gross, S., Meier, L. L., and Semmer, N. K. (2013). Latent growth modeling applied to diary data: The trajectory of vigor across a working week as an illustrative example. In A. B. Bakker and K. J. Daniels (Eds), *A Day in the Life of a Happy Worker* (pp. 114–131). Psychology Press.

Heck, R. H., and Thomas, S. L. (2015). *An Introduction to Multilevel Modeling Techniques: MLM and SEM Approaches Using MPlus* (3rd ed.). Routledge.

Houben, M., Van Den Noortgate, W., and Kuppens, P. (2015). The relation between short-term emotion dynamics and psychological well-being: A meta-analysis. *Psychological Bulletin, 141*(4), 901–930. https://doi.org/10.1037/a0038822.

Ilies, R., Liu, X.-Y., Liu, Y., and Zheng, X. (2017). Why do employees have better family lives when they are highly engaged at work? *Journal of Applied Psychology, 102*(6), 956–970. https://doi.org/10.1037/apl0000211.

Kahn, W. A. (1990). Psychological conditions of personal engagement and disengagement at work. *Academy of Management Journal, 33*(4), 692–724. https://doi.org/10.2307/256287.

Luta, D., Powell, D. M., and Spence, J. R. (2019). Entrained engagement? Investigating if work engagement follows a predictable pattern across the work week and the role of personality in shaping its pattern. In N. M. Ashkanasy, W. J. Zerbe, and C. E. J. Härtel (Series Eds), *Research on Emotion in Organizations: Vol 15, Emotions and Leadership* (pp. 89–109). Emerald Publishing. https://doi.org/10.1108/S1746-979120190000015009.

McArdle, J. J. (2009). Latent variable modeling of differences and changes with longitudinal data. *Annual Review of Psychology, 60*(1), 577–605. https://doi.org/10.1146/annurev.psych.60.110707.163612.

Meade, A. W., and Craig, S. B. (2012). Identifying careless responses in survey data. *Psychological Methods, 17*(3), 437–455. https://doi.org/10.1037/a0028085.

Mitchell, T. R., and James, L. R. (2001). Building better theory: Time and the specification of when things happen. *Academy of Management Review, 26*(4), 530–547. https://doi.org/10.5465/amr.2001.5393889.

Nesselroade, J. R. (1991). The wrap and the woof of the developmental fabric. In R. Downs, L. Liben, and D. Palermo (Eds), *Visions of Developments, the Environment, and Aesthetics: The Legacy of Joachim F. Wohlwill* (pp. 213–240). Lawrence Erlbaum.

Nesselroade, J. R., and Ram, N. (2004). Studying intraindividual variability: What we have learned that will help us understand lives in context. *Research in Human Development, 1*(1–2), 9–29. https://doi.org/10.1080/15427609.2004.9683328.

Newman, D. A. (2014). Missing data: Five practical guidelines. *Organizational Research Methods, 17*(4), 372–411. https://doi.org/10.1177/1094428114548590.

Ohly, S., Sonnentag, S., Niessen, C., and Zapf, D. (2010). Diary studies in organizational research: An introduction and some practical recommendations. *Journal of Personnel Psychology, 9*(10), 79–93. https://doi.org/10.1027/1866-5888/a000009.

Preacher, K. J., Zhang, Z., and Zyphur, M. J. (2016). Multilevel structural equation models for assessing moderation within and across levels of analysis. *Psychological Methods, 21*(2), 189–205. https://doi.org/10.1037/met0000052.

Preacher, K. J., Zyphur, M. J., and Zhang, Z. (2010). A general multilevel SEM framework for assessing multilevel mediation. *Psychological Methods, 15*(3), 209–233. https://doi.org/10.1037/a0020141.

Raudenbush, S. W., and Bryk, A. S. (2002). *Hierarchical Linear Models: Applications and Data Analysis Methods*. Sage Publications.

Reis, H. T., and Gable, S. L. (2000). Event-sampling and other methods for studying everyday experience. In H. T. Reis and C. M. Judd (Eds), *Handbook of Research Methods in Social and Personality Psychology* (pp. 190–222). Cambridge University Press.

Rich, B. L., LePine, J. A., and Crawford, E. R. (2010). Job engagement: Antecedents and effects on job performance. *Academy of Management Journal, 53*(3), 617–635. https://doi.org/10.5465/AMJ.2010.51468988.

Schaufeli, W. B., and Bakker, A. B. (2004). Job demands, job resources, and their relationship with burnout and engagement: A multi-sample study. *Journal of Organizational Behavior, 25*(3), 293–315. https://doi.org/10.1002/job.248.

Singer, J. D., and Willett, J. B. (2003). *Applied Longitudinal Data Analysis: Modeling Change and Event Occurrence.* Oxford University Press.

Sonnentag, S. (2003). Recovery, work engagement, and proactive behavior: A new look at the interface between non-work and work. *Journal of Applied Psychology, 88*(3), 518–528. https://doi.org/10.1037/0021-9010.88.3.518.

Vandenberg, R. J., and Lance, C. E. (2000). A review and synthesis of the measurement invariance literature: Suggestions, practices, and recommendations for organizational research. *Organizational Research Methods, 3*(1), 4–70. https://doi.org/10.1177/109442810031002.

Venz, L., Pundt, A., and Sonnentag, S. (2018). What matters for work engagement? A diary study on resources and the benefits of selective optimization with compensation for state work engagement. *Journal of Organizational Behavior, 39*(1), 26–38. https://doi.org/10.1002/job.2207.

Voelkle, M. C., Oud, J. H. L., Davidov, E., and Schmidt, P. (2012). An SEM approach to continuous time modeling of panel data: Relating authoritarianism and anomia. *Psychological Methods, 17*(2), 176–192. https://doi.org/10.1037/a0027543.

Young, H. R., Glerum, D. R., Wang, W., and Joseph, D. L. (2018). Who are the most engaged at work? A meta-analysis of personality and employee engagement. *Journal of Organizational Behavior, 39*(10), 1330–1346. https://doi.org/10.1002/job.2303.

Zhang, Z., Zyphur, M. J., and Preacher, K. J. (2009). Testing multilevel mediation using hierarchical linear models: Problems and solutions. *Organizational Research Methods, 12*(4), 695–719. https://doi.org/10.1177/1094428108327450.

14. Profiles of engagement dimensions and targets: applications and opportunities for person-centered analytic techniques

Matthew J. W. McLarnon, Alexandre J. S. Morin, and David Litalien

Engagement plays a central role in employee commitment, well-being, and performance (e.g., Crawford et al., 2010; Harter et al., 2002). It is therefore not surprising that employee engagement is among the most widely researched workplace attitudes (see Macey & Schneider, 2008; Meyer & Gagné, 2008). Although employee engagement has been primarily used in reference to focal work or job-relevant tasks, engagement can also be represented by multi-target conceptualizations. Saks (this volume) noted that engagement might be experienced differently across distinct work-related targets, such as tasks, occupation, organization, and team, as well as across targets external to work, like family and leisure activities. Moreover, within targets, engagement is often conceptualized as having multiple facets, or dimensions (see Xanthopoulou & Bakker, this volume). The adoption of multidimensional and multi-target conceptualizations clearly provides many novel theoretical and empirical opportunities for engagement scholars.

In this regard, the present chapter was guided by three potential research questions which might be worth considering when exploring the nature of employee engagement within and across targets. First, do employees differ in the extent to which they experience engagement to different targets (e.g., job, team, organization, occupation, family)? Put differently, this question asks whether there are distinct subpopulations, or profiles, of employees characterized by distinct configurations of engagement within and across targets. Second, do these different profiles of employees differ in terms of outcomes (e.g., job satisfaction, commitment, turnover intention), and can membership in these profiles be predicted, or explained, by theoretically important antecedents (e.g., tenure, work demands, leadership)? Third, do these profiles demonstrate change over time? In other words, how stable are these distinct configurations, and which shape best characterizes change over time?

We believe these research questions are crucially important, and provide a guide and foundation for a person-centered research agenda into employee engagement. However, little guidance is available on the data-analytic techniques that are able to leverage the advantages of multi-target data. Thus, a major goal of this chapter is to introduce person-centered analyses to highlight how they may be applied to the study of engagement within and across targets. Importantly, person-centered approaches can be applied in multidimensional and/or multi-target research studies. We begin by briefly outlining engagement, providing background detail on multi-target approaches. Next, we introduce person-centered analyses, which are specifically designed to help researchers identify employees characterized by distinct configurations, or patterns, of engagement. The use of person-centered analyses may afford researchers unique insights into the structure and function of employee engagement within and across multiple targets. When considering the approaches outlined here, it is, however, important to keep in mind that person-centered analyses represent only one potential means for examining employee engagement, which is likely to be relevant for some research questions but not for all. Then, we briefly review past person-centered engagement research before discussing person-centered methods that can be used in single- or multi-target engagement investigations. Finally, we highlight potential measurement issues surrounding the multidimensional nature of engagement when multiple targets are considered.

Nature of employee engagement

Engagement has been defined in a number of ways (e.g., Mäkikangas et al., 2012). One common conceptualization is that engagement reflects "a positive, fulfilling, work-related state of mind that is characterized by vigor, dedication, and absorption" (Schaufeli et al., 2002, p. 74). This framework is reflected in the Utrecht Work Engagement Scale (UWES; Schaufeli & Bakker, 2010), which assesses the three-dimensional structure of vigor, dedication, and absorption. These can be characterized as experiencing the target of engagement as stimulating and energizing (vigor), personally significant and meaningful (dedication), and emotionally, physically, and mentally engrossing (absorption).

An alternative conceptualization stems from Rich et al.'s (2010; based on Kahn, 1990) representation of job engagement as encompassing physical, cognitive, and affective dimensions seen as important for optimal performance. Physical engagement reflects behavioral involvement with one's tasks, cognitive engagement reflects attention on one's tasks, and affective engagement denotes emotional connection to one's work and to others. Although we use the UWES framework in our examples, we do not necessarily advocate for this specific definition of engagement, nor do we prefer a specific set of engagement targets. Relevance of particular definitions, dimensions, and targets should be informed by appropriate theory and specific research questions.

Multi-target approaches

A major tenet of multi-target approaches is that engagement can be experienced dissimilarly across different targets in an employee's environment. Saks (this volume) provides insight into the different engagement targets of work tasks, profession and occupation, and work team, and to external targets such as the family. Within multi-target approaches, the nature of engagement can correspond to any of the above definitions or conceptualizations and can be applied to any target present in an employee's environment. For instance, the vigor, dedication, and absorption employees feel towards their work may be different from the vigor, dedication, and absorption they simultaneously feel towards their colleagues and occupation.

Emphasizing multi-target approaches, Rich et al. (2010) noted that engagement reflected multiple involvements, operating in a connected, holistic manner in an employee's life. Recently, a multi-target approach was proposed by Newton et al. (2020), who developed a task-level theory of engagement to suggest that engagement demonstrated dynamicity across tasks (see Sonnentag et al., this volume, for further discussion on dynamic issues). Using NASA astronaut trainees, they provided evidence for how engagement in a previous task influenced performance and engagement in a subsequent task. Their results broadly underscored the need to consider stability and change in the study of engagement across targets. This perspective also highlighted the importance of adopting a multi-target (e.g., multi-task) perspective because not all engagements are equal, and different engagements may have differential antecedents and/or outcomes, and may influence each other.

Introduction to person-centered analyses

Person-centered analyses are designed to classify cases (individuals, teams, etc.) based on the assumption that a sample includes a *mixture* of unobserved subpopulations presenting distinct configurations of scores on a set of focal variables. In other words, person-centered analyses assume that observed data reflect a "mix" of parameters (e.g., means, variances, and even relations among variables) that stem from the presence of discrete subpopulations of cases. Person-centered analyses are part of the mixture modeling framework, and offer insight into how multiple variables simultaneously and holistically co-occur within subpopulations. For instance, it may be possible for a subpopulation of employees to have very strong task and team engagement, but weak organizational engagement, whereas another subpopulation of employees might present weak task engagement, coupled with strong organizational and team engagement. These subpopulations could have distinct relations with antecedents and outcomes, leading to different interpretations and, importantly, different practical implications. It is important to emphasize that the purpose of mixture models is to explore the presence and nature of these discrete subpopulations across a set of focal variables, rather than focusing on the variables themselves (at least until predictors and/or outcomes are included).

In this way, and in contrast to factor analyses, which estimate continuous latent variables (i.e., the factors), mixture models rely on the estimation of a categorical latent variable (i.e., the profiles) of which the categories reflect discrete subpopulations. Mixture modeling also differs from factor analyses in that the latter are variable-centered. Variable-centered analyses assume population homogeneity (i.e., all cases drawn from a single population) and result in a single set of quantitative estimates (i.e., means, regression coefficients, factor loadings) that apply equally to all population members. Mixture models relax this homogeneity assumption, potentially allowing for any model parameters to differ across discrete subpopulations.

In mixture models, these unobserved subpopulations are called *latent profiles* or *latent classes*. Although the terms "latent profile analysis" (LPA) and "latent class analysis" (LCA) are often used interchangeably, the former seeks to identify subpopulations presenting distinct configurations of a set of continuous variables, whereas the latter relies on binary or categorical variables. Given that modern mixture modeling can incorporate many types of ratings (i.e., ordinal, nominal, continuous, count, etc.) we hereafter use *LPA* to summarize both approaches.

LPA makes it possible to examine the combined effects of a set of variables that would be challenging to examine within typical variable-centered approaches like multiple regression and factor analysis (e.g., Morin et al., 2011). Although moderated multiple regression can assess how effects of one variable change according to another variable, thus potentially providing insight into the combined influence of different engagement dimensions and targets, the nature of interactions can be difficult to interpret when three or more interaction terms are considered, especially in the presence of nonlinearity. Instead, mixture modeling provides a holistic perspective on the combined influence of a set of variables within and between cases. It is also important to recognize that mixture modeling is not the only person-centered framework. For instance, modern cluster analysis techniques (Brusco et al., 2011; Hofmans et al., 2018) may provide alternatives for addressing person-centered research questions. However, mixture modeling provides a more flexible approach to the integration of latent subpopulations in models that contain predictors, outcomes, and complex chains of relations (i.e., mediation, moderation; see McLarnon & O'Neill, 2018), as well as longitudinal or multilevel components. Readers interested in gaining further background on LPA may find the following resources useful: Morin et al. (2020), Morin and Litalien (2019), and Morin and Wang (2016).

Employee engagement through a mixture modeling lens

Though focused on a single target of engagement (work in general), one of the most cutting-edge examples of person-centered analyses as applied to employee engagement (using the UWES) comes from Gillet et al. (2019). Using LPA across two time points, Gillet et al. (2019) identified five subpopulations of employees:

1. Engaged, yet distant, corresponding to employees with moderate levels of overall engagement, vigor, and dedication, coupled with very low levels of absorption (we discuss how overall and specific dimension scores can be included in the same model in the *Multidimensional issues* section);
2. Normatively engaged, corresponding to individuals with average levels of engagement across dimensions;
3. Vigorously absorbed, corresponding to individuals with high levels of vigor and absorption;
4. Disengaged-vigorous, corresponding to individuals with low levels of dedication, absorption, and overall engagement, but high levels of vigor;

5. Totally disengaged, corresponding to individuals with low levels across all engagement facets.

Notably, these profiles demonstrated differential relations with stress, turnover intentions, and satisfaction. Specifically, engaged yet distant individuals had the highest job satisfaction, and the lowest stress and turnover intentions. More recently, Gillet et al. (2020) applied a similar method to the job engagement measures of Rich et al. (2010) and identified globally disengaged, globally engaged, globally but not emotionally engaged, and moderately engaged profiles.

Several other studies have applied person-centered analyses to employee engagement. However, much of this work has explored profiles based on combinations of engagement with other variables (e.g., burnout – Mäkikangas et al., 2017; and workaholism – Gillet et al., 2018). Thus, despite their importance, these studies remain limited in their ability to provide a direct interpretation of the unique effects of engagement. Accordingly, future studies on multi-target conceptualizations may wish to solely focus on indicators of engagement when conducting LPA. This will allow researchers to concentrate on the structure and function of engagement configurations within and across targets, without needing to interpret the resulting subpopulations in relation to other constructs. With that said, researchers should use their theoretically informed judgment when determining the set of variables to include, and inclusion of other constructs may indeed be worthwhile in many studies.

Typical person-centered approaches

We now present key person-centered approaches, illustrated in Figure 14.1, that are suitable to the analysis of cross-sectional and longitudinal data. For cross-sectional data, we highlight LPA and mixture regression analyses (MRA). For longitudinal data, we discuss latent transition analyses (LTA) and growth mixture analyses (GMA). We also highlight multiple-group and longitudinal tests of profile similarity, multilevel models, and methods to examine covariate effects (e.g., predictors, outcomes). Extensive *Mplus* syntax for these models is provided in Morin et al. (2020) and Morin and Litalien (2019).

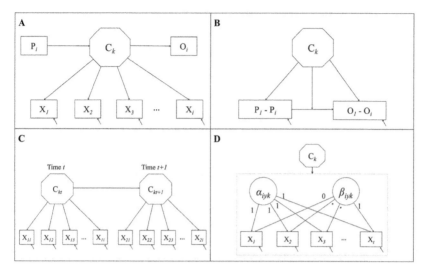

Figure 14.1   Key person-centered approaches

Note: Panel A is the LPA model. This model shows k latent profiles, C_k, derived on the basis of scores on X_1 to X_i indicators. Predictors, P_i, and outcomes, O_i, can be examined, where the predictors influence likelihood of profile membership, and where profile membership influences mean differences in the outcomes across subgroups. Panel B is the MRA model. MRA estimates *k* latent profiles, C_k, based on differing regression relations between a set of P_i to P_i predictors and O_i to O_i outcomes. MRA can also be combined with LPA to identify subgroups that differ on the configuration of indicators, as well as on the strength of relations between indicator variables (see Chénard-Poirier, Morin, & Boudrias, 2017). Panel C is the LTA model. LTA estimates k latent profiles at two time points, C_{kt} and C_{kt+1}, from repeated measures of the same set of X_i items. LTA can assess the probabilities of cases transitioning between C_{kt} and C_{kt+1} profiles over time. LTA can also assess the similarity of a profile solution over time, however, the model at Time t+1 (i.e., C_{kt+1}) does not need to be equivalent the model at Time t (i.e., C_k). In other words, it is not required that C_k and C_{kt+1} have the same structure or number of profiles. Panel D is the GMA model. C_k profiles of differing longitudinal trajectories (i.e., discrete intercepts/slopes) over time. Trajectories are estimated within a latent curve model, of which any part can vary across profiles (i.e., means/variances of growth factors, slope factor loadings [as in a latent basis model], etc.), hence the dashed line around the entire model.

Latent profile analysis

LPA is designed to identify subpopulations characterized by quantitatively and qualitatively distinct configurations of scores on a set of focal variables. For example, LPA can be used to identify subpopulations of employees who demonstrate different configurations of the engagement dimensions (e.g., vigor, dedication, absorption) within and across targets. The LPA model is shown in Figure 14.1, Panel A, where the octagon represents the latent profile variable, C, with k latent profiles (i.e., $C_1 \ldots C_k$) derived from a series of indicators ($X_1 \ldots X_j$; e.g., vigor, dedication, absorption). In a basic formulation, LPA is expressed as (see Masyn, 2013, for technical details):

$$\sigma_i^2 = \sum_{k=1}^{K} \pi_k (\mu_{ik} - \mu_i)^2 + \sum_{k-1}^{K} \pi_k \sigma_{ik}^2 \qquad (1)$$

LPA decomposes the variance, σ_i^2, of each i indicator into between-profile (the first term) and within-profile (the second term) components. Profile-specific means, μ_{ik}, and variances, σ_{ik}^2, operate as a function of π_k, which reflects the proportion of cases assigned to each profile. Despite this relatively straightforward decomposition, the complexity of LPA and other mixture models can increase the chance of converging on improper models (e.g., with negative variances) or models that fail to converge, which may occur when a model is overparameterized (e.g., too many profiles or free parameters estimated). Should this occur, more parsimonious models with profile-invariant variances ($\sigma_{ik}^2 = \sigma_i^2$) can be explored. We recommend starting with "optimal" models (i.e., use σ_{ik}^2) and then reducing complexity as needed.

LPA can be used to explore questions related to engagement as it functions simultaneously across dimensions *and* targets. Consider an example in which a researcher has customized two versions of the UWES: one where the vigor, dedication, and absorption items are tailored to reflect task engagement, and a second version where the items reflect engagement in one's occupation. Such an approach could provide six indicators (three dimensions for each target), allowing for the estimation of profiles reflecting vigor, dedication, and absorption in one's task *and* occupation. This might reveal highly distinct profiles demonstrating, for example: (a) a configuration mirroring the engaged, yet distant pattern mentioned above for task engagement, but a normatively engaged configuration for occupation engagement, and (b) a configuration corresponding to the vigorous absorption profile described earlier for task engagement, but a totally disengaged configuration for occupation engagement. In this way, a parsimonious, holistic approach to assessing engagement within and between targets can be achieved. Further illustrations of LPA are available, for instance, in the motivation (Howard et al., 2016), organizational commitment (for a review, see Meyer & Morin, 2016), and team-conflict literatures (O'Neill et al., 2018).

LPAs are also flexible enough to accommodate the examination of profile similarity across samples. A comprehensive framework for assessing similarity in multi-group LPA was developed by Morin, Meyer, et al. (2016; see also Morin, 2016; Morin & Litalien, 2017, 2019; Morin, McLarnon, & Litalien, 2020). Assessing the extent to which a core set of engagement profiles emerge across samples from different organizations, for example, can provide evidence for generalizability and construct validity, but can also enable discussion of the contexts that enable unique, peripheral subpopulations. For an illustration of this framework, see Litalien et al. (2017).

Mixture regression analysis

Whereas LPA identifies subpopulations presenting distinct configurations of a series of indicators, MRA (Figure 14.1, Panel B) identifies subpopulations that differ from one another in the way variables relate to other variables (i.e., on the basis of differing regression relations between variables). MRA freely estimates the regressions' relations, as well as the means and variances of the outcome variables, to identify profile-specific regression equations (i.e., differing slopes, intercepts, and residuals across profiles; $y_{ik} = b_{ik} \times x_{ik} + \varepsilon_{ik}$). More precisely, in this classical approach to MRA, the profiles function as moderators of predictor–outcome relations. Unfortunately, we are not aware of any engagement research that has used classical MRA, so we direct readers to other research areas. For instance, Hofmans et al. (2013) used MRA to examine relations between pay satisfaction and job satisfaction. They found two profiles of employees: 80 percent of employees had a significant positive relation between pay and job satisfaction, whereas 20 percent of employees had a non-significant relation. Despite the lack of classical MRA applications to the study of engagement, examples can be imagined. Referring back to the previous example of engagement dimensions directed at one's task and occupation, MRA-based analyses could be designed to assess how the six engagement variables can predict burnout and stress. Here, MRA could reveal profiles differing in terms of the relations observed between the six engagement indicators and the two outcomes. For example, a profile could present strong negative relations between engagement and the outcomes, another profile could present null relations, and/or another profile could present negative relations from some predictor–outcome pairs but not others.

Moving beyond the classical MRA model, Chénard-Poirier et al. (2017) developed a more flexible hybrid MRA–LPA approach that allows for the identification of subpopulations presenting distinct configurations on a set of predictors (as in LPA) but also characterized by distinct predictors–outcomes relations (as in MRA). This approach was applied by Gillet et al. (2018) to study the combined effects of work engagement and workaholism, allowing them to identify a mainly workaholic profile, a mainly engaged profile, and an engaged-workaholic profile, each of which was characterized by a distinct pattern of relations between the predictors (workaholism and engagement) and outcomes (sleeping difficulties and work–family conflict). Importantly, this hybrid framework makes it possible to differentiate outcome relations on the basis of between-profile predictor–outcome associations (i.e., profiles that are characterized by distinct configurations of predictor and outcome levels) from within-profile predictor–outcome associations (i.e., profiles that are each characterized by distinct sets of predictor–outcome relations).

Latent transition analysis

LTA (Figure 14.1, Panel C) combines a series of time-specific LPAs into a single model. For example, a LPA describing Time 1 profiles can be combined with a second LPA estimated at Time 2 from repeated measures of the same set of indicators. LTA helps to assess stability and change over time in terms of profile definition (within-sample stability) and membership (within-person stability), enabling consideration of the effects of important time-related events (e.g., organizational changes, promotions). Within-person (in)stability represents individual transitions, or lack thereof, across profiles over time and is specifically assessed via LTA. In contrast, within-sample stability is first assessed within longitudinal LPAs (see Morin, 2016; Morin & Litalien, 2017, 2019; Morin, McLarnon, & Litalien, 2020) to test for temporal consistency in the number, nature, and relative size of profiles, as well as longitudinal equivalence of predictors and outcomes. Ideally, LTAs should be derived from the most *similar* longitudinal LPA to maximize parsimony and comparability (Gillet et al., 2017).

As noted, Gillet et al. (2019) examined engagement profiles longitudinally, finding that over a four-month period profile membership was stable for more than 90 percent of employees. Extending this approach to examine multiple targets would also be relatively straightforward. For instance, the measures of task and occupational vigor, dedication, and absorption can be measured at multiple time points, and modeled using a LTA representation incorporating multiple time-specific LPAs (as described previously). This would enable comprehensive investigations into the stability of profiles characterized by multiple engagement dimensions and targets.

Other examples of LTA are available in the area of organizational commitment (Kam et al., 2016), and respondent faking (McLarnon et al., 2019), among others. Though we have discussed LTA as incorporating time-specific LPAs, LTA is sufficiently flexible to estimate transitions between different mixture models (Nylund-Gibson et al., 2014). For example, LTA can be used to explore how an LPA at Time 1 relates to an MRA at Time 2.

Growth mixture analysis

GMA (Figure 14.1, Panel D) extends latent curve models (LCMs; Bollen & Curran, 2006) to identify subpopulations characterized by distinct longitudinal trajectories. LCMs use indicator variables assessed on multiple occasions (i.e., three or more), and estimate trajectories via intercept (initial level) and slope factors (change over time). GMAs are highly flexible for modeling different trajectories, and may be useful for investigating dynamic engagement processes (see Sonnentag et al., this volume). The most common trajectory reflects a single, linear slope, though more complex trajectories can also be estimated.

Linear and quadratic models

Linear GMAs estimate profiles with different average intercept and slope factors, such that the profiles reflect different trajectories (e.g., steady increases, decreases, or static levels over time). Quadratic GMA, which requires four or more measures, incorporates an additional slope factor, representing a curvilinear trajectory. More complex GMAs can be designed to allow profiles to follow trajectories of higher-order polynomial functions (e.g., cubic, quartic).

Piecewise models

Piecewise GMAs estimate trajectories before and after a transition point (potentially reflecting an intervention or notable life event, like a promotion). Piecewise models incorporate two or more slopes, representing the pre- and post-transition trajectories. Linear piecewise models with two slope factors require ≥2 measures before the transition, ≥2 after the transition point, *and* a total of at least five measures. Additional measures can allow for the estimation of curvilinear functions before or after the transition. Piecewise models require knowledge of when the transition occurs (though see Kwok et al., 2010).

Latent basis models

A limitation of typical GMA is that all profiles are assumed to follow a trajectory characterized by the same shape (e.g., linear, quadratic, piecewise). The latent basis model provides a workaround. GMA (and LCM, by association) requires only two time codes (slope factor loadings) to be fixed to identify the model. Commonly, the first measure, X_1 (see Figure 14.1, Panel D), is fixed to 0 to designate the trajectory start, and the final measure, X_p, is fixed to 1. The remaining time codes can be freely estimated (as in typical factor loadings). In this 0,1 coding, the slope represents the total change between the measures coded 0 and 1. In a GMA with this coding, the freely estimated time codes can differ across profiles and reflect the proportion of total change that occurred at each measurement occasion, thus allowing each profile to follow distinctly shaped, non-linear trajectories.

Non-linear models

GMA can also incorporate other non-linear forms (i.e., exponential, logistic, Gompertz, etc.), and descriptions of these trajectories are available in Grimm et al. (2016).

Growth mixture analysis summary

We presented GMA in many of its different forms because they could be useful for longitudinal multi-target engagement studies. However, GMA may be better suited for exploring a limited set of engagement variables in a single model (see, for example, De Wind et al., 2017; Upadyaya & Salmela-Aro, 2015). For instance, GMA may be an option for examining trajectories of vigor across task and occupation targets. Unfortunately, GMA with six constructs (vigor, dedication, and absorption across two targets) would have at the least 12 factors (intercept and slope for each engagement construct), leading to an extremely complex model, which would likely have convergence issues and lengthy computation time. If interest is on the combined experience of vigor, dedication, and absorption within and across targets, then LTA may be better suited. Of course, choice of an analytical model must be guided by theory and relevant research questions. Given our relatively brief survey of analytical options, readers should consider Morin et al. (2020) and Morin and Litalien (2019) for more thorough discussions of GMA.

Auxiliary variables and covariates

Once an optimal person-centered model is determined, the next stage of data analysis often addresses how covariates have an influence on membership (i.e., predictors), or how profile membership influences outcomes. Covariates are considered *auxiliary* variables because they are external to the focal mixture model. These approaches allow exploring whether, for example, tenure is a predictor of a set of engagement profiles, and also whether engagement profile membership results in meaningful differences in performance and burnout.

Recent work on using auxiliary variables has suggested that an optimal, uncon-ditional profile structure should be determined before covariate relations are examined. Of covariate methods available, the approach of directly including the covariates into the optimal model is one of the most straightforward, and can reduce Type 1 errors and limit bias (see Bolck et al., 2004). When covariates are directly included, care should be taken to ensure that the nature of the optimal unconditional model is unchanged. Asparouhov and Muthén (2014) suggested that if covariates change the unconditional model, the latent categorical variable could have lost its meaning. Techniques such as using the starting values from the optimal unconditional model may help remedy this, but caution must still be exercised (see Morin et al., 2020).

Because of the chance that direct inclusion can change the meaning of a profile, several methods have been developed to help circumvent this issue. Best practice recommendations currently suggest using Mplus' R3STEP procedure for predictors, the DCAT procedure for binary, categorical, and nominal out-comes, and either the DU3STEP, DCON, or BCH procedures for continuous outcomes (for additional details, see Morin et al., 2020).

Whether direct inclusion or the R3STEP procedure is used, predictor relations involve multinomial logistic regression, in which k-1 effects for each pairwise comparison of profile membership are estimated (k=number of profiles). The multinomial logistic coefficients, typically transformed into odds ratios (ORs) to assist with interpretation, give the probability of membership in one profile versus another (e.g., an OR=2.00 suggests that for a 1-unit increase in the predictor, a case is twice as likely to be a member of a target profile versus a comparison profile). Outcome relations are somewhat more straightforward. Regardless of direct inclusion or Mplus' auxiliary procedures, outcome rela-tions are estimated as tests of mean differences across profiles.

LPAs and mixture models can also be used within mediated and/or moderated models. These possibilities can be facilitated with direct inclusion, or through the manual approaches associated with Mplus' R3STEP/DU3STEP and BCH procedures (McLarnon & O'Neill, 2018; Nylund-Gibson et al., 2014).

Multilevel approaches

LPAs can also be used with multilevel data. Although examples of multilevel mixture models are relatively rare, Mäkikangas et al. (2018) provided an overview of multilevel LPAs, and they are presented as a candidate for use in engagement research. A multilevel LPA of multi-target engagement would allow researchers to account for the nesting of employees in teams, and could allow for estimating distinct employee- and team-level profiles. For example, team engagement can be modeled alongside task engagement, resulting in (individual-level) multi-target profiles, whereas the multilevel framework allows for estimating team-level profiles that represent the relative occurrence of individual-level profiles within each team. Conceivably, teams that comprise individuals with strong team engagement profiles might have more positive team outcomes than teams with members who have different multi-target engagement patterns. Readers should consult González-Romá (this volume) for greater detail on multilevel engagement issues and models.

Multidimensional issues

Gillet et al. (2019, 2020) noted that vigor, dedication, and absorption, just like physical, cognitive, and affective engagement, tend to be quite highly correlated. High correlations can suggest redundancy, multicollinearity, and conceptual overlap between variables, but also unmodelled multidimensionality. High correlations are even more likely for multi-target approaches. For example, two measures of vigor – one assessing task engagement, and another corresponding to occupational engagement – would likely be highly correlated. This would stem from the similarity of the constructs, but also from the similarity in contexts in which these forms of engagement would be enacted, as well as from the reliance on similarly worded items across vigor scales.

Unfortunately, highly correlated variables can obscure unique profile configurations, potentially negating the added value of person-centered methods. As a potential solution, a close examination of preliminary measurement models and factor analyses has been advised (Morin, Boudrias et al., 2016, 2017). Specifically, exploratory structural equation modeling (ESEM), integrated with bifactor models, can provide superior variance decomposition for multidimensional measures (Morin, Arens, et al., 2016). ESEM functions similarly to exploratory factor analysis, allowing for measured variables to be indicators of multiple latent factors. ESEM, however, when paired with target rotation, reflects a confirmatory approach, leveraging researcher knowledge of the hypothesized factor structure. In this way, ESEM can better represent the construct-relevant psychometric multidimensionality (Morin, Arens, et al., 2016), reducing factor correlations. As well, integrating a bifactor model, in which a global factor defined by all items included in a measure (e.g., all task engagement items) is estimated in conjunction with a series of specific factors (e.g., task-related vigor, dedication, and absorption) reflecting variance left unexplained by the global factor, has recently been shown to result in a more accurate depiction of employee engagement (Gillet et al., 2020).

After identifying an optimal multidimensional measurement model, factor scores can be exported from this model for use in LPA or other mixture model (Gillet et al., 2019). Factor scores partially control for measurement error by differentially weighting more reliable items (i.e., those with stronger factor loadings). As well, factor scores preserve the underlying measurement model, which can include global and specific factors, and/or longitudinal and multi-group invariance. Together, bifactor-ESEM with target rotation might be strongly advantageous for studying the multidimensional structure of employee engagement within and between targets. The application of this approach to the UWES measure would equip subsequent LPAs with four engagement variables for each target – one global factor, and one each for the specific factors of vigor, dedication, and absorption (for illustrations, see Gillet et al., 2019, 2020). Therefore, researchers should view person- and variable-centered analyses as complementary. When paired together, these approaches can enable comprehensive investigations of employee engagement and of many other organizational phenomena.

Sample size issues

A final point worthy of consideration concerns sample size requirements for person-centered analyses. The mixture models discussed here are generally best suited to large sample sizes. Large samples of employees not only provide greater statistical power, but more importantly enhance the ability of mixture models to converge on proper numerical solutions that may reveal theoretically important profiles (Meyer & Morin, 2016). However, no clear guidelines are currently available on sample size requirements for the models we have described. To this end, we echo Meyer and Morin (2016) and suggest that researchers be cognizant of two contrasting perspectives on sample size. On one hand, although researchers should aim to access large (~500 cases) or very large (~1,000 cases) samples, which enable the application of the more complex models highlighted in this chapter, large samples might reveal statistically significant differences that have weak practical significance, or may identify subpopulations that have low theoretical importance. On the other hand, lower sample sizes (e.g., <300) may only allow researchers to apply mixture models of moderate complexity, thus potentially requiring them to make adjustments to their focal model.

Conclusion

Person-centered analyses, like LPA, may be ideally suited for investigating research questions on employee engagement as it functions within and between targets. We provided readers with a brief overview of person-centered approaches that could be applicable to studying engagement through a multidimensional and/or multi-target lens. We are confident these analytical techniques will afford researchers unique opportunities to investigate important questions on the role of employee engagement from single- and/or multi-target perspectives.

Acknowledgements

The second and third authors were supported by funding from the Social Sciences and Humanities Research Council of Canada (435–2018–0368) in the preparation of this chapter.

References

Asparouhov, T., and Muthén, B.O. (2014). Auxiliary variables in mixture modeling: Three-step approaches using M*plus*. *Structural Equation Modeling*, *21*, 329–341.

Bolck, A., Croon, M., and Hagenaars, J. (2004). Estimating latent structure models with categorical variables: One-step versus three-step estimators. *Political Analysis*, *12*, 3–27.

Bollen, K.A., and Curran, P.J. (2006). *Latent Curve Models: A Structural Equation Perspective*. Hoboken, NJ: Wiley.

Brusco, M.J., Steinley, D., Cradit, J.D., and Singh, R. (2011). Emergent clustering methods for empirical OM research. *Journal of Operations Management*, *30*, 454–466.

Chénard-Poirier, L.-A., Morin, A.J.S., and Boudrias, J.-S. (2017). On the merits of coherent leadership empowerment behaviors: A mixture regression approach. *Journal of Vocational Behavior*, *103*, 66–75.

Crawford, E.R., LePine, J.A., and Rich, B.L. (2010). Linking job demands and resources to employee engagement and burnout: A theoretical extension and meta-analytic test. *Journal of Applied Psychology*, *95*, 834–848.

De Wind, A., Leijten, F.R., Hoekstra, T., Geuskens, G.A., Burdorf, A., and van der Beek, A.J. (2017). "Mental retirement?" Trajectories of work engagement preceding retirement among older workers. *Scandinavian Journal of Work, Environment & Health*, *43*, 34–41.

Gillet, N., Caesens, G., Morin, A.J.S., and Stinglhamber, F. (2019) Complementary variable- and person-centred approaches to the dimensionality of work engagement: A longitudinal investigation. *European Journal of Work and Organizational Psychology*, 28, 239–258.

Gillet, N., Morin, A.J.S, Jeoffrion, C., and Fouquereau, E. (2020). A person-centered perspective on the combined effects of global and specific levels of job engagement. *Group & Organization Management*, 45, 556–594.

Gillet, N., Morin, A.J.S., and Reeve, J. (2017). Stability, change, and implications of students' motivation profiles: A latent transition analysis. *Contemporary Educational Psychology*, 51, 222–239.

Gillet, N., Morin, A.J.S., Sandrin, E., and Houle, S.A. (2018). Investigating the combined effects of workaholism and work engagement: A substantive-methodological synergy of variable- centered and person-centered methodologies. *Journal of Vocational Behavior*, 109, 54–77.

Grimm, K.J., Ram, N., and Estabrook, R. (2016). *Growth Modeling: Structural Equation and Multilevel Approaches*. New York, NY: Guilford.

Harter, J.K., Schmidt, F.L., and Hayes, T.L. (2002). Business-unit-level relationship between employee satisfaction, employee engagement, and business outcomes: A meta-analysis. *Journal of Applied Psychology*, 87, 268–279.

Hofmans, J., De Gieter, S., and Pepermans, R. (2013). Individual differences in the relationship between satisfaction with job rewards and job satisfaction. *Journal of Vocational Behavior*, 82, 1–9.

Hofmans, J., Vantilborgh, T., and Solinger, O.N. (2018). K-centres functional clustering: A person-centered approach to modeling complex nonlinear growth trajectories. *Organizational Research Methods*, 21, 905–930.

Howard, J., Gagné, M., Morin, A.J.S., and Van den Broeck, A. (2016). Motivation profiles at work: A self-determination theory approach. *Journal of Vocational Behavior*, 95–96, 74–96.

Kahn, W.A. (1990). Psychological conditions of personal engagement and disengagement at work. *Academy of Management Journal*, 33, 692–724.

Kam, C., Morin, A.J.S., Meyer, J.P., and Topolnytsky, L. (2016). Are commitment profiles stable and predictable? A latent transition analysis. *Journal of Management*, 42, 1462–1490.

Kwok, O., Luo, W., and West, S.G. (2010). Using modification indexes to detect turning points in longitudinal data: A Monte Carlo study. *Structural Equation Modeling*, 17, 216–240.

Litalien, D., Morin, A.J.S., and McInerney, D.M. (2017). Generalizability of achievement goal profiles across five cultural groups: More similarities than differences. *Contemporary Educational Psychology*, 51, 267–283.

Macey, W.H., and Schneider, B. (2008). The meaning of employee engagement. *Industrial and Organizational Psychology: Perspectives on Science and Practice*, 1, 3–30.

Mäkikangas, A., Feldt, T., Kinnunen, U., and Tolvanen, A. (2012). Do low burnout and high work engagement always go hand in hand? Investigation of the energy and identification dimensions in longitudinal data. *Anxiety Stress & Coping*, 25, 93–116.

Mäkikangas, A., Hyvönen, K., and Feldt, T. (2017). The energy and identification continua of burnout and work engagement: Developmental profiles over eight years. *Burnout Research*, 5, 44–54.

Mäkikangas, A., Tolvanen, A., Aunola, K., Feldt, T., Mauno, S., and Kinnunen, U. (2018). Multilevel latent profile analysis with covariates: Identifying job characteristics profiles in hierarchical data as an example. *Organizational Research Methods*, 21, 931–954.

Masyn, K. (2013). Latent class analysis and finite mixture modeling. In T.D. Little (Ed.), *The Oxford Handbook of Quantitative Methods in Psychology* (Vol. 2, pp. 551–611). New York, NY: Oxford University Press.

McLarnon, M.J.W., DeLongchamp, A.C., and Schneider, T.J. (2019). Faking it! Individual differences in types and degrees of faking behavior. *Personality and Individual Differences, 138,* 88–95.

McLarnon, M.J.W., and O'Neill, T.A. (2018). Extensions of auxiliary variable approaches for the investigation of mediation, moderation, and conditional effects in mixture models. *Organizational Research Methods, 21,* 955–982.

Meyer, J.P., and Gagné, M. (2008). Employee engagement from a self-determination theory perspective. *Industrial and Organizational Psychology: Perspectives on Science and Practice, 1,* 60–63.

Meyer, J.P., and Morin, A.J.S. (2016). A person-centered approach to commitment research: Theory, research, and methodology. *Journal of Organizational Behavior, 37,* 584–612.

Morin, A.J.S. (2016). Person-centered research strategies in commitment research. In J.P. Meyer (Ed.), *The Handbook of Employee Commitment* (pp. 490–508). Cheltenham, UK, and Northampton, MA: Edward Elgar Publishing.

Morin, A.J.S., Arens, A., and Marsh, H.W. (2016). A bifactor exploratory structural equation modeling framework for the identification of distinct sources of construct-relevant psychometric multidimensionality. *Structural Equation Modeling, 23,* 116–139.

Morin, A.J.S., Boudrias, J.-S., Marsh, H.W., Madore, I., and Desrumaux, P. (2016). Further reflections on disentangling shape and level effects in person-centered analyses: An illustration aimed at exploring the dimensionality of psychological health. *Structural Equation Modeling, 23,* 438–454.

Morin, A.J.S., Boudrias, J.-S., Marsh, H.W., McInerney, D.M., Dagenais-Desmarais, V., Madore, I., and Litalien, D. (2017). Complementary variable- and person-centered approaches to exploring the dimensionality of psychometric constructs: Application to psychological wellbeing at work. *Journal of Business and Psychology, 32,* 395–419.

Morin, A.J.S., and Litalien, D. (2017). *Webnote: Longitudinal Tests of Profile Similarity and Latent Transition Analyses.* Montreal, QC: Substantive Methodological Synergy Research Laboratory.

Morin, A.J.S., and Litalien, D. (2019). Mixture modeling for lifespan developmental research. In B. Knight (Ed.), in *The Oxford Encyclopedia of Psychology and Aging.* Oxford, UK: Oxford University Press.

Morin, A.J.S., McLarnon, M.J.W., and Litalien, D. (2020). Mixture modeling for organizational behavior research. In Y. Griep and S. Hansen (Eds), *Handbook on the Temporal Dynamics of Organizational Behavior* (pp. 351–379). Cheltenham, UK, and Northampton, MA: Edward Elgar Publishing.

Morin, A.J.S., Meyer, J.P., Creusier, J., and Biétry, F. (2016). Multiple-group analysis of similarity in latent profile solutions. *Organizational Research Methods, 19,* 231–254.

Morin, A.J.S., Morizot, J., Boudrias, J.-S., and Madore, I. (2011). A multifoci person-centered perspective on workplace affective commitment: A latent profile/factor mixture analysis. *Organizational Research Methods, 14,* 58–90.

Morin, A.J.S., and Wang, J.C.K. (2016). A gentle introduction to mixture modeling using physical fitness data. In N. Ntoumanis and N. Myers (Eds), *An Introduction to Intermediate and Advanced Statistical Analyses for Sport and Exercise Scientists* (pp. 183–210). London: Wiley.

Newton, D.W., LePine, J.A., Kim, J.K., Wellman, N., and Bush, J.T. (2020). Taking engagement to task: The nature and functioning of task engagement across transitions. *Journal of Applied Psychology, 105*, 1–18.

Nylund-Gibson, K.L., Grimm, R., Quirk, M., and Furlong, M. (2014). A latent transition mixture model using the three-step specification. *Structural Equation Modeling, 21*, 439–454.

O'Neill, T.A., McLarnon, M.J.W., Hoffart, G.C., Woodley, H.J., and Allen, N.J. (2018). The structure and function of team conflict state profiles. *Journal of Management, 44*, 811–836.

Rich, B.L., Lepine, J.A., and Crawford, E.R. (2010). Job engagement: Antecedents and effects on job performance. *Academy of Management Journal, 53*, 617–635.

Schaufeli, W.B., and Bakker, A.B. (2010). Defining and measuring work engagement: Bringing clarity to the concept. In A.B. Bakker and M.P. Leiter (Eds), *Work Engagement: A Handbook of Essential Theory and Research* (pp. 10–24). New York, NY: Psychology Press.

Schaufeli, W.B., Salanova, M., González-Romá, V., and Bakker, A.B. (2002). The measurement of engagement and burnout: A two sample confirmatory factor analytic approach. *Journal of Happiness Studies, 3*, 71–92.

Upadyaya, K., and Salmela-Aro, K. (2015). Development of early vocational behavior: Parallel associations between career engagement and satisfaction. *Journal of Vocational Behavior, 90*, 66–74.

15. Employee engagement in the new world of data

Alexis A. Fink and William H. Macey

Employee surveys have been a core part of human resources strategy for decades; by the end of the twentieth century, 70 percent of US organizations were surveying their populations regularly (Paul & Bracken, 1995). Advances in technology have moved engagement surveys from cumbersome, time-consuming paper-and-pencil exercises to lightweight, engaging and flexible tools, complemented by the potential for highly personalized action planning. In this chapter, we explore the roots of sensing for employee engagement via employee surveys and new opportunities created by data sources and methods, and address risks posed and future research needs as this field evolves. Importantly, the study of engagement, its antecedents and consequences using the newer big data sources and methods at times requires a leap of faith because much of the data that might be subject to analysis were never intended to be relevant to the engagement construct and there is little evidence presently available to place those data in a nomological net.

In what follows, we first briefly set up a critical tension in conducting research on employees. We then review the traditional approaches to the measurement of employee engagement. Then we explore the kinds of new data sources available that might contribute to the understanding of engagement, its antecedents and consequences. Data management and analysis (both quantitative and qualitative) is covered next in some detail. We close with a more detailed section on the privacy and ethics issues associated with these new data sources. Throughout, we suggest some avenues for future research using these newer data sources and analytic approaches.

Balancing privacy with insight

One of the core tensions in studying employees at work is the balance between honoring the obligation to privacy and honoring the need for insight that helps improve well-being, engagement, performance and other important outcomes at work. In the early days of engagement research, engagement projects were typically stand-alone pieces of work, and joining data to other data sources was generally cumbersome. Further, the data available were typically restricted in number and scope – for example, attributes such as location, tenure, job type and perhaps level and performance history. In this chapter, we will explore some new sources of information that can provide insight into engagement and work outcomes. However, as data complexity increases, so does the need to ensure that employee consent is unambiguously obtained and data sources are used only in appropriate ways. Essential considerations involve both awareness and control (Adams, 2017). This is much more easily said than done when the precise nature of the data included in a consent agreement may be unclear, and when the temptation is great to use analytic techniques that promise to create useful insight out of large volumes of data. Further, new privacy legislation, such as the European Union (EU) General Data Protection Regulation (GDPR), expands the requirements for how organizations store and use data; more on this important issue later.

The traditional practice of measuring employee engagement

Gathering feedback from employees in service of morale and employee relations dates back a century, to the 1920s (Jacoby, 1988). Since the early 2000s, the main focus of these surveys has been "engagement", although the specific meaning of the word among survey practitioners has been varied and largely embracing constructs such as satisfaction, commitment, pride and discretionary effort.

Garrad and Hyland (2020) outline a core set of activities that characterize effective organizational surveys: careful measurement, robust data analysis and collective feedback and action planning. Countless studies, published and unpublished, have explored the impact of engagement and related constructs. And, indeed, engagement has been shown to have effects across every conceivable aspect of organizational life (Del Duco et al., 2020) with those relationships tested at the organization (Schneider et al., 2017), team (González-Romá, this volume), and individual (Halbesleben, this volume) levels of analysis.

New data sources and new contexts

Over the past decade, information technology has advanced tremendously. Processes that formerly took weeks can be completed in an instant. Products and experiences can be delivered with high degrees of customization and personalization. These advances have created new opportunities and expectations; employees have come to expect experiences at work to be comparable to experiences they receive as consumers in terms of speed, flexibility, personalization and elegance (e.g., Ng et al., 2010). These advances create new opportunities for employee research, and excitement in this space has invited many new entrants into the commercial space. However, despite new sophistication, practitioners must remain vigilant to key risks and errors that often plague survey research: overlooking limitations of cross-sectional designs, ignoring common method bias and the necessary conditions for claiming causality, and surveying only the evaluating and remembering self (Garrad & Hyland, 2020). Happily, emerging techniques and sources of data can help address these challenges.

The first few decades of the twenty-first century have brought dizzying new capabilities for measuring employee performance, attitudes and experiences. These originate in the use of both more frequent "pulse" surveys (Jolton & Klein, 2020) and the ambient data captured from the interaction of employees with each other and their environment. Increasingly, data about where we are, who we are with and what we are doing can be captured and mined for insights, simply as a by-product of doing our jobs (Chakrabarti & McCune, 2020). Many workplaces now use collaboration platforms such as Microsoft Teams, Slack, Jive or Workplace that enable teams to work in new, more efficient ways, but also create a digital record of who is working on which projects at what frequency, and who is talking to or reacting to whom about what. This in-depth social graph of interactions was previously cumbersome to gather manually, and relied on the (fallible) remembering self for reporting – one of Garrad and Hyland's (2020) risk factors in sensing. This so-called digital exhaust – data that are generated as a by-product of working and interacting with computer systems – can be combined with other data to identify patterns that were previously unknowable, or, at best, difficult to discover, such as whether some types of interactions are more important to key outcomes (e.g., Cross & Prusak, 2002) and work motivation (Gagné, Parker & Griffin, this volume). For example, Bernstein and Waber (2019) note that organizations that moved to open-office plans have surprisingly seen a drop in face-to-face interactions. Similarly, the increasing use of social media suggests changes in the way workers communicate (McFarland & Ployhart, 2015). Findings such as these have enormous implications for how group norms develop and engagement behaviors (e.g., helping others) might be manifested. As we will discuss later, however, consideration of ethics and data privacy are paramount; with great power comes great responsibility.

New data sources also open up possibilities for tracking outcome variables as well as processes and the relationships among them. Where previously researchers were often constrained to supervisor ratings or performance reviews, in many cases performance can now be captured and quantified as a natural part of executing one's job. A simple example might be the speed with which a grocery store checker can scan items. Further, where until recently a single, global measure of performance was often all that was available, opportunities to harvest ambient data make it possible to capture outcome variables, such as the time to complete various full performance goals, with a reasonable level of precision.

Novel data sources, such as biometrics and location, can also now be captured with a fair degree of accuracy. While these must be carefully considered in each unique context for appropriateness, certainly in some situations they may be highly useful. For example, it may be possible to measure biometrics like heart rate and breathing of new police academy graduates in response to potentially dangerous situations as a result of different training approaches. These data-capturing techniques provide some unique opportunities for the assessment of worker engagement as well as for establishing linkages among the different kinds of data. As another example, Watts (2016) describes an effort at Microsoft to predict several employee survey outcomes at the team level of analysis using email response times. Watts showed that the best predictor of employees' satisfaction with the manager is the amount of time taken by the managers to respond to emails. While in this instance actual email responsiveness might not be directly causing satisfaction with the manager, it is clearly capturing something important. Unfortunately, while there are many anecdotal and vendor accounts of successful applications of the use of these kinds of data to organizational problems, at present few examples exist in the peer-reviewed literature. But it is very clear in the world of practice that existing or potential behavioral data can be informative about employee engagement and useful for perhaps suggesting interventions that might improve both engagement and job performance. Practitioner–scholar partnerships seem to be very much worth pursuing.

New approaches to collecting, managing and using engagement data

Traditionally, each engagement survey was a project bookended by survey design and survey feedback. Survey data were compartmentalized, stored in a file separate from other human resources (HR) and operational records. Connecting records from one data system to another often involved laborious, time-intensive data cleaning and matching. Data management strategies have since improved and expanded dramatically, from highly structured and efficient data cubes to unstructured, expansive data lakes (e.g., Inmon, 2016). Data access approaches have similarly evolved, so that data can be present or connected, but only accessible to those few specified through individual or role-based permissions. Additionally, entirely new data architectures have emerged to complement and augment traditional, tabular structures such as relational and object databases. Notably, graph databases, which center on a person and "decorate" that individual's record with a variety of information, such as survey responses, promotion history, shift assignment and so forth, create opportunities for faster, more complex forms of analysis without the laborious joining and cleaning of the past (e.g., Angles & Gutierrez, 2008).

The increased volume, variety and velocity, the original Vs of Big Data (King et al., 2015; Laney, 2001), also create an opportunity, and in some cases a requirement, to use different analytical methods. Many of these fall under the broad category of machine learning (such as random forest analysis, a bootstrapping method applied to regression trees where the result is the mean prediction of the different trees; Hastie et al., 2009). While the underlying calculations may be different than those used in familiar techniques such as linear regression, they are quite similar in purpose, and often quite similar in outcome. Researchers employing multiple methods will often find that the results converge fairly well.

In some cases, the volume of data is such that the most efficient and compelling analysis is not a statistic at all; when dealing with very large data sets, statistical significance can approach meaninglessness as very small differences meet that criterion. In those cases, a clear data visualization can be much more illuminating than a tabular presentation of results (e.g., Sinar, 2020).

Quantitative analysis

For many who are coming to work with people data via data science training rather than social science training, techniques such as those discussed above (machine learning and random forests) might be more familiar than the inferential statistics of social science. Additionally, those accustomed to ingesting and managing very large data sets may find utility in data processing techniques such as map-reduction techniques (e.g., Lammel, 2008; Wickham, 2011) to help bring order to a data set. Here, the brute force of substantial computing power is harnessed to test hundreds or thousands of relationships within a data set to discover very specific relationships among variables, using parallel processes to filter (map) and summarize (reduce) patterns within the data. Statistical purists will likely argue that this approach will capitalize on chance, and generate spurious results. However, discipline around separating out training data sets and analyses from validation data sets and analyses from within the data can help put those concerns to rest. These procedures are of course reminiscent of the validation and cross-validation models used in traditional validity studies within Industrial/Organizational Psychology.

The possibilities created through these new data types and methods invite the question of how engagement is operationally defined in ambient data (George et al., 2014). With the increasing variety of data available, there is the increasing risk of using what are at best weak proxies for engagement as a psychological state. For example, ambient data might include things like response times and interaction length (Chakrabarti & McCune, 2020), and some might see these as indicators of engagement. But theory building relevant to the existing literature will be difficult even if the data patterns recognized are compelling illustrations of some seemingly engagement-related phenomena.

Simsek et al. (2019) note how big data research often begins with the availability of data as opposed to theory. Big data research regarding engagement-related phenomena should be valued to the extent that those phenomena are tightly linked either to the context in which engagement emerges and/or to strategically-relevant engagement outcomes at the individual, unit or organizational levels. That said, abductive research strategies have their place. Consider, for example, the possibility of exploring the role of internal employee interaction patterns on the emergence of engagement climate (see Albrecht, this volume). Matusik et al. (2019) demonstrate the construct validity of interpersonal data captured using wearable Bluetooth sensors. Their research clearly speaks to the viability of big data for expanding engagement theory vis-à-vis the dynamics of interpersonal behavior over time (see also Sonnentag et al., this volume). Research methods that gather ambient, biometric or social interaction data, as opposed to remembered experiences or judgments, offer the possibility of unobtrusively studying engagement micro-behaviors by capturing data *in vivo* at (relatively) high sampling rates (Klonek et al., 2019), thus allowing for the identification of temporal patterns such as the reciprocation of discretionary within-group helping behaviors and allowing for team-level measurement of engagement.

New sources of data, increased analytic power, and an expansion of engagement to include the broader employee experience can also lead to more integrated insights. For example, organizations may work to predict attrition, promotion and transfer rates based on personal profiles encompassing engagement, performance and skills appraisals, and match human capital availability to strategic human capital requirements. This might extend to include broader economic data along with individual employee attributes such as time since last promotion, performance history and pay fairness perceptions. Organizations might tie together their offer acceptance rates and their attrition rates to understand their employment brand equity and thereby identify potential risks to company performance. At the employee level, organizations may seek to identify patterns in data that signal threats to personal well-being. Some organizations may already be doing these kinds of analyses, but they remain proprietary and the academic research literature is pretty much devoid of such attempts – which are eminently doable given available data analytic techniques. Here are a few examples of what is possible.

Subjective well-being as an engagement outcome

Subjective well-being (SWB) has been demonstrated to be clearly identifiable in text such as in social media posts and is considered an important outcome of work engagement (Halbesleben, this volume). Luhmann (2017) notes that relevant data on mood can extend beyond text to include data available from fitness trackers and mobile phones. That said, he notes that Twitter data have been a particularly common source of SWB data. It is important to note that each organization should carefully consider the privacy and employee-trust implications of including non-work sources in their data feeds for analysis of employees; many organizations prioritize employee trust above the insight they might gain from examining employees' personal Twitter feeds or fitness tracker data, and decline to include such data in their studies and models. Additionally, technologically savvy employees may effectively manage the privacy settings on their social media platforms such that very little information is publicly available, thus rendering these strategies less effective.

Beyond studying the dynamic relationship between engagement measures and SWB at an individual level, it would also seem useful to explore changes in SWB in relation to specific contextual events, such as changes in leadership or supervision. As part of the large-scale United States Army Comprehensive Soldier Fitness Program, Lester et al. (2011b) investigated the resilience of army officers promoted early compared to those promoted at normal schedules. Those promoted early were significantly and meaningfully better in terms of a number of resilience measures, including work engagement. In a separate study, Lester et al. (2011a) found that certain resilience measures, not consistently including engagement, differentiated soldiers on three negative behavioral outcomes. Vie et al. (2013) detail the broad economic and organizational effectiveness implications of using big data to improve the well-being of soldiers and their families.

Qualitative analysis

Big data are inherently messy, and this is particularly true of text analytics. Broadly, text analytics refers to the use of data analysis techniques to make sense of written expression. These techniques range from the relatively simple, such as the closed-ended search for key words in a body of text, to the very complex (e.g., the identification of the grammatical structure of text to aid in automated question-answering using natural language processing (NLP) techniques). These latter methods include topic identification and the evaluation of the sentiment (valence) in the text. Text analytics thus represents a mixed qualitative–quantitative paradigm by which free-form data can be analyzed to link what people say to various antecedents and outcomes. Text analytics is in some ways a new label for the automation of content analysis as traditionally applied in organizational research.

Big data techniques are considered largely exploratory and are inductive in nature. However, text analytics more generally, and NLP more specifically, are relevant to engagement research in multiple ways, including:

1. Identifying narrative themes and their importance relevant to the larger work experience;
2. Determining the emotions and sentiment associated with specific elements of the work context;

3. Determining worker predispositions to engage (Hough & Oswald, this volume), and how those predispositions effect the interpretation of work experiences and work behavior; and
4. Capturing the practical advice and collective wisdom of employees that can be of enormous practical benefit to organization leaders.

Each of these are discussed below in turn.

Topic modeling and theme identification

Thematic analysis is a challenging undertaking yet essential to the interpretation of free-form text. Topic modeling, which generally refers to the use of machine learning to identify themes, is particularly useful when very large amounts of data are available, in contrast to the forms of content coding that are typically applied in the intensive analysis of rich and complex narratives that are common to qualitative studies (Macey, this volume). Topic modeling relies on methods normally associated with big data and is typically applied to large data sets.

Topic modeling involves fitting a probabilistic model to data to identify groups of words that are likely to co-occur. Multiple methods exist, but arguably latent Dirichlet allocation (LDA) is the most popular. It is useful to think of topic modeling as a procedure analogous to factor analysis in that it is used to identify the latent structure that the words in a body of text reflect. Banks et al. (2018) outline in great detail the data-handling steps needed to implement LDA, and Kropp et al. (2017) offer a helpful tutorial. As an alternative, Schmiedel et al. (2019) provide details for using structural topic modeling (STM), which has the advantage of incorporating document metadata as covariates (e.g., "star" ratings accompanying employee reviews).

The choice of a particular topic model requires interpreting how words cluster together. In practice, different solutions are typically evaluated iteratively, guided by both relevant statistical criteria and interpretability. This is somewhat akin to what qualitative researchers do when developing thematic categories. The difference between text analytics as described above and traditional qualitative research is that in the latter the researcher is continually evaluating new content, testing the adequacy of the coding scheme, and revising the coding structure as necessary. The researcher necessarily challenges the evolving structure so that both new and existing information can be accommodated. Implicit here in traditional qualitative research is the likelihood of a deeper and perhaps more thoughtful consideration of the emerging themes. That said, topic modeling has the advantage of practical applicability to very large data sets and the relatively easy transportability of any final coding scheme to new data sets.

Sentiment analysis

Workers do not always speak in neutral terms when describing their employment experiences. Sentiment analysis is used to illuminate the valence associated with a body of text (often at the sentence level) and, with greater difficulty, the opinions on specific topics. It is particularly valuable in the employee survey context as it provides for an evaluative capability applied to open-ended survey comments.

Nonetheless, sentiment analysis is a considerably more complex process than it would seem to be when initially thinking about it. Moreover, the achieved accuracy is often less than practically useful. Liu (2015) details the challenges associated with sentiment analysis, among the most notable being issues with sarcasm, negation and modality. Many of the available cloud-based sentiment-analysis platforms have difficulty dealing with idioms (e.g., "tear you down" or "like family") that are common in employee-related narratives. Practically useful sentiment analysis requires means of handling not only a large number of potential idioms and modalities but also a significant number of semantic composition rules (Liu, 2015). While much of the work done in this area is proprietary, several studies in the information-processing literature demonstrate the capability of sentiment analysis based on employee reviews provided on Glassdoor. For example, Chamberlain (2015) demonstrated that investment returns for companies on Glassdoor's "Best companies to work for list" outperformed a portfolio comprised of companies otherwise listed on the New York Stock Exchange. Sull et al. (2019) describe the joint effort of *MIT Sloan Management Review*, CultureX, and Glassdoor to offer a web-based tool allowing site visitors to compare the positive sentiment attached to nine different corporate values as represented in over one million Glassdoor employee reviews. This tool may be useful to researchers who wish to contrast and compare their engagement data against those evaluations of sentiment. For example, this might be particularly relevant to the various survey group consortia (such as the Mayflower Group).

Measuring the predisposition to engage

Macey and Schneider (2008) proposed that trait engagement can be "regarded as an inclination or orientation to experience the world from a particular vantage point (e.g., positive affectivity characterized by feelings of enthusiasm)" (p. 5; see Hough and Oswald, this volume). Bakker and Oerlemans

(2011) characterized work engagement within the circumplex model of affect as representing high levels of both pleasure and activation. Both trait affect and the Big Five personality factors are identifiable in text (see Boyd & Pennebaker, 2017, for an overview). Exploratory analysis of rich blog content focused on employee work experiences would seem particularly relevant to understanding variability in interpretations of employment work experiences. Arguably, individual reports of work experiences such as those gathered in survey comments reflect both trait and state engagement. Thus, mixed methods may well be necessary to make sense of the organizational implications of reported work experiences.

Capturing prescriptive comments

One particularly interesting recent development is the identification of prescriptive survey comments that provide very useful information on which managers can take action. Prescriptive in this context does not simply mean identifying need on the basis of topic or aspect frequency characterized by negative sentiment (e.g., "There is not a lot of cross training"), although that may indeed be relevant. Rather, it involves the use of (1) targeted questions asking specifically for advice; and (2) the identification of modal auxiliaries in written expression (e.g., "ought", "should"). Text analytics have a particularly valuable role in guiding organizational stakeholders in the effective use of survey comments.

Privacy and ethics

All of the above discussion presupposes that researchers have taken the appropriate steps and precautions to ensure that the data that exist across various systems are in fact available to analyze ethically. As digital privacy has gained attention and protection, it cannot be assumed that all data that exist in a system are appropriate to include. In general, data collected for one purpose cannot be used for other purposes, absent specific consent from the participants; for organizations covered by the EU GDPR, substantial fines can be levied for violating this principle.

Expanding research to include some of the ambient data sources discussed in this chapter creates such questions. In particular, biometric data, such as pulse rate or pupil dilation, hold the potential to yield fascinating insights. However, if these responses are involuntary, the question of consent may be important. Let us say that a group of employees grant consent for a study on collaboration that uses a small, wearable device. If the consent was granted to examine location and proximity, but the device also detects biometrics such as heart rate, is it appropriate to include the additional variables? What if the additional variables yield information that leads to identification of fraud on the part of some employees? Ethical standards (e.g., National Commission for the Protection of Human Subjects of Biomedical and Behavioral Research, 1979) would command that only those data points for which consent was granted, and for the explicitly stated purpose, should be retained and analyzed. Saari and Scherbaum (2020) provide a useful reference to the key considerations in protecting employee privacy and ethics in an evolving data landscape.

Similarly, organizations must carefully consider the ethics of scraping data from the public internet. In addition to considering employee privacy, and the appropriateness and relevance of publicly available information, organizations must also consider the terms of service for the various websites they might access. While much research has focused on sources such as Twitter, there are numerous blogging sites where people may share insights or experiences that may or may not be professionally relevant. Further, some clearly professionally- or engagement-relevant sources – such as LinkedIn, Glassdoor or Blind – may forbid automated scraping, but permit manual review of content on their sites. Additionally, there are a number of sites that offer services akin to background checks, purporting to identify a variety of personal records that might not be legally appropriate to consider in an employment decision but nonetheless might bias a hiring manager or recruiter. Even where organizations may have thoughtful policies regarding privacy practices, individual employees or managers may not be aware of these policies as they access the web.

Conclusion

Engagement remains an important and nuanced area for research in organizations. New data sources and new methods of analysis provide opportunities for researchers and managers to discover previously hidden patterns and to help support workplaces that support both individuals and organizational outcomes. Organizational scientists can partner with data scientists to discover and utilize new insights, but must carefully protect the privacy of the employees whose data are being explored.

We are in a period of rapid change, technologically and socially. These changes are felt in the workplace as well, as more employers consider expanding remote and flexible work, jobs are reconfigured to take advantage of automation, and fairness of employment practices comes under increased scrutiny (see Boudreau, Cappelli & Eldor and Gagné et al., this volume). These workplace changes are significant, and will invite deep investigation of employee performance and engagement as approaches are refined. As the world of work and the field of employee engagement evolve, researchers can provide greater insight and benefit to their organizations through exploration of ambient data (e.g., pulse, response times) alongside frequent pulsing and larger "traditional" surveys and HR data from HR information systems (HRIS). They can examine peer and hierarchical interaction patterns that previously would have been ephemeral, garnering insights about effective behavior and patterns of inclusion. They can understand nuances in onboarding to speed up time to full performance, and identify subtle patterns that suggest increased attrition risk. To preserve the trust of employees and organizations, as well as to meet legal requirements, researchers must thoughtfully guard employee privacy as they delve into additional data streams in search of increased performance and competitive advantage.

Much research remains to be done to determine the important explanatory and predictive relationships among those different data streams. A better understanding of how engagement, as measured in these various ways, plays out in effective individual and team performance, as well as the contributions of those predictors to attrition, will help (a) inform practitioners as they build their measurement strategies and as they design organizational systems and interventions to absorb and effectively respond to the data, and (b) enrich the employee engagement construct with further understanding of antecedents and outcomes. Further, the commercial availability of employee, financial and other corporate data scraped from the web will make it quite feasible to pursue research agendas exploring the relationship between engagement and business and operational criteria across many companies.

References

Adams, M. (2017). Big data and individual privacy in the age of the Internet of Things. *Technology Innovation Management Review, 7,* 12–24.

Angles, R., and Gutierrez, C. (2008). Survey of graph data base models. *ACM Computing Surveys, 40*(1), 1–39.

Bakker, A. B., and Oerlemans, W. (2011). Subjective well-being in organizations. In K. Cameron and G. Spreitzer (Eds), *Handbook of Positive Organizational Scholarship* (pp. 178–190). Oxford University Press.

Banks, G. C., Woznyj, H. M., Wesslen, R. S., and Ross, R. L. (2018). A review of best practice recommendations for text analysis in R (and a user-friendly app). *Journal of Business and Psychology, 33*(4), 445–459.

Bernstein, E., and Waber, B. (2019). The truth about open offices. *Harvard Business Review, 97*(6), 82–91.

Boyd, R. L., and Pennebaker, J. W. (2017). Language-based personality: A new approach to personality in a digital world. *Current Opinion in Behavioral Sciences, 18*, 63–68.

Chakrabarti, M., and McCune, E., A. (2020). Is the engagement survey the only way? Alternative sources for employee sensing. In W. H. Macey and A. A. Fink (Eds), *Employee Surveys and Sensing: Driving Organizational Culture and Performance* (pp. 219–235). Oxford University Press.

Chamberlain, A. (2015, March). *Does Company Culture Pay Off?* Glassdoor. www .glassdoor.ca/research/app/uploads/sites/2/2015/05/GD_Report_1.pdf.

Cross, R., and Prusak, L. (2002). The people who make organizations go – or stop. *Harvard Business Review, 80*, 104–12.

Del Duco, S. M., Hyland, P. K., Reeves, D. W., and Caputo, A. W. (2020). Linkage analysis: Tying employee attitudes to business outcomes. In W. H. Macey and A. A. Fink (Eds), *Employee Surveys and Sensing: Driving Organizational Culture and Performance* (pp. 272–287). Oxford University Press.

Garrad, L., and Hyland, P. (2020). Employee survey research: A critical review of theory and practice. In W. H. Macey and A. A. Fink (Eds), *Employee Surveys and Sensing: Driving Organizational Culture and Performance* (pp. 374–389). Oxford University Press.

George, G., Haas, M. R., and Pentland, A. (2014). Big data and management. *Academy of Management Journal, 57*, 321–326.

Hastie, T., Tibshirani, R., and Friedman, J. (2009). *The Elements of Statistical Learning: Data Mining, Inference, and Prediction.* Springer Science & Business Media.

Inmon, B. (2016). *Data Lake Architecture: Designing the Data Lake and Avoiding the Garbage Dump.* Technics Publications.

Jacoby, S. M. (1988). Employee attitude surveys in historical perspective. *Industrial Relations, 27*(1), 74–93.

Jolton, J. A., and Klein, C. (2020). Exploring the universe of pulse surveys and continuous listening opportunities. In W. H. Macey and A. A. Fink (Eds), *Employee Surveys and Sensing: Driving Organizational Culture and Performance* (pp. 53–67). Oxford University Press.

King, E. B., Tonidandel, S., Cortina, J. M., and Fink, A. A. (2015). Building understanding of the data science revolution and IO psychology. In S. Tonidandel, E. B. King, and J. M. Cortina (Eds), *Big Data at Work* (pp. 15–30). Routledge.

Klonek, F. E., Gerpott, F., Lehmann-Willenbrock, N., and Parker, S. (2019). Time to go wild: How to conceptualize and measure process dynamics in real teams with high resolution. *Organizational Psychology Review, 6*, 63–91.

Kropp, A., Kind, C., and Yost, A. (2017, April 26). *NLP and Text Mining for I/O Psychologists* [Master tutorial]. Conference of the Society for Industrial and Organizational Psychology, Orlando. https://github.com/andreakropp/SIOP2017 -NLPTutorial.

Lammel, R. (2008). Google's MapReduce programming model – Revisited. *Science of Computer Programming, 70*(1), 1–30. https://doi.org/10.1016/j.scico.2007.07.001.

Laney, D. (2001, February 6). 3-D data management: Controlling data volume, velocity and variety. https://blogs.gartner.com/doug-laney/deja-vvvue-others -claiming-gartners-volume-velocity-variety-construct-for-big-data.

Lester, P. B., Harms, P. D., Bulling, D. J., Herian, M. N., and Spain, S. M. (2011a). *Evaluation of Relationships between Reported Resilience and Soldier Outcomes Report #1: Negative Outcomes. United States Army Comprehensive Soldier Fitness Program.* US Government Printing Office.

Lester, P. B., Harms, P. D., Bulling, D. J., Herian, M. N., Beal, S. J., and Spain, S. M. (2011b). *Evaluation of Relationships between Reported Resilience and Soldier Outcomes Report #2: Positive Outcomes. United States Army Comprehensive Soldier Fitness Program.* US Government Printing Office.

Liu, B. (2015). *Sentiment Analysis: Mining Sentiments, Opinions, and Emotions.* Cambridge University Press.

Luhmann, M. (2017). Using big data to study subjective well-being. *Current Opinion in Behavioral Sciences, 18,* 28–33.

Macey, W. H., and Schneider, B. (2008). The meaning of employee engagement. *Industrial and Organizational Psychology: Perspectives on Science and Practice, 1,* 3–30.

Matusik, J. G., Heidl, R., Hollenbeck, J. R., Yu, A., Lee, H. W., and Howe, M. (2019). Wearable Bluetooth sensors for capturing relational variables and temporal variability in relationships: A construct validation study. *Journal of Applied Psychology, 104*(3), 357–387.

McFarland, L. A., and Ployhart, R. E. (2015). Social media: A contextual framework to guide research and practice. *Journal of Applied Psychology, 100*(6), 1653–1677.

National Commission for the Protection of Human Subjects of Biomedical and Behavioral Research (1979). *The Belmont Report: Ethical Principles and Guidelines for the Protection of Human Subjects of Research.* www.hhs.gov/ohrp/regulations -and-policy/belmont-report.

Ng, E. S. W., Schweitzer, L., and Lyons, S. T. (2010). New generation, great expectations: A field study of the millennial generation. *Journal of Business and Psychology, 25,* 281–292.

Paul, K. B., and Bracken, D. W. (1995). Everything you always wanted to know about employee surveys. *Training & Development, 49*(1), 45–49.

Saari, L. M., and Scherbaum, C. A. (2020). From identified surveys to new technologies: Employee privacy and ethical considerations. In W. H. Macey and A. A. Fink (Eds), *Employee Surveys and Sensing: Driving Organizational Culture and Performance* (pp. 391–405). Oxford University Press.

Schmiedel, T., Müller, O., and vom Brocke, J. (2019). Topic modeling as a strategy of inquiry in organizational research: A tutorial with an application example on organizational culture. *Organizational Research Methods, 22*(4), 941–968.

Schneider, B., Yost, A. B., Kropp, A., Kind, C. and Lam, H. (2017). Workforce engagement: What it is, what drives it, and why it matters for organizational performance. *Journal of Organizational Behavior, 39*(4), 462–480.

Simsek, Z., Vaara, E., Paruchuri, S., Nadkarni, S., and Shaw, J. D. (2019). New ways of seeing big data. *Academy of Management Journal, 62*(4), 971–978.

Sinar, E. (2020). Data visualization. In W. H. Macey and A. A. Fink (Eds), *Employee Surveys and Sensing: Driving Organizational Culture and Performance* (pp. 306–323). Oxford University Press.

Sull, D., Sull, C., and Chamberlain, A. (2019, June 25). Measuring culture in leading companies. *MIT Sloan Management Review* and Glassdoor. www.glassdoor.com/ research/mit-culture-500/.

Vie, L. L., Griffith, K. N., Scheier, L. M., Lester, P. B., and Seligman, M. E. P. (2013). The Person-Event Data Environment: Leveraging big data for studies of psychological strengths in soldiers. *Frontiers in Psychology*, 4, Article 934. https://doi.org/10.3389/fpsyg.2013.00934.

Watts, D. (2016). The organizational spectroscope. *Medium*. https://medium.com/@duncanjwatts/the-organizational-spectroscope-7f9f239a897c#.

Wickham, H (2011). The split-apply-combine strategy for data analysis. *Journal of Statistical Software*, *40*, 1–29.

Conclusion

16. Learnings and future directions

Benjamin Schneider and John P. Meyer

And we thought we knew quite a bit about engagement! After all, one does not decide to edit a book on a topic where one is a novice. We are wonderfully appreciative of what we have learned currently exists in this literature and the potential for answering exciting research questions with useful research methods going forward. In this concluding chapter, we want to reflect on the impressive insights and recommendations for future research offered throughout this book. On that note, we add this thought: the conceptualization and study of engagement is barely 30 years old but it has produced a wealth of studies because (a) it is a fascinating way to think about human experiences and behavior in the work role, and (b) it has "grabbed" the business world, so that world has been supportive of the research effort.

Our goal in this conclusion was to identify and integrate key themes reflected across the chapters, not to write another review of the engagement research literature. We took on the role of discussants as if the chapters were presentations at a conference on the future of engagement research. In this mode, we discuss what we learned and what the future research efforts might look like based on our chapter authors' efforts. Though we divide these topics into two major sections there is of course lots of overlap between them.

Learnings

Focus

Engagement has many foci (Alan Saks calls them targets), many of them not much explored. Most engagement research has focused on the job or the work as a whole identifiable entity and not something that can be further segmented into components or facets. The ultimate example of this focus concerns the most often-used measure of engagement, the Utrecht Work Engagement

Scale (UWES)—with the focus on the whole job in the items that assess three work engagement facets: vigor, dedication and absorption. But Saks, as well as Matthew McLarnon, Alexandre Morin and David Litalien, show us that a job certainly has numerous facets to it, some perhaps more engaging than others. Given this fact, a set of job facets are amenable to study for the degree to which they each deplete or enhance engagement. In his chapter on the impact of technology on engagement, John Boudreau uses this notion of work facets, or work elements, to advantage. For example, when introducing technology into the workplace, organizations might consider what elements employees find most and least engaging, and, where possible, redesign the work so that the least engaging elements are automated.

Of course, chapter authors did not always conceptualize the work people do as the target of engagement. Saks, as well as Marisa Salanova, for example, notes that targets of engagement reside both within (e.g., work teams, organization) and outside (e.g., family, hobbies) the work domain. Marylène Gagné, Sharon Parker and Mark Griffin also raise the issue of the degree to which jobs in the future will require increasing levels of interdependence—suggesting, as did Saks, that those with whom we work are, and must be, central to our more complete conceptualization of "work" engagement.

There was less emphasis in the chapters on behavioral manifestations of engagement compared to the engagement experience (state engagement). So, rather than the target being how people experience their social and work environment, targets might also be behavior. A clear example of what we mean is the chapter by Simon Albrecht, who writes about change engagement, engagement reflecting enthusiasm for organizational change initiatives. The other major discussion of behavioral foci for engagement is in Jonathon Halbesleben's chapter, where he focuses extensively on targeted engagement (e.g., for creativity, safety, job crafting) from the Conservation of Resources (COR) theory perspective. Indeed, in his discussion of safety he shows that safety engagement has validity against behavioral safety outcomes; we turn to outcomes of engagement next.

Outcomes of engagement

Halbesleben provides a rich portrait of the many outcomes (at the individual level of analysis) that have been shown to be related to engagement. These outcomes generally fall within the broad category of "job performance" that is so often written about, but subsume important distinctions. So, just like engagement has facets, and just like jobs have facets (foci), so do the potential outcomes have specificity. Halbesleben shows, for example, that the following,

at a minimum, have solid support in the literature as positive outcomes correlated with engagement: innovation, creativity, well-being, job crafting and
safety. But, as he shows, not all outcomes of greater engagement are positive,
with some replicated research studies revealing that the more engaged people
are in their job, the more conflict they experience in their work–life balance.

While there is more research on outcomes at the individual level of analysis
as summarized by Halbesleben, there has recently been considerable research
interest in higher levels of analysis—both in and of themselves and in various
cross-level efforts. For example, Salanova reveals considerable evidence for
performance outcomes for team and organizational levels of engagement, and
Despoina Xanthopoulou and Arnold Bakker include multi-level performance
outcomes in their evaluation of a multi-level nomological network of engagement antecedents and outcomes. Finally, Leaetta Hough and Frederick Oswald
raise some interesting questions—without definitive answers yet—about how
personality can accrue to the team and even perhaps the organizational levels
of analysis to influence engagement and performance at those levels of analysis.

Engagement in a changing world of work

Studies of work engagement generally view work and the job as constants. Such
a model of the job as non-changing is convenient for researchers who do not
then have to fret about changes that may alter their findings. But at least three
chapters in the present book alert us to the fallacy of such a view. Peter Cappelli
and Liat Eldor, for example, write about engagement in work when many of
the usual features of the broader work role are no longer present, including the
organization as the employer or the collaboration of co-workers. When one is
a contractor or gig worker, one is legally one's own boss working for one's own
organization (take a bricklayer or an Uber driver). Cappelli and Eldor in fact
raise issues like the pride in one's clients (those who provide the contract) as
a source of potential engagement for contract workers. Importantly, Cappelli
and Eldor note that about 15 percent of all workers in the U.S. and Europe are
now working as contract or gig workers, with that percentage likely to increase
as companies find the use of such work relationships beneficial—like Google
with its 10,000 contract workers or many universities with their contract
teachers.

John Boudreau's chapter, and the chapter by Gagné and her colleagues, explicitly raise the following question: As technology, especially AI, is introduced
into the workplace, what does this do to the nature of work, work relationships, the relationship between workers and their employing organizations—
and engagement? Both chapters provide rich conceptual maps for thinking

through the antecedents and consequences of engagement, and where engagement fits in the future studies of work. Boudreau is especially concerned with which facets of existing jobs are likely to disappear in the future, reaching the conclusion that, while some facets of jobs may no longer be done by humans, the thought that jobs and the workers who do them will disappear is probably an overstatement. He provides the example of how the introduction of ATMs in the financial world has not decreased employment in banks. He is not sanguine about the struggles workers will have as they are asked to upskill to meet new job requirements brought on by new technologies. As we noted earlier, the specific work elements on which people will be asked to work as these changes occur has implications for how engaged people will be in their work.

Gagné et al. provide an updated model of work motivation based on self-determination theory (SDT) that includes the possible future changes in work. This chapter is a tour de force in explicating the potential negative consequences of increased technology in the workplace, but also a strong call to action in companies to enhance engagement. Their conceptual model of future work design as a result of technology is explicit in noting both the uncertainties about additional changes that might take place and the interdependency required to get the work done. They propose that, to combat the potential negative consequences of technology, the new work must be designed to be stimulating, offer opportunities for mastery and autonomy in getting the work done, and be accompanied by organizational and co-worker support (they call this the SMART framework). These are the kinds of task or work elements that yield engagement but only if they become part of the plan for the introduction of new technology. The guiding notion here is that companies must introduce new technology in ways that meet employee needs for autonomy, competency and relatedness that will, in turn, yield the autonomous motivation that is equated with engagement. But workers themselves also have responsibilities, as they are required to alter the way they approach work, being more proactive and adaptive as change is introduced.

Multi-level

Who knew there were so many levels at which engagement could be studied? For example, Salanova showed how her HERO (healthy and resilient organizations) model works at individual, team and organizational levels of analysis as an aid to understanding well-being both within and across levels. More specifically, it is important for us to note that, while Salanova focused on engagement as an indicator of well-being, she has a much broader definition of well-being than engagement—though engagement is a key facet of it. So, her HERO model includes self-efficacy and resilience also as indicants of well-being—and these also exist at multiple levels of analysis.

Xanthopoulou and Bakker summarized evidence that exists regarding their proposed cross-level nomological network of antecedents and consequences of engagement. They conclude that the nomological network seems to hold true across levels of analysis—and that there are cross-level effects too. Both Xanthopoulou and Bakker, as well as Salanova, provide substantial evidence for a group or team engagement construct, and the former chapter shows, as we noted earlier, that the antecedents and consequences of such an aggregate engagement construct replicate across levels.

And then there is the multi-level issue raised cleverly by Saks as the referent for engagement. So, it is one thing to speak of the focus or target of engagement and another to speak of the referent for engagement, as in engagement for whom. Sample items might be: I am enthusiastic about my job; members of my team are enthusiastic about their jobs; members of this organization are enthusiastic about their jobs. "Job" in these examples can be replaced by other targets. If you take the referents and array them against the potential targets of engagement and then overlay that matrix with three facets of engagement (vigor, dedication and absorption) one obtains a portrait of how interestingly complex the work of multi-level engagement research can be.

Personality

Hough and Oswald show us that an exclusive focus on contextual issues vis-à-vis engagement is a narrow approach to understanding the antecedents of engagement. They note that several meta-analyses reveal quite sizeable relationships between people's personalities and their engagement at work, some in the 0.60 range (see their Table 5.1). We mention their chapter here because, with few exceptions, it is the only one in which individual differences play a role. For example, Halbesleben introduced the notion that Conscientiousness might serve as a moderator of relationships of engagement to outcomes. We will have more to say about this issue of personality later in our section on future research needs.

Leadership

We were somewhat surprised at the relative lack of attention to leadership in the chapters. Of course, people wrote about topics we asked them to write about but, even so, people wrote about lots of antecedents in the work context without much attention to leadership. The two chapters with the most evidence supporting a leadership effect on engagement were the ones by Salanova and Albrecht. In Salanova's HERO model, leadership behavior is an important antecedent of well-being, and of course of engagement as a facet of well-being. Indeed, her presentation included evidence that a leadership coaching intervention produced at least short-term effects on follower engagement.

Albrecht's approach places great weight on leadership as an antecedent of both employee engagement in work and employee engagement in change through its impact on engagement climate and change climate. His framework proposes that focused leadership behaviors—behaviors focused on engagement and change—produce the corresponding climates which, in turn, yield the intended engagement outcomes. An interesting point about Albrecht's model is that it is a leadership model focused on a specific outcome—employee engagement—which is not much found in the general leadership literature. So, as Halbesleben showed, the focus or target of engagement has been studied quite a bit now, but leadership research has focused on leadership style (transformational, transactional, servant), more than the accomplishment of specific goals—like innovation, creativity or inclusion.

Methodology

Engagement scholars certainly have been adventurous in the varieties of methods used to study engagement. We were very fortunate to have five chapters explicitly about methods useful in studying engagement. In addition, of course, the remaining chapters are filled with methodological insights and approaches. William Macey's exposition of qualitative methods for the study of engagement is an appropriate place to begin since it was Kahn's early qualitative studies that played such an important role in advancing interest in the study of engagement—though not through the methods he used. Thus, the survey method of study took over quickly—independently but quickly via the UWES, which has dominated studies, at least in the peer-reviewed published literature. On the other hand, we are quite familiar with qualitative studies that have been done in companies via in-house and consulting practitioners. The goal of such company-specific studies is to illuminate the specific details for a company that may require attention for enhancing engagement. Indeed, some such projects are actually accomplished as follow-ups to surveys that yielded more general data that were useful for cross-company comparisons but which did not contain the details necessary for specifically focused change.

Perhaps the central methodological issue raised throughout the book, and particularly in our chapters focused on methods, concerned the multi-level issue in engagement. Vicente González-Romá carefully introduced readers to the analytic issues surrounding multi-level research and then explicitly focused on the details. In his chapter, it becomes clear that the quality of the data used in multi-level modeling is critical, and that care must be taken in having data at the appropriate level when doing such analyses. More specifically, González-Romá noted how survey data used for multi-level research must meet certain criteria (frame of reference in the items) prior to being useful for testing hypotheses about multi-level models. Interestingly, Salanova and Albrecht also raise the issue of the survey data meeting certain requirements for analysis, the bottom-line message being that the data submitted for multi-level analyses is the critical starting point.

Sabine Sonnentag, Monika Wiegelmann and Maike Czink also write about the care that must be exercised in multi-level modeling, and focus especially on assessing change over time using such models. Together, the chapters on the future of work by Boudreau, Cappelli and Eldor, and Gagné and her colleagues certainly make it very clear that tracking engagement over time as the nature of work and its contexts change will be important, and Sonnentag and her colleagues offer models for conducting such analyses.

McLarnon et al. introduce us to a very different "person-centered" approach to data analysis than is typical in most engagement research. Here the objective is to identify different patterns in the ways that individuals can be engaged at work. For example, rather than considering the mean levels of vigor, dedication and absorption within a sample, using a person-centered approach we might identify some clusters of individuals with high levels of vigor, dedication and absorption, but others with high levels of vigor and dedication and low levels of absorption. In this case, the interest might in determining whether the level of absorption makes a difference in terms of performance. Similarly, we could look for different patterns of engagement across targets. For example, are there differences in levels of engagement across tasks within a job, or differences in the relative strength of engagement in the job, organization, team, project, and so on? Again, if there are differences, do they have implications for where these individuals direct their efforts? And this is just the beginning. Person-centered analytic techniques can be used to investigate differences in the relative importance of different antecedents of engagement to identify different patterns in the trajectories of change in engagement, or to examine changes in patterns (profiles) of engagement over time.

Interestingly, Fink and Macey in their chapter on what they call "the new world of data" implicitly suggest that the breadth of the kinds of data now available for study could also be studied over time. What some call "big data" is really "breadth of data" existing in vast consulting firms' and companies' databases.

Alexis Fink and William Macey raise two important cautions as we think about future research with big data. First, the issue of ethics/privacy is a concern, especially when using data from people in a way they have not expressly agreed to. This includes wearable monitors, use of cell-phone tracking data, personal data stored in human resource information systems (HRIS) and, of course, the use of data scraped from the web. Second, they suggest the importance and utility of data scientists working with organizational scientists to explore large databases because the former might just crunch the numbers but the latter can help in defining conceptually-based questions important for both theory and practice.

Summary

We have learned a great deal about engagement, its antecedents and consequences, and how these are, and might be, studied. The terms multiply about what we have learned vis-à-vis engagement: the focus, the referents, the levels, the patterns, the change, the multi-level models, and so forth, and these all provide a sound base on which to build future research efforts, the topic to which we turn next.

Future research needs

Chapter authors were asked to have a separate section, as you saw, with regard to future research directions. Our goal here is to provide an integrative summary of the suggestions made for future research necessary for further understanding of the engagement construct. We derived two main foci for future research, and we explore these in some detail based on chapter authors' thoughts: change issues and levels issues. In addition, we also provide a brief set of our own thoughts for future research.

Change

Essentially all chapter authors discussed how important it is for us to study engagement over time. There were chapters specifically focused on change that discussed the issue from three different vantage points:

1. A conceptual standpoint as in Gagné and her colleagues;
2. From a statistical/methodological perspective, as in González-Romá and Sonnentag and her colleagues; and
3. From the perspective of what is actually happening in the world of work, as in the Cappelli and Eldor as well as Boudreau chapters.

Cappelli and Eldor, as well as Boudreau, note how changes in the workplace have not received the attention required in studies of engagement. More specifically, Cappelli and Eldor argue for the need to study the engagement of non-traditional contract workers. They argue persuasively that not having a boss and not having regular co-workers, and frequently working for many different clients rather than a single employing organization, makes engagement different and requires new approaches and measures to expose those differences. They ask: Are the expectations and resources provided to contract workers different from those given to employees? When contract workers and organizational employees work side-by-side at the same jobs, do they differ in the work engagement they experience—and on what bases? The way Cappelli and Eldor frame future research needs regarding contract work makes us think that the qualitative approaches detailed by Macey, rather than mass administration of surveys to contract workers, might be a fruitful place to begin.

Boudreau, with his focus on the effects of technology and automation on work, notes that jobs are changing even when regular employees of an organization are the focus. He asks for research on the elements of the work people do because technology is likely to change some work elements and not others. He will be delighted when he reads Saks' chapter to see his emphasis on the different facets or foci of engagement—and across levels of analysis (referents) as well. Similarly, Saks would be delighted to see how important task engagement is to Boudreau as an approach to deconstructing and reinventing jobs. Boudreau makes it clear that the changes that will happen as a result of technology and work automation will not be one-time changes, but that they will be continuously changing (he refers to "perpetually deconstructed and reinvented work"). This makes it important to not only study overall engagement over time but to study changes in engagement as linked to the specific work elements (tasks) being done—and changes in them. His notion of time and timing of change raises the issue of the levels of uncertainty likely experienced by employees going forward, a topic of future engagement research raised by Gagné and her colleagues.

Gagné and her colleagues effectively conceptualize the issue of change, focusing not only on technology but also the uncertainty associated with it, and the likely increased inter-connectedness (relatedness) of people it yields. For them, the best kind of research would be to take advantage of natural experiments occurring in companies to explore the different ways change is approached and the consequences for engagement. For example, they note that when employees did not trust their managers, change in their jobs was accompanied by increased levels of distress. If companies have existing engagement survey programs, they might randomly choose some units or situations to begin making changes and have others as hold-out samples for comparison. Following their SDT-based model, Gagné and her colleagues also propose that research would be valuable to understand the effects of increases in job autonomy on increased opportunities for employees to engage in job crafting and the increased engagement that can yield. And Sonnentag and her colleagues provide us with the statistical models for conducting such analyses of change over time—and across time and levels of analysis.

Gagné and her colleagues also propose that the education of managers to take a more psychological approach to change in jobs might yield a host of positive engagement consequences for employees, as well as job performance enhancement. They note that managers frequently are not educated to think about the psychological impact of change on employees and that studies of the effects of such education would be useful—a view that both Albrecht and Salanova would share. Albrecht also writes about change, proposing that we need more research on the degree to which senior leaders and their employees are engaged in change (not just engaged, but engaged in change). Salanova notes that her projects on the coaching of leaders yielded some improvements but that she was only able to follow up with them for three months.

To this point, we have emphasized how change in people's work and work worlds may get reflected in engagement, but we have not explored the issue of time lags—for how long do these effects we have discussed last? Salanova demonstrated in her intervention research that we cannot assume that short-term gains will be maintained without additional efforts, and we need more research to determine what these might be. Halbesleben devoted considerable room to the need for future research to map relationships between engagement and its outcomes over time, and for different time periods in people's lives. McLarnon and his colleagues, in their person-centered approach, caution us that changes might not be uniform across people. Just as individuals can have different patterns of vigor, dedication and absorption, and/or patterns of engagement with different targets, they might experience different patterns of change in these facets of engagements over time. We need to gain a better understanding of why these differences exist, and whether they occur naturally over time (e.g., in response to maturity or experience) or are in response to interventions.

If Macey was commenting on future research needs about change, he would for sure emphasize how useful it could be if more qualitative studies were conducted on all of the different kinds of changes we have just noted. Diary studies, participant–observer studies, and interviews (both of individuals and teams) might expose engagement-related experiences that are not being tapped by standard surveys—and which could yield new measures of these. Given that change is happening at different levels of analysis, we turn to research needs regarding levels next.

Levels of analysis

We open this section with this caution: There is no correct level of analysis, or multiple levels of analysis, except those designed to answer the question(s) of interest. Schneider has struggled with the levels issue for years and reached the following conclusion: There is no best or right one and psychological concepts—like engagement—aggregate up meaningfully to higher levels of analysis. Indeed, we have in these chapters levels of analysis ranging from the within-person level, to the between individual, to the between team, the unit and the organization—and some that cut across all or most of these.

Perhaps the most ambitious attempt at the simultaneous study of engagement across level is the chapter by Xanthopoulou and Bakker. They conclude that there is some beginning evidence indicating common relationships among engagement and its antecedents and consequences across levels. But they are not sanguine, and note that there is research needed, especially on the stability of engagement over time at different levels of analysis and how that stability, or the lack thereof, gets played out reciprocally across levels. Saks, of course, would add the thought that there is research needed on the different targets of engagement (task elements) as well; that focusing only on overall work engagement across levels will not suffice as the field develops.

A few additional chapter authors also raise the issue of reciprocity both within and across levels of analysis. Doing so, they note that future research on this issue is necessary for developing the engagement construct. As a side note, it is our perception that reciprocal relationships are not much studied in any of our literatures. Saks, for example, notes a need for research on what he calls the spillover effect—how engagement in one target (the job) has an impact on engagement in another target (family), and vice versa. He notes, for example, that there is a need for such spillover research across targets and, of course, across levels—between individuals and teams as referents or between units and organizations as referents. Halbesleben also notes a need for research relevant to reciprocity. In his case, the issue is one of reciprocal relationships between engagement and its antecedents (resources in his COR framework). So, if one has positive resources to get one's work done then it leads to engagement—and that engagement in turn can lead to obtaining increased resources. Clearly there is a need for such research because what happens in organizations goes in more directions than left to right arrows, like many of our models. He also notes that increased performance can have negative consequences as well—increased performance can yield pressure from the boss for even higher levels of performance—and these need to be studied as well. Again, we note that Macey would see such research questions as an opportunity for qualitatively assessing how people actually experience these reciprocal relationships since qualitative approaches are especially valuable in exploring new research questions.

In Salanova's chapter, the issue of the need for reciprocity-like research emerges explicitly when she discusses contagion in teams. Here she notes that individual-level engagement can influence the level of team engagement and vice versa. Hough and Oswald make precisely the same point when they present the need for research on personality composition in teams and groups and the impact of these on both individual engagement and team performance. Further they suggest how it would be useful to assess not only employee personality vis-à-vis engagement but the personality of leaders and the effects of a leader's engaging personality on employee engagement. In short, reciprocity among the variables involved in engagement research, both within and between levels of analysis, is important and necessary.

From a research perspective, Xanthopoulou and Bakker also briefly, but importantly, raise the issue of the data submitted to analysis across levels. They focus on the common method issue wherein the collection of data about engagement, its antecedents and its consequences emerge from the same data source. Many researchers—but not all—see this "common method bias" as raising questions about the magnitude of relationships observed when data (e.g., predictor and criterion) come from the same source. Fink and Macey tell us that the use of large databases analyzed over time can do much to remove these common method biases because the data contained in "data lakes" will be there from numerous sources (HRIS systems as well as employee survey data), and may even include data from outside the organization itself—zip codes and such, for example. They note that research is also needed, possibly via big data sets, regarding a very large number of variables at multiple levels of analysis, including differences between organizations in selection processes and data on onboarding processes and their relationship to engagement. It is certainly worth recalling that Fink and Macey note that the variables available in "data lakes" may not match existing conceptual constructs. This will necessitate the creation of proxy variables and it will be a question of how close to the theoretical idea the proxy variables will be.

The quality of the data being analyzed across levels of analysis—actually at any level of analysis—is raised also in the more technical data-analytic chapters by González-Romá and Sonnentag and her colleagues. González-Romá, in particular, devotes considerable effort to documenting the need to have appropriate data collected in order to carry out multi-level analyses. He is especially concerned with the framing of items in survey research so that the focus of the survey items is at that level to which the data will be aggregated. For example, when studying team-level engagement, are the items worded with reference to what is happening in the team? Such cautions are not new, but he then raises a question for future research at team and higher levels of analysis concerning the variance (not just the mean) in the aggregated engagement data. More specifically, he asks this question: What effect does the degree of variance in aggregated data have on relationships observed within and across levels of analysis? He refers to this issue as one of multi-level configural analyses such that (team, unit, organizational) variability is introduced as a potential moderator of relationships using only the means of the aggregates. Such research is needed, and he presents the statistical models and an example for readers for doing precisely these analyses.

The co-editors' wish list for additional future engagement research

To this point, we have attempted to highlight some of the key recommendations for research suggested by our expert authors. Of course, we cannot do them complete justice here, and strongly encourage readers to go to the chapters for more detail. Here we add some additional research questions and recommendations that occurred to us from the unique vantage point of having read all of the chapters, helping us to appreciate the richness of the "big picture." As we thought through these wonderful chapters and our authors' suggestions for future research, we had some additional ideas about potentially useful and important research questions. Chapter authors may not have specifically suggested what follows, but then again we had an opportunity to read all of the chapters and they did not!

- More comparative research is needed on correlates of engagement to round out the multi-level focus represented in the chapters. For example, studies of differences in engagement associated with age cohort, gender, socio-economic status and culture would expand the conceptual space for future engagement research. Questions like these might be explored:
  - Are people who are planning to retire early less engaged than those who wish to continue to work past typical retirement age?
  - Are women who earn less than their male counterparts less engaged in their work?
  - Do employees in precarious "jobs" care less about engagement than those with stable "careers"?
  - Do people who live in tighter societal cultures experience less engagement than those who live in looser societal cultures?

- More research is needed on the role of leadership vis-à-vis engagement. We hinted at this issue in describing Albrecht's research in which he explored the role of change-oriented leadership in influencing the engagement of followers in the change process. Studies of leadership focused on engagement in service to customers or on safety or on innovation and creativity might reveal improved validity for the relationship between leadership style and engagement against such specific outcomes. So, rather than studying the relationship between global leadership style and engagement, we might study the relationship between outcome-focused leadership and outcome-focused engagement—and achievement of those specific outcomes.

- Research on person–situation interaction and person–organization fit and engagement is also required. Reviews of the engagement literature have focused on either the contextual or personal antecedents of engagement but not the two together. In addition, the specific issue of person–environment "fit" as a correlate of engagement is to our knowledge rare. But fit is one of the most ubiquitous constructs in psychological science and deserves to play a role in our understanding of engagement. In addition, there are few if any studies that look at anything like a person–situation approach to understanding the antecedents of engagement. Are some contextual antecedents more important than others as a function of the personality of the people involved? Who knows? Do some personalities fit better into, and become more engaged in, some contexts than others? We do know that person–situation interactions and person–situation fit effects have been found in research on job satisfaction and organizational commitment, so they are also likely to affect engagement. Consideration of both person and situation simultaneously is needed.

- More research needs to be accomplished on the potential dark side of engagement. Halbesleben reported finding that highly work-engaged people had more work–life conflicts and were more prone to work-arounds that might result in accidents; more research on this kind of possibility could be important. So, while there can be positive spillover effects of individual onto team engagement, there may be negative spillover effects of engagement in family and engagement in work—and vice versa. The assessment of engagement via surveys like the UWES grew out of research on burnout, and the issue is the degree to which high levels of engagement—and with regard to which targets or foci—can in fact yield burnout.

- More cross-fertilization of research across the arenas where engagement is being studied would enhance understanding of the construct. Engagement has become a construct of interest in more than the work world: in education, sports and recreation, civil action and more. And, even in a work context, OB/HR/I-O (Organizational Behavior/Human Resources Management/Industrial-Organizational Psychology) researchers are not the only ones studying it, with folks in marketing beginning studies of customer engagement. How engagement is conceptualized and assessed, and its role as an antecedent of important behavior, across these venues could prove insightful.

- More intervention/field experimental research is certainly called for. We hinted at this issue several times but declare it here as a central way to more firmly establish presumed causal arrows in engagement models. Much of our research on engagement has been one-shot cross-sectional survey in style, and the use of more time-based panel designs and experimental or quasi-experimental designs to trace through causal issues is important.

- More academic research and business partnerships for engagement research could be useful. For example, research involving both large business-based databases and academics with conceptual models to test could yield both theoretically important and practical evidence of engagement and its management. Such collaborations in our field are rare but they exist—with even some consulting firms with large databases (especially Gallup) occasionally publishing results of their research.

Summary

Anyone who thought we knew everything we need to know about engagement must be disappointed by this consideration of the kinds of research still needing to be done. For sure we have learned a lot and the rule is that the more we know, the more we know what we do not know. Our chapter authors were wonderful in summarizing the literatures we asked them to work with—but then to add their thoughts about what is still left to do. In this final chapter we summarized some of what we know and focused in on some of the ways we can learn what we do not yet know. Have fun pursuing these ideas!

Index[1]

Note

1. This index includes a selected group of authors who appear either cited several times in *A Research Agenda for Employee Engagement in a Changing World of Work* or across several chapters. Please see the individual reference sections for each chapter for all authors cited across this title.